NEITHER CRYSTAL NOR GOLD

ROBERT W. ARTIGO

Neither Crystal
nor Gold

LIGHTHOUSE PUBLISHING

Cover Design by Enrique J. Aguilar

Cover photograph:
Christ Cathedral by Challenge Roddie

Inside front flap:
Christ Seated in Glory as the Lord of Creation
Tapestry in Christ Cathedral by Brother Martin Erspamer,
a monk of Saint Meinrad Archabbey
Photograph by Challenge Roddie

For my wife, Melissa

CONTENTS

FOREWORD

by Tim Busch

It has been a joy to commission the writing of a great history that weaves the lifetime work of Dr. Robert and Arvella Schuller, who developed an extraordinary televangelist program that led to building the campus that is now the Christ Cathedral of the Diocese of Orange. The Schullers came to California in the 1950s and began the novel method of preaching at a drive-in movie theater. Worshipers would pull up in their cars, attach a speaker to their windows, then listen to Dr. Schuller preach from the snack-bar roof.

Over the ensuing sixty years, Dr. and Mrs. Schuller, along with their family, assembled over thirty acres of property that became the world-renowned Crystal Cathedral. It was not crystal and it was not a cathedral, but what is interesting is that he named it as such even though it was not part of the Roman Catholic diocese, which is a church that exclusively uses the term *cathedral* for the primary house of worship where the bishop cathedra (chair) is housed.

As Dr. and Mrs. Schuller aged, they began to pass their ministry on to the children, starting with the son, Dr. Robert A. Schuller, and then to the eldest daughter, Sheila Schuller Coleman, and ultimately to their grandson, Bobby Schuller.

Dr. Schuller was quite a dreamer, a magnanimous man who loved the Lord and relied on His providence, prayer, and grace.

Then, the 2008 and 2009 financial downturn hit; the contributions from the televangelist audience, which represented 90 percent of their revenue source, dried up, and Dr. Schuller was unable to pay his bills. Ultimately, the ministry filed for bankruptcy, which led to numerous lawsuits and a foreclosure by the bank. It was at that time that a small group of benefactors suggested to the bishop of Orange, Tod D. Brown, that he shelve his idea of building a ground-up cathedral in Santa Ana and focus on the purchase of the Crystal

Cathedral. Although Bishop Brown was cool to the idea at the out-set, he listened and began to become more interested. Initially, the offer was covert because he was concerned about a possible holy war regarding the Catholic Church trying to buy a Protestant facility, although the transfer of church property between faiths—Christian, Muslim, and Jewish—has gone on for centuries.

Then, as a turning point, Dr. Schuller's son-in-law offered to sale a portion of the property to an apartment developer. It was at this point that I ran to the bishop to advise him that the diocese needed to publicly offer to purchase the property for worship, which was originally intended. He still was skeptical that Dr. Schuller would be open to this idea.

As providence would have it, Dr. Schuller was not only open to it but he welcomed the Catholics with open arms, as he became very excited that the legacy of Robert and Arvella's life's vocation would now be held, as he stated, by the Church of Peter, and that it would be run by his bishop, Bishop Tod D. Brown. This was quite novel for a Protestant minister to look at the local Catholic bishop as his bishop. It is also true, but not usually recited by a Protestant minister, that the Catholic Church was founded by Jesus and the first pope was Peter, appointed by Jesus Christ Himself, and that the popes of today are the lineage from Peter.

I found all of this very fascinating because we were fearful that he would nix the deal but, in fact, he advanced the cause.

What I also found fascinating was that Dr. and Mrs. Schuller had been alienated by the children and the rest of the leaders of the church when the financial struggle began. Somehow between that time and when the final decision was made, they were returned as voting members of the governing board. There were nine members, and the vote to support the purchase by the Roman Catholic Church of Orange was 5–4, with Dr. and Mrs. Schuller voting in favor. The offer by Chapman University was higher and, in many ways, much more accommodating because its offer allowed the cathedral build-ing to be rented for one dollar per year for thirty years on Sundays. This was not a possibility for the Roman Catholic Church, as it is their primary place of worship.

This is a story of God's providence, of God's mercy, of God's grace. It is the story of each person, from Bishop Brown, who oversaw the purchase of the campus, and his successor, Bishop Kevin Vann, who oversaw the renovation, to all of the lay and ordained who were involved—people of goodwill but born with Original Sin, people who were struggling with each other to advance the cause of the cathedral purchase and its renovation, yet in some instances, resisting it because they did not believe it aligned with the long-term objectives of the Diocese of Orange. Ultimately, through the Holy Spirit, the acquisition was done at an incredible price of $55.7 million, the mere value of the land. The property was completely entitled for the uses that the cathedral needs, and it saved a decade of entitlement delay to build. All of the infrastructure was in place. The land was flat and located in the center of the county, which is also the diocesan boundaries, where cathedrals should be located, with multiple freeways accessing the cathedral to all of Orange County and to San Diego to the south and Los Angeles to the north.

From the day Dr. Schuller began, he saw God's plan for his life-time work to build a cathedral campus for the Diocese of Orange, sixty years in advance of its actual purchase and thirty-five years before the diocese was formed from its neighboring Archdiocese of Los Angeles.

The story is a case study relying on the providence of the Holy Spirit. Jesus used parables to teach. The parable of the sixty-year case study of the campus being bought, built, and transferred should convince anyone how God works through cooperating hands.

As you read through the story, think of how people were work-ing for the benefit of their church and woke up to realize that the Holy Spirit had been collaborating with all of the different factions of interest, to effectuate what was intended all along—that the Dio-cese of Orange would have its cathedral in a location much more dynamic, bigger than was ever dreamed. Had the diocese built a ground-up cathedral in Santa Ana, it would have had a cathedral in an average location—there would be no chancery offices, there would be no school, there would be no office building for lay apos-tolates and a EWTN television station, no expansive cemetery and mausoleum (which over time would endow the cathedral expenses). It would have been on fifteen acres not thirty-two, with no imme-diate access to freeways, and the cost would be twice at about $250 million versus $125 million. There would be no extra land to build future retreat centers, retirement homes, or whatever the presiding Ordinary and his advisers may deem appropriate.

The location of this property is the most diverse part of Orange County, where Asian and Latino immigrants have settled, yet is still accessible to the origin of the Anglo population. Today, every weekend, twelve Masses are celebrated in four languages (English, Spanish, Vietnamese, and Mandarin) and are attended by as many as twelve thousand people. That would not have occurred at the other location that was originally identified if not for the convenience of the cathedral to the diverse populace.

Because the property was so expansive and all-inclusive, the diocese was also able to sell the Chancery Office at a significant profit to help fund the acquisition and renovation. They were able to sell off part of the original cathedral campus and retain a parish church facility for the neighborhood. They were able to finance an existing facility with the very bank who held the mortgage with Dr. and Mrs. Schuller, Farmers and Merchants Bank of Long Beach, California, who, albeit not Catholic, were a proponent of the Roman Catholic diocese buying the campus.

It is also interesting that other suitors such as Hobby Lobby, Saddleback Church, Dutch Reformed Church, and others that were allegedly interested in purchasing the property never came to the table—just Chapman University, whose objective was to convert the cathedral itself into an auditorium and pharmaceutical and veterinarian schools. This did not sit well with Dr. Schuller, because he had raised money to use it for a house of worship. How could all of his labors end up in a secular cause?

This is that story. Between these pages there is movement, action, leaps of faith, and big dreams that became reality for love of one thing: the spreading of the Gospel of Jesus Christ. If at the end you do not see the tapestry, then the creators of this book pray that you will some day and that you will know that the little works you weave each day in service to God may be contributing to something unimaginable that can transcend the centuries. Think big. The details, as remarkable as they are, contained in the following pages, will go down as some of the greatest things that I have ever witnessed in my life—the acquisition and renovation of this amazing facility went far beyond the legendary cathedral. Enjoy reading, and I hope it will bring great confidence to witness the will of God prevailing.

ₐₒ ₐₒ ₐₒ

ACKNOWLEDGMENTS

I give thanks to Robert W. Artigo, the author of this book. He dutifully researched the story of the purchase of the Crystal Cathedral and choreographed an incredible written performance. He worked tirelessly during the pandemic with the support of his wife, Melissa. His work, like the story of the Crystal Cathedral itself, is surely guided by the Holy Spirit.

I give thanks to my wife, Steph, and children, Garrett and Kenzie, who stood by me during the acquisition process from the moment I began the long journey in 2010.

I give thanks to Catholic prelates who played prominent roles in this story. Bishop Tod Brown, the Ordinary of the Diocese of Orange, undertook the long and complex task of acquiring a televangelist's iconic facility—setting the stage for the Crystal Cathedral's transformation into the Christ Cathedral. Archbishop José Gomez, the metropolitan of the Archdiocese of Los Angeles, supported the purchase of the cathedral from the start. Cardinal James Harvey, the Prefect of the Papal Household, also supported the acquisition and rallied many in the Vatican to do likewise. Cardinal Dolan of New York who, as President of the United States Conference of Bishops, intervened with the Vatican to assure them that this was a worthy and noble cause. Bishop Kevin Vann, the current Ordinary of the Diocese of Orange, and his auxiliary, Bishop Timothy Freyer, who have overseen the renovation of the campus and reviewed this work, to assure its accuracy. They all have my prayerful gratitude.

I give thanks to Monsignor Lawrence Baird, who was on the Cathedral Steering Committee and quickly and fully supported the acquisition of the Crystal Cathedral.

I give thanks to the early donors and supporters who advised Bishop Brown and the diocesan board on the acquisition, especially Jim Tecca, Mike Hagan, Rob and Berni Neal, Dennis and Lynne Jilot and John L. Curci.

I give thanks for Bill Close, as well as Cardinal Roger Mahony who shepherded the building of the Our Lady of the Angels Cathedral in Los Angeles twenty years before and gave me great encouragement in this endeavor.

I give thanks to the two Apostolic Nuncios during the tenure of acquiring and renovating the Christ Cathedral including Archbishop Carlo Maria Vigano arriving just as the acquisition required an important Vatican approval and Archbishop Christophe Pierre who served during the renovation and dedication. I give thanks to Father Robert Spitzer, S.J., now housed on the Christ Cathedral campus, who gave me unsurpassed spiritual guidance and direction during an often difficult process. I give thanks to my own spiritual director, Father Luke Mata, who has been faithfully directing me for many years in discerning the will and whispers of the Holy Spirit.

Finally, I give thanks to all those who came to support the Christ Cathedral project and joined the work to complete it in a spirit of Christian unity. It is because of them, many of whose names will never be known, that Christ Cathedral officially opened in July 2019, providing a place of spiritual refuge and refreshment for the Catholics of Orange County and all who seek the truth and face of God.

Ruby

What brought twenty-two-year-old Ruby Rinker to the drive-in movie theater in Orange, California, that gorgeous Sunday morning was not in itself totally clear. It was not a feature film like *East of Eden* starring James Dean playing, one of 1955's top motion pictures. Rather, it was a Christian preacher on the marquee, a man Ruby had never heard of until she saw his photo and the article about him in the local newspaper. He was going to preach outdoors and, unbelievably, from the roof of the snack bar. He had no money to build a church, so the drive-in was going to get it started. She was curious, but that was not in itself enough to inspire her to get behind the wheel of her green-and-white 1955 Chevy Bel Aire and drive thirty miles from Torrance to Orange, just to listen. Nevertheless, that is what she did. She took literally the minister's invitation to "come as you are ... in the family car"[1] and wore a T-shirt and jeans.

Ruby was just nineteen when she moved to California from Dayton, Ohio, and became a self-described beach girl who hung out at the beach and coffee shops—a long way from Dayton, a small town where she had a very strict Christian upbringing in the Assemblies of God church. At the time, the religion governed all her activities—most notably, what *not* to do. There was no roller skating, no dancing, and certainly no skirts above the knees. There was so much to fear from the wrath of God; she had soured on religion.

She always believed in God the Father, God the Son, and God the Holy Spirit, but organized religion, like the one she was raised in, was just not for her. She prayed daily and asked God to guide her; but once in California, she stopped going to church. That was just how it was—until after a few years without church she picked up the *Orange County Register* and saw the man pictured next to a tall handmade crucifix. *Why not?*

She parked the Chevy among the other cars facing the snack bar, then placed the drive-in audio box on the glass of her car door. She

15

rolled up the window to secure it in place. It was quiet in her car, like she had driven to some secluded place. Then the organ music started, and the organ player was on the roof too! Ruby found herself just listening. She did not know all the songs, but there was something familiar and appealing about it. Then the large figure robed in black stood at the podium—and indeed he was on the roof of the snack bar just as advertised. He wore glasses and a tie. His voice came right into the car.

He was not a fire-and-brimstone evangelist like the ones popular at roadside tent revivals. His voice boomed, and his hands went up in grand gestures.

"God loves you and so do I!" he thundered.

The preacher quoted the Bible and continued to emphasize God's love. It was a foreign message to Ruby. She had heard so much about a punishing God to be feared—the kind of God that would strike with lightning if she had veered from someone's concept of perfection. Here, she was hearing the word *perfection* in a different way, a perfect love for her no matter what. This was the love of Jesus Christ, she learned, and she was called to love in return.

She did not recall the exact Bible quote, but it was the kind of message stated in First John 4:18: "There is no fear in love, but perfect love casts out fear. For fear has to do with punishment, and he who fears is not perfected in love."

She liked the young preacher and was inspired by the sermon. After the closing prayer, this unusual man who so profoundly articulated a message of God's love that resonated with her walked up to her open window. He introduced himself and talked with Ruby. He was kind, with an infectious personality and a broad smile that filled Ruby with the urge to return the smile. Of course, she did, and when he urged her to return, she blurted out a commitment to do so. She did not even think before the words jumped out of her mouth.

The drive-in was thirty miles from her home. When she left to attend the service that morning, she did not really know why she wanted to go and what that drive would mean. Ruby's Christian faith was forever changed that day as the simple concept that God loves her energized her connection to Jesus through the Holy Spirit.

A few years later, Ruby moved to Florida and missed the drive-in sermons. It was an experience destined to never fade from her memory. She would have been shocked to know how that humble ministry would become a huge part of her life.

It was another one of those Sunday mornings a decade after settling into Floridian life when Ruby was inspired to write a letter to the preacher from the drive-in. Ruby was in front of the TV changing the channels and stopped when she saw a preacher in a gray and black robe with a burgundy collar speaking to a crowded church. He was high up in front of a wide white podium, and when he spoke with big grand gestures, Ruby thought, *Could this be the preacher from the drive-in?*

He was a little older, a little grayer, and the TV made the already larger-than-life figure that much larger. As he spoke, the camera angle changed and revealed that he was standing next to an opening in the wall that peered out over a parking lot. The pictured dissolved to an image of people sitting in their cars, watching from the parking lot.

Ruby was pretty sure, but not totally, that this was the preacher from the drive-in. She picked up a pen and wrote a letter and sent it to the address on the TV. She asked, "Are you the minister from the drive-in?"[2] She did not know if she would ever get a response nor what that response would mean for the rest of her life.

The answer was yes. The minister's rapid response and kind words surprised Ruby. She wrote again, and he wrote back. Then again, and he wrote back. That went on for years.

By the mid-1980s, Ruby Rinker and the reverend were good friends. They genuinely liked each other. Ruby also got to know the preacher's wife, whom she saw as a full partner in the ministry. When Ruby married Marshall E. "Doc" Rinker Sr., a Florida building materials magnate, she introduced the men. The TV preacher visited Florida, and they all went to dinner together in Fort Lauderdale. Eventually, she was invited to sit on the board of a growing international ministry. The friendship between Ruby and the minister had nothing to do with money. When she met him and began their long friendship, she had little money of her own. It was not until she married "Doc" that she had the means to help the ministry, so she did on occasion.

Doc was ninety-one when he died of cancer in Palm Beach in 1996. Ruby recalled how the preacher made a special trip across the country to be at her husband's bedside in his last days. He knelt by the bed, tears pouring from his eyes as he prayed for God to comfort the dying man.

Ruby was left with the job of carrying on Doc's prolific philanthropy, and that is what she did. Among many grants and donations to various causes, Rinker made a sizable gift to the preacher's ministry in 2004. The ministry dedicated a lobby and plaque in her name. She eventually left the board; her religious focus had changed over the years. After becoming friends with her neighbor's priest, she became Catholic. But she still followed the preacher and his ministry through the decades, all the way to the mountaintop and back down again.

In early 2010, her phone rang.

The caller was the minister—his voice still strong, but with a hint of changes that came with aging. The ministry was in financial straits. Bankruptcy was a possibility. There was turmoil, confusion, and fear about what would come next. It could come down to all that the minister had built, including the lobby bearing Ruby Rinker's name, being lost through auction.

The preacher asked for one final favor from Ruby Rinker. He wanted her to return to the International Board of Directors to be a full voting member. It would not be a long assignment. He did not say what he expected of her; perhaps he did not know for sure at the time. Ruby read the subtext—the preacher wanted to have friends around him, people he could trust.

Ruby hung up the phone. Her old friend was in need and there was no way she was going to say no. She dropped her head in silence for a moment, and her eyes welled up. Then she prayed for God to give her strength to know what to do whenever the time came.

The Preacher

The cows made untillable Alton, Iowa, farmland useful. The wet, marshy, sloppy ground was a favorite flood area of the Floyd River, ideal for grazing the milk cows, when not flooded, and little else. The sprawling farm belonged to Anthony and Jennie Schuller (pronounced "Skull-er") and boasted hogs, chickens, and horses among the dairy cows. Robert H. Schuller would one day surrender to popular demand and just accept that he would always be known as Schuller (pronounced "Shoo-ler"). The Schullers were themselves both children of Dutch immigrants. With five offspring, they numbered seven as a family; the youngest by seven years was Robert. By eighth grade, in the 1930s, he knew all corners of the farm intimately, especially the back pastureland. He knew the cows far more than he would like to admit. Milking them daily was torture. When he ventured out to the squishy terrain, the chore was unpleasant, but comparatively easy. All he had to do was go out and get the cows back to the farm proper. But his older sister Violet began to wonder why the cows often returned long before Robert. She was not surprised by what she discovered.

"He was out in the back of the pasture, sitting atop a high bank," Violet Mouw remembered, "pretending he was a preacher."[1]

Robert was sending his sermons out across the Floyd River, literally until the cows came home. It was the only other use he had for the back pastureland, and he made good use of it to transport himself away from the Depression-era farm and to hone his skills. He was not cut out for farm work, so he was just doing what he was cut out for: preaching. He had known it from the age of five.

Robert's uncle Henry Beltman, his mother's brother, was legendary in Alton, Iowa. The former-soldier-turned-Christian-missionary saw parts of the world both exotic and harrowing and was returning from work in China. As evidence of just how much the family, and the small church community, had anticipated Henry's return in 1931, there were weeks of preparation, including multiple visits to the tailor so that Robert could be properly fitted into his new Sunday suit. It had been eight years since Robert's mother had seen Henry, and that was even before Robert was born! On the big day, the excitement was enough to make Robert burst. The sky was a crisp blue; the summer corn stalks were alive with the morning sun.

The Schuller farmhouse was at the end of a long dirt driveway. Butterflies and excitement swirled inside Robert's belly as a dust cloud appeared on the distant road coming toward the farm. It turned onto the driveway and kept coming. *Had to be him! It just had to be!*

Robert jumped up and down yelling, "Uncle Henry, Uncle Henry!"[2]

Henry walked up, looked at the nearly breathless child, and placed his hands on the boy's head, saying, "So, you're Robert Harold." Schuller recalled the words and the feeling of solemn stillness coming to him inside. "He said, 'You will be a preacher when you grow up!'"[3] Schuller explained. "And I bought it, hook line and sinker."[4]

That night, Robert added a line to his nightly prayers, affirming his willingness, and asked God to make him a preacher, like Uncle Henry, when he grew up. The next morning during the family breakfast, after Uncle Henry had gone to Grandpa's house, Robert made his intentions official. He was going to be a preacher. To his surprise, the news made his father cry. The mystery of the emotional moment was only cleared up two decades later, when Schuller learned that his father had had his own boyhood dream of becoming a minister, only to have his parents die when he was in sixth grade.

"I had to quit school and get a job as a farm hand," the elder Schuller told Robert. "So, I prayed, 'God make me a minister, through one of my sons someday.'"[5]

Although he was named Harold Robert Schuller at birth on September 16, 1926, he was called Robert. His father was one of the few who addressed him as Harold in such intimate moments as this. His siblings preceded Robert by several years, and the age gap made it seem as though he was growing up as an only child. At the very least it made him fiercely independent. For his father and mother, the late addition to the family was a bit of a surprise; his father had given up hope that he would have a son who would become a minister. Schuller was moved to tears to hear his father's confession.

"Take him, Lord," the elder Schuller said he'd prayed, "and make him your preacher." But there was more, and the elder Schuller fought through more tears. "I never, never, never wanted you to know how I felt. It had to be an honest call from the Lord."[6]

From the moment he attended his first elementary school classes, in a one-room schoolhouse, Robert attacked his schoolwork with an inspired zeal. He was not at the farm, and that was a welcome change, but he was also on a mission to fulfill his calling. He set seminary college in his mind as a goal and pursued it like little else. He was a chubby kid, and sports seemed to pass him by; but as he moved through the grades, school theater and music programs quickly attracted him as he was drawn to entertaining, speaking, and performing in front of groups. The more the better. It was all much more appealing than slopping the hogs or milking cows.

School was a refuge and a place for growth. The farm offered only disgusting toil. Like any kid his age at that time, it was the radio that drew much of his interest in the evenings. One of his favorites was *Jack Armstrong: The All-American Boy*. The radio adventure was popular from 1933 to 1951. The program originated at WBBM in Chicago on July 31, 1933. If he scrambled, he could get chores done before the program started and get an hour of uninterrupted listening. But sometimes, chores pulled him away and he would grumble about milking the cows. There were three milk cows, and every night one needed milking.

Pail in hand, he would go out to the barn and begin the dirty process. There were flies, and tails slapped him in the face. Trouble was, the tails were peppered with cockleburs, which were thorny with long, slender spines and found all over the pasture. That irritation was nothing compared to the intimate details of milking—confined spaces, awkward angles from a seated position on a stool, and managing udder manipulation for maximum production. When the milker was in such a precarious position, it was not uncommon for a cow to spread her legs, lift her thorny tail, and relieve herself. The disgusting splatter went everywhere.

"I'm sure glad I'm not going to be a farmer when I grow up!"[7] Schuller would say to himself. This familiar refrain was well observed on the Schuller farm. His brother, Henry, was fond of pointing out just how unfit for the job Robert really was, and his father also recognized the boy's displeasure with the life. Schuller's father was always there to encourage him to work hard and that he could achieve the goals he set for himself. That kind of encouragement was helpful but did not numb the pain of some farm experiences. He once lost a bucket of fresh eggs and received a nasty gash on his chin when a horse hoof hit him in the face and knocked him to the ground. Still, life was not all a kick in the head.

Robert enjoyed theater and acting when he was not involved directly in his studies, and by all accounts, he was a happy child—when not forced to do chores.

Schuller attended Hope College in Holland, Michigan. It was a small Christian university founded in the 1860s by Dutch immigrants affiliated with the Reformed Church in America. After completing four years at Hope, he moved on to Western Theological Seminary.

As Schuller neared graduation from seminary school, he noticed how many of his peers, the graduating seniors, struggled with something he called the "green eyed monster of jealousy."[8] It seemed everyone was obsessed with building the largest church, even to the point of criticizing already successful ministers like Norman Vincent Peale. Peale was in New York and had the largest Reformed church congregation in the country—a job some coveted, but knew they would never have. It frightened Schuller because he feared his own "potentially demonic" "secret ambitions."[9] Schuller says he prayed for immunity against it, and the answer came quickly in the form of a writing assignment. He procrastinated to the point that a professor directed him to write about a minister named George Truett. Schuller learned that Truett wrote about how he started his congregation with just a few people on the promise to "spend his whole life with these people and to never, ever look for, ask for, pray for, or long for a larger church."[10] Four decades later, he was at the top of the largest Baptist church in the world.

Schuller added a new prayer to his own growing list.

"God give me the chance to go anywhere—start with nothing if you wish—and let me spend forty years building a great church for Jesus Christ!"[11] Now he had a new goal, a forty-year goal.

Schuller married Arvella Dehaan, a woman he had met a few years earlier when he gave his first sermon at his local church. She introduced herself as his organist for the service. While Schuller was at seminary, they carried on a successful long-distance relationship and spent their vacations together. They married June 15, 1950, and shortly thereafter headed off to Ivanhoe, Illinois, a Chicago suburb where Schuller was ordained and took a position as pastor of a small church.

Ivanhoe Reformed Church of Dolton had thirty-five members in a fractured congregation. Healing that divide and finding his footing as pastor was a learning experience and a maturing process. He learned from his mistakes and focused on crafting his Sunday messages the way he used to cram for exams. Meanwhile, financially, life was a challenge. The Schullers struggled to pay for essentials, including gasoline and utilities. By April 1951—when they had their first child, Sheila—the hard work was paying dividends. The church, which had seats for 150, was full on Sunday, and Bible study had grown so much that they began an effort to expand the chapel and borrowed class space from a neighbor. Schuller learned about fundraising to meet those modest goals and met a very good local architect. Shortly after the birth of Robert A. "Bobby" Schuller, in 1954, a letter arrived from the regional leader of the Reformed church in Los Angeles. The board there had voted to open a church in Orange County and approved an invitation to Schuller to take on the task.

Schuller was not so sure. He certainly wanted to get back to California. A choir trip there when he was in school left him with a deep appreciation for the area. But so much was left to be done in Ivanhoe. He had imagined himself spending forty years, just working on that church. The invitation surprised him, and he could not help but think about how far away California was from everything he and Arvella had ever known. It was not just Arvella and Robert anymore. There were two children. Still, he contemplated a trip, just to check it out. The problem was he could not afford the expense.

A friend at the Ivanhoe church, the one man in whom he had confided about the offer, worked for Santa Fe Railroad. He gave Schuller a round-trip ticket.

What Schuller learned on that trip was that the city the church was eying for expansion was Garden Grove. There were not any Reformed church members in the area. The city was largely made up of orchards, but new houses were going up and the population was growing. Schuller would be tasked with not just building a church but recruiting. He was comfortable with that idea. Back in Illinois he had walked door to door inviting people to church. And there was something else. He had left the gray-and-white Chicago area in the dead of winter and arrived in a world filled with sunshine and flowers under a warm sun. It was intoxicating natural beauty.

Arvella met him at the train station when he got back a few days later. There was no doubt about it. They were moving to California. Saying goodbye to his congregation was the hard part. As testimony to how he had impacted the Ivanhoe church, when he made the announcement the crowd numbered about five hundred.

The Schullers packed everything they owned and headed for the Golden State.

The Drive-In

There was something in the light breeze that Sunday morning. It seemed to be calling to the orange blossoms, sweet eucalyptus, and the many spring flowers as if commanding them to come alive. Robert H. Schuller, just twenty-eight years old, had the scent of nature in his nose, but it was the Holy Spirit who moved him in the nearly empty drive-in movie theater. He thought of himself as blessed and he was thankful. There was no shining vision of a tall, glittering spire in the distance for which to set his sights. There was not a voice calling, "If you build it, they will come." Instead, he stood in the open space surrounded by orange orchards and eucalyptus absolutely assured in the belief that "this is the day that the Lord has made, let us rejoice and be glad in it." In just a few hours the stage would be set, and the cars would come. The music would play and the choir would sing, and he had spread the Good News just as he had been called. Chicago was so many miles ago, if not so many days. Remarkably, it was all happening just two weeks after he rolled into town with his little family.

There were two giant movie screens on opposite ends of the vast open space that was shaped like a pair of baseball fields connected right field to left field. The lot had elongated mounds and undulations for better viewing angles. Each screen was built into towering walls. On the other side of the walls were large marquees, above them the letters identifying the location as the Orange Drive-In. The newest congregation in Orange County ... *In a drive-in?*

A drive-in theater was not his first choice. Not his second or even his seventh. Schuller had scribbled the list on a napkin as his wife and daughter perused a menu at a Route 66 café in Albuquerque, New Mexico. Bobby, the baby, was oblivious as Daddy added to the list. Schuller might have added more, but in his frustration and focus he dismissed some options before he could get them onto paper. Schuller was still bristling a bit at the words his wife, Arvella, had read as they drove along the highway only hours before.

"I checked the whole town of Garden Grove, and it's *impossible* to find an empty hall," she had read.[1] The letter was from the regional missionary of the Reformed church, a man who would be Schuller's supervisor. Schuller urged Arvella to continue. So, she did. "You're just going to have to spend the first year building a structure on the two acres we found for a church site."[2]

That reality seemed more like a hurdle than a wall to Schuller, so the word *impossible* was digging at him. It made him cringe to hear it every time. In the café, the list was coming together inspired by an idea that action was far preferable to a delay of a year. In his autobiography, *My Journey: From an Iowa Farm to a Cathedral of Dreams*, Schuller was resolute. "I didn't come to spend my time building buildings; I came to preach the Good News, to comfort a hurting world," he wrote.[3] To do that he needed options of already constructed, logical, and affordable venues.

Renting a schoolhouse, warehouse, and even a mortuary chapel all made it onto the list—as did a movie theater and putting up a tent for an old-fashioned tent revival in a field. There were ten options. Each had pluses and minuses. Some could be crossed off because of legal problems. For example, schools were forbidden to rent to religious organizations. Other choices were crossed off because further research showed that there were no such buildings. For one, there were no Masonic lodges in the area. In fact, the list came down to just a few realistic options. Tucked away at number nine, just after "Rent a Jewish" synagogue (there were none) and just before "Tent," was "Rent a Drive-in."[4] A tent seemed uninspired, but a *drive-in?* Arvella, as an important part of whatever the ministry looked like, would have a say a few days later.

Over a cup of coffee at their new Garden Grove home, Schuller turned to Arvella and reminded her of a drive-in service they had attended while honeymooning in Iowa. It took a while to gain her full attention, because she was playing with the infant Bobby. But she finally focused and said, "I do remember the service. It was beautiful. There was something special about worshipping God outdoors."[5]

The drive-in service the newlyweds had attended in Iowa was not a completely novel idea. There had been a few. For example, the

Neptune Drive-In in Daytona Beach, Florida, began hosting worship services in 1953 on Atlantic Avenue.

Arvella imagined the perfect weather in Garden Grove, and they both thought of the orange blossoms in the air. The blossoms surrounded the senses in the spring of 1955 in Orange County. Every year they bloomed easily and abundantly as warm spring weather arrived. In sunny Southern California, free of frost early in the year, orange trees flourished in endless orchards. On the branches there were dense groupings of blossoms, each with brilliant white petals and rich nectar, to draw in honeybees and other pollinators. The sweet scent that came with spring was a pleasant tease, which called for patience. It was the promise of an awe-inspiring crop of bright orange fruit that would be enough for all, but the trees would not bear ripe fruit until winter. Schuller saw the setting and the drive-in as an opportunity that would bear a harvest. But how much? Only God knew.

The Orange Drive-In theater had opened in 1941 near what is now Highway 5 and Chapman Avenue in the city of Orange. By 1955 it was still the only drive-in in the entire county and just a few miles from the Schullers' humble new home.

It took a long impatient week of wondering, but finally the phone rang. On the other end of the line was Norman Miner, the manager of the drive-in. He had called with an answer to Schuller's inquiry about renting the drive-in. He said Schuller could rent the drive-in for ten dollars each Sunday. It was a price he decided on based on how much it cost to put the union sound technician on the job who would turn on the lights and power for the service and operate the sound system. Norman Miner's heart must have been in the right place; he became a member of the church and a longtime volunteer who taught Bible studies.

Schuller promoted the big day in the paper with an ad describing the service as part of an inspiring new Protestant church and included the first use of his famous slogan "Come as you are in the family car!" The service would be as welcoming as it was well planned, and Schuller decided he'd ask for outside help. He borrowed a choir from a neighboring church, towed an organ he had bought on a budget to the drive-in, and left the sound engineering to the pro. Each car would have its own speaker to hear the sermon and the music. Arvella organized the song list and was the official rooftop organist. It was all set.

But Robert Schuller's drive-in church was not without its critics: with one week until the big day, a member of his own denomination, another minister no less, attacked Schuller as perpetrating an evil and operating a passion pit. It was personal, and it rocked Schuller's confidence to his core.

The next day, Sunday, Schuller was stuck in an emotional turmoil, drenched in self-doubt and insecurity. So, the Schullers decided to attend a church that they had heard good things about and to just enjoy the day.

The sermon was on God's formula for self-confidence and centered on Philippians 1:6: "He who began a good work in you will bring it to completion."

But the preacher emphasized that "God will complete it!" and it ignited Schuller. He was overcome by a deep sense of relief as the doubt washed away, replaced by calm self-assurance. The preacher said the foundation of confidence should be built, not on might, money, or magic, but on the mercy of God. When the Schullers left the church, they drove immediately to a lumber store where they picked up the supplies and wood needed to build the cross that would stand as the rootop focal point at the drive-in.

Schuller began the week as a carpenter and planned to finish the week as pastor of a new church—barring unforeseen problems. There were only a few worries—not the least of which was attendance. He remembered meeting with the theater manager and joking that attendance at the service would be two, including himself and Arvella. But then he wondered seriously about the message it would send if only a few cars sat in the vast parking lot during the sermon. With such fanfare, a choir, and energetic worship, what would it say to the surrounding community when the story appeared in the paper the next day? *Religion in the drive-in was a bust.* So, he called on the borrowed choir director with an unusual request. He asked if it would be okay if each member of the choir could drive their own car. "If there are fifty of you, then there we can count on at least fifty cars being in the lot," he insisted.[6] Schuller got the answer he wanted. The drive-in would not be empty. But as Sunday grew near, there were rare clouds in the sky.

Rain would ruin everything. Schuller pictured Arvella getting soaked while playing the organ. His confidence could be the size of Orange County itself, but he could do nothing about rain. It was a worry so intense that it began to distract him from every other thought—that is, until he got some assurances in the form of what Schuller felt was a directive from God. The message to the new pastor was simple. Focus on the sermon and not on things that are not in Schuller's department. The weather was God's responsibility. So, Schuller accepted that instruction.

On Saturday, March 26, 1955, Schuller picked up the local newspaper. The *Orange County Register* was the paper of record for his new home. The Saturday edition, a day before that all-important first Sunday sermon, Schuller got a dose of both excitement and cautionary reflection in the form of two *Register* articles: one exhilarating, and the other (little did anyone know at the time) prophetic.

He had paid out of his own pocket for an advertisement in hopes of spreading the word about the drive-in church, and he had prayed it would be the start of something big. So, imagine his surprise when he saw a picture of himself, one hand on his hip, and the other gently caressing a sixteen-foot-high crucifix atop the tar-papered snack-bar roof. The caption read: "... with Reverend Schuller in the pulpit. Church goers do not have to get out of their cars. They flick on the loudspeaker and the church is brought to them."[7]

He knew, of course, that the newspaper man and photographer had visited while he set up a few days before, but he had no idea a picture that big would be published or that valuable newspaper-page space would be dedicated to a full nine-paragraph column.

"As cars arrive, they will hear the vibrant tone of organ music pealing through the hundreds of speakers in the field, filling the air," Schuller was quoted in the paper.[8]

He was also thrilled to see that the article included the detail about the Bethel Radio Choir of Long Beach singing on opening day. The free publicity was just what the new drive-in church needed, and what he prayed for to buoy attendance. That article was the first of many that would mention his name over the next six decades. But it was the second article he read that day, the one that did not mention his name, that had a remarkable meaning only fully understood decades later.

Schuller was fascinated with psychology as much as he was with preaching and saw them as not mutually exclusive. Psychology was not at odds with his Christian faith, and it remained part of his life-long education. So, a column from a psychologist about preaching would not have escaped his notice. Not when the very first words of the column were "Bishop Sheen and Dr. Peale typify the clergymen who don't need ecclesiastic crutches to lean upon in order to inspire a congregation."[9]

Theologian and bishop Fulton Sheen was a household name with thirty million viewers to his weekly TV program *Life Is Worth Living*. Minister Dr. Norman Vincent Peale, a nationally renowned speaker, had a runaway bestseller with his 1952 book, *The Power of Positive Thinking*. Bishop Sheen was a Catholic. Peele, like Schuller, was from the Reformed church. They were two irresistible names in bold type, and Schuller would have been hooked.

Case N-378, as Dr. George W. Crane preferred to number "The Worry Clinic" syndicated columns, focused on describing how aging orators can fall into a trap of ineffectual laziness, by relying too much on props and ornate art. His point was that props, art, and flash were used by clergy who had lost their edge as orators.

"We psychologists do not indict the use of art in churches. We don't insist on the austere simplicity of the Quaker meeting house," wrote Crane. "We do, however, recognize that many clergymen grow fat and lazy in their advanced years."[10]

Crane suggested that as virility waned, second-rate orators relied on gimmicks to achieve results. He pointed out that Jesus needed only an unpretentious place to deliver the Sermon on the Mount. Jesus relied, "as Dr. Peale and most of the other virile clergymen, on the power of the spoken word."[11]

"Stand Upright," Cane closed out. "For someday they may be asked to preach out in the open air as Jesus did.... A topnotch clergyman, such as Bishop Sheen or Dr. Norman Vincent Peale, can speak in the open air and soon take an audience to a mountain-top experience where you feel uplifted and so inspired that your face will almost glow as did that of Moses when he saw God atop Mt. Sinai."[12]

For the young and unknown Robert H. Schuller—whose own preaching skill and notoriety would rival that of Peale and Bishop

Sheen, and whose enormous ministry and architectural marvels would embrace the open air like no one else in modern times—the climb to the mountaintop was a giant leap of faith, and it had to begin somewhere.

On Sunday, March 27, 1955, the weather was mostly clear, and the temperature was a perfect seventy degrees at 11:00 a.m. The humble mountaintop was the tar-paper roof of the snack bar at the center of the drive-in complex. The small altar was a plywood-constructed box, four feet by four feet by six feet, and the cross was towering sixteen feet high and bolted to the back of the altar. The cross was adorned with decorative molding. It was all hand-constructed by Schuller. To the right and left, palms filled out the makeshift dais. The choir stood up and sat as needed from folding chairs on the roof. Arvella played the organ, not entirely on the roof, but down a little in the front, her back to the congregation. She wore a black church robe, like a judge's garment, and a hat adorned with a long feather.

As the first of the scheduled hymns faded, Schuller took a deep breath and lifted his hands in the air, palms out as if embracing the gathering of cars. He wore a long black church robe and tie. Fifty bumpers, grills, and a hundred headlights faced him, unlike any audience he had ever addressed. Twenty cars belonged to the choir. Probably a hundred people were in attendance. But he had no eye contact, ten feet above the ground, so he made the gesture big to connect with them and began with a welcoming invocation.

The drive-in churchgoers adjusted the volumes on their speakers. Schuller's voice crackled through as if each had him on a personal radio. There was no survey of who parked that first day to attend. No explanation from where they had come or from how far. They were, as expected, mostly not dressed in any special Sunday attire, not gripping dog-eared Bibles or whispering about big Sunday gatherings. Instead, they were as they had arrived, quietly attending a drive-in church service, in some state of privacy and curiosity and in varying levels of past exposure to Christian teaching. Similarly, there was no scale by which to judge exactly what they got out of that first service or how many would return. Few, if any, had a single notion of what it took for Robert Schuller to post the organ safely near the top of the snack-bar roof, let alone how plans for the entire service came together as they had. And it did not rain.

Schuller had already defied the odds by launching a church service on a shoestring, and only two weeks after arriving in the area. He had been told repeatedly that it was impossible, but there he was. He had come to Orange County with a single lofty hope: to bring the Good News to a spiritual wasteland he had been told so much about. He wanted to reach the "unchurched," and as he faced some of them in the relative anonymity of car-windshield reflections, the word *impossible* flashed through his mind. *Fine*, he may have thought at the time, *I'm prepared for you.*

The sermon focused on Matthew 17:20: "If you have faith as a grain of mustard seed, you will say to this mountain, 'Move from here to there,' and it will move; and nothing will be impossible to you."

Choir member Anne Waltz was looking on from her choir seat. "I knew then that I was in the midst of something very special," she said. "It was an exciting and inspiring time."[13]

The Builder

In Garden Grove, California, quiet evenings in the Schuller household were infrequent, but since moving the Garden Grove Community Church administration out of the house and into a physical church office, some sense of privacy and solitude had finally arrived. Once each week, Robert Schuller and sometimes Arvella would retire to their small living room and turn on the black-and-white television. The show was *Life Is Worth Living*, the lecture program hosted by the Venerable Archbishop Fulton J. Sheen.

Sheen was a Catholic scholar, educator, and orator who started out on radio, and by 1952, just after he was ordained auxiliary bishop of the Archdiocese of New York, he had become a staple on American television. As mentioned previously, his regular weekly audience would reach thirty million viewers—the most ever for such a program in the United States. He was considered the first televangelist and widely regarded as the greatest orator of the twentieth century. None of this was lost on Schuller, who did not have the remotest inkling that television was even a possibility for himself. As he watched, Schuller marveled at Sheen's commanding presence, grand robes, and deep instruction mixed with humor. Schuller wrote of Sheen's influence on him, pointing out the skill with which he "blended the truths of psychology, philosophy and theology" with greater skill and creativity than anyone he had ever seen.[1]

Sheen was known for a lively stage presence and humor that was expressive across the medium, drawing a connection with his audience with a friendly smile just before looking into the camera to make a deep, serious point. His subjects ranged from the true meaning of evil to the Virgin Mary and prayer. Any given week, Schuller was drawn to the study of Fulton's powerful subject matter and monologue. One of those nights, he might have heard Sheen offer an example of prayer of petition. The bishop related a story about how as a young priest he was studying philosophy in New

33

York. He had decided he wanted to mark the fifth anniversary of his ordination by visiting Lourdes, France, and the famous grotto where Bernadette Soubirous said an apparition of the Virgin Mary appeared to her. Sheen's goal was to offer a novena, which is a recitation of prayers and devotions over nine consecutive days. He had enough money to travel there, but not enough money to pay for lodging or get home. He decided to leave that up to God through prayers of petition to Mary.

"If I had faith enough to get to Lourdes to celebrate the fifth anniversary of my ordination, it was up to the Blessed Mother to get me out," he told the audience.[2] That was to say, it was God's help he sought through the love and mercy of the Mother of Jesus.

Sheen went to Lourdes and arrived broke. He found himself a hotel and settled in. By day six, he was still broke, and he had begun to imagine the French police at his door and jail in his future. Without much choice, he stuck it out to complete the novena prayer at the grotto, which totaled nine days. On the ninth and final morning, he went down to the grotto and nothing happened. The ninth day at noon, nothing happened. Then, that evening nothing happened, and it had "gotten serious." Late that night Sheen decided to go to the grotto one more time. At around 10 p.m., he was praying the Rosary when a man tapped him on the shoulder. He wanted to know if Sheen were an American priest and if he could speak French. The answer to both questions was yes. So, the man asked Sheen if he would be willing to travel to Paris with his family and speak French. Sheen agreed. Then the man asked, "Have you paid your hotel bill yet?"

Even if that message were the one broadcast Schuller missed, petition and faith was the story of his church's expansion beyond anything the young minister could have planned. It came together—one prayer and one gift at a time—as if God concealed His goals to protect the results. As Bishop Sheen was fond of pointing out, "The tapestry is woven from the back."

It would not have been an unheard-of act of a loving father to inspire without revealing the tapestry before it is complete. Schuller's own father said it plainly when explaining why he did not tell his son that he had prayed his boy would one day be a preacher. "I never, never, never wanted you to know how I felt. It had to be an honest call from the Lord."[3]

Robert H. Schuller had already proven that he had the faith enough to build a humble outdoor church, and it did not take him long to feel the next steps tugging at him. The drive-in services had struck a chord. Every week there were more cars rolling into the drive-in, hooking up the speakers, and rolling out again—passengers feeling inspired, entertained, or with the satisfaction they had experienced something new and unusual.

Among the first to notice the preacher's success were the owners of a nearby fruit stand who found the road packed with cars on Sundays. The line of cars would seem to be a boon to business, but the family-run fruit stand struggled to see much benefit of a blocked road. On the other hand, the grandson of the owner of that fruit stand found it all very fascinating. With Grandma and Grandpa living right next door to the drive-in and the fruit stand not far away, six-year-old Christopher Smith and his older brother and sister would venture out to watch Schuller preach. Their view was from the line of eucalyptus trees, and they could hear the sermon crackle from the speakers mounted on car windows.

Christopher Smith later recalled, "We saw what we thought was this crazy preacher having church outside, all these cars right in the middle of the day, in the same place where we had watched the movie the night before. We thought, oh my gosh, how cool to have church outside."[4] The Smiths were a Catholic family. For kids, the novelty of going to church in a drive-in did seem exciting. "We used to love going out and watching." Six decades later, Christopher's own faith journey into Christian ministry would intersect with Reverend Robert H. Schuller and the church he built in the most unlikely of ways.

"We used to ask Mom and Dad, 'Why can't we just go to that church where you just stay in your car?' They'd say, 'Don't get any ideas, kids.'"

The line of cars proved little Christopher was not the only one thinking about going to church in a car. Although the rolling congregation expanded, some cars rolled in on Sunday morning and rolled out, never to return. That was what happened with the Jacksons, another Orange County Catholic family. Dad had seen the article about Robert Schuller and the drive-in in the *Orange County Register*. The novelty piqued his interest. Randy Jackson, who was twelve years old in 1955, recalled the excitement of going to a drive-in when a movie was not playing.

"Would they still have popcorn?" he recalled thinking at the time.[5]

Mr. Jackson, the patriarch, was behind the wheel of the family station wagon. It was a bulging, light-blue Ford, with his four sons aboard for the adventure. Little Randy recalled riding in his pajamas and that his mother was not there because she was home with his newborn sister. It was fun, but one time was enough. They never went back.

"Being able to go to church in your pajamas was cool," he said.

Come as you are.

Randy Jackson does not remember much else, but he never forgot his early connection to Robert Schuller as Schuller's ministry and fame grew into a megachurch and a worldwide ministry. Like Christopher Smith, Jackson's path would cross again with Schuller's decades later. That was when Jackson had become a prominent Orange County architect tasked with a critical job related to the restoration of the Crystal Cathedral campus. But that was a long way from the Orange Drive-In—not in distance but in years.

It started with Schuller facing one need at a time, then finding one solution at a time and building one structure at a time. When a congregation grew quickly under normal circumstances, it was exciting to watch the affirmation of the Good News—to see the pews fill, the bright energetic smiles of altered new Christian lives, and the financial support that paid to keep the lights on. It was almost as satisfying as to feel blessed just to spread God's Word to His increasing flock. A congregation grew into its space. That was under normal circumstances.

While it was still very exciting and satisfying, Robert Schuller started with next to nothing, without the luxury of even an office with a phone outside his own home. There was no space to grow into other than parking spaces at the drive-in. Everything else was done in the office at home. For Schuller this "office" was metaphorical, an office that was made up of the living room and the only telephone in the neighborhood. It was twenty-four hours a day. Bible studies, counseling, choir practice—all happened in the Schullers' home. Even for a family passionate about their labor for God, it was a strain. The only solace was in knowing that land had already been prepped for a physical chapel. After just six months, the congregation had grown to the point that it was recognized as an official church. For the California State Charter, Schuller provided the name Garden Grove Community Church. It was intentionally vague to avoid a denominational bias that might discourage the unchurched he was trying to reach.

Three miles west of the drive-in on Chapman Avenue, there was a plot of land that the Reformed church had purchased, two acres that one day would be just fine and give the fledgling congregation something to grow into. When it came time for that next leap of faith, Schuller went to the denominational committee with the idea that he had to hire an architect. The reaction was anything but enthusiastic. Instead of expressing confidence in Schuller, the committee instead focused on the financial burden. Calling an architect frivolous, members insisted that a known local dairy farmer could design and erect a barn in no time.

But Schuller could not forget the advice from an architect friend back in Chicago. He had told Schuller never to compromise on design, that it was art, not money, that should have the last word.

"If you don't have the money, then you're not ready," said the friend.[6]

Schuller was realistic. He knew what the two acres could handle, but a barn? He had always had a keen interest in and love for the great cathedrals scattered across the European continent, although he had only seen them in pictures. Even the beautiful churches he had seen in America were examples of art fitting the glory and honor of God. On the advice of another friend, and without asking the committee permission, Schuller reached out to architect Richard Shelley at the American Institute of Architects. He explained what he was planning to do and made it clear he had no money. But he promised that, whatever the architect charged, Schuller would pay him some day.

The architect accepted, and the design not only pleased Schuller; it was embraced fully by the once-skeptical committee. The architect was paid in full without debate. A quick bank loan put construction underway, and it didn't take long for the new home of Garden Grove Community Church to rise from nothing to become a 250-seat chapel with a stained glass cross as the focal point built into the wall surrounded by stained glass. The cross was as visible outside as it was inside. Just eighteen months after the first drive-in service, the Richard Shelley stained glass chapel was complete. It had stained glass fitting for its purpose on three sides. There was an office, rooms for Bible study, and space for other services, including a dedicated suicide prevention line.

The help line was the church's first full-time missionary service and was formed out of an unexpected tragedy. A mother of three had been battling depression, and when the church office was in the Schuller home, she called a few times in the middle of the night. Each time, Arvella and Robert responded. One time she was found unconscious and near death from an overdose after calling with a plea for help to pick up her children. Although she recovered, it was not long before she called again. The phone rang in an empty house. The Schullers were out of town, and the call went unanswered. Tragically, the woman died. But the legacy of that unfortunate event was the twenty-four-hour suicide hotline, which helped countless others. It was the first outreach ministry of Schuller's church.

Schuller's early successful recruiting efforts were in no small part due to the growing population of Orange County. The postwar years made the area lucrative and affordable. This rising tide boosted other ships as well. For example, the footprint of the Catholic Church in Orange County was small in 1956. The only active parish was St. Boniface, five miles away in Anaheim. St. Boniface had been in continuous operation for nearly one hundred years. It was part of the Archdiocese of Los Angeles, which was in the process of expanding in Orange County, including a new parish in Garden Grove at the corner of Lewis Street and Garden Grove Boulevard. The location was five miles from Schuller in the other direction. For the Archdiocese of Los Angeles, St. Callistus Parish was aimed at meeting the needs of the area's growing Catholic population. Cousins in the Christian church, St. Callistus's and Schuller's ministry were to coexist for decades without much interaction. But their destinies would one day intersect. On that journey, it was Robert H. Schuller who had the head start. His next inspiration cut the physical distance between his ministry and the future location of St. Callistus to just one mile.

The Richard Shelley stained glass chapel was set to be dedicated on September 23, 1956. Amid planning those first services, Schuller looked at the wonderful building on Chapman and Seacrest and was suddenly struck by an obvious flaw he was saddened he had neglected to notice before. He thought of the Grays. They were a married couple who attended the first service at the drive-in and were there every Sunday afterward without fail. At first, Schuller had not met them, because the green Buick would leave just early enough to avoid Schuller's after-service greeting. He knew the regulars by the cars they drove. But that one was always gone moments before the service ended. It made the people in the green car quite mysterious. Eventually, Warren Gray, the driver of the green Buick, called and introduced himself. As it turned out, his wife, Rosie, had been stricken with a serious stroke some time before, and it left her without the ability to walk or speak. The drive-in church had been a lifeline, a miracle in their lives. The couple wanted to be formal church members and Christians, baptized by Schuller. They were.

But now, Schuller was disturbed that the Grays would be left without a church if they could not go to the drive-in. Wheelchairs were just too uncomfortable for Rosie, so the chapel was out of the question. Schuller was heartbroken that it had not occurred to him sooner. So it was decided that as long as the Grays were attending the drive-in service, it would be scheduled every Sunday. Rosie Gray's health was such that it could be weeks or months before she died. No one knew for sure.

Schuller delivered his sermon twice to meet the needs of the growing congregation: one indoors, and one outdoors. With ninety minutes in between, they had enough time to move the choir and the organ to the drive-in and set up. It worked. Sunday after Sunday, attendance grew at the chapel. All 250 seats were filled. At the drive-in, a year on Rosie Gray was still there with the other two hundred worshippers. It was a remarkable spurt of growth and, certainly in the case of Rosie Gray, a miracle. A lot of work paid off, but it was exhausting. Schuller was at once grateful and blessed, while being burdened and overworked. He contemplated just resigning from the chapel and continuing his Sunday sermons outside at the drive-in. Perhaps the other way around.

Just when Schuller stalled at the crossroads the answer hit him: "The message God was trying to get into my thick Dutch head through Rosie, 'Schuller, why not build a walk-in/drive-in church to accommodate both those who can walk in and those who can't?'"[7]

Schuller sketched out the plans himself all the way down to how he would be able to address the people inside and the people in their cars outside all at the same time. He decided it would take ten acres of land and require selling the stained glass chapel and land. It was exciting and risky; Schuller accepted it as a calling and directive from God. But that did not make things easy. Instead, it made life exceedingly difficult—enough to make him wonder if he had not just headed down a path leading away from heaven and not toward it.

While the Schuller family was away on a short camping trip, a church elder hired a young seminary graduate to help Schuller. It was not a move that helped, but rather it divided church leadership when Schuller was trying to forge ahead with the indoor/outdoor church. With the new associate minister, there were rumors, gossip, and negativity about "grandiose" plans. Schuller found himself isolated and questioning everything, even to the point of depression. In Reformed church tradition, Schuller was president of the corporation and chairman of the board, but the associate pastor dismissed him with an eye on taking over. A half year later, the whole thing came to a head with charges by the new associate that Schuller was not preaching the Gospel. He also faced a battle with night terrors to the point that he prayed God would just take him away in the night—until one night when he offered a different prayer with tears streaming from his eyes: "Jesus, if you're really alive, heal me before it's too late. Remove this obsession. Deliver me from my negative thinking. Amen."[8]

Schuller insists he experienced a physical sensation in his head, as if a giant finger inserted and when pulling out took something with it. His anxiety and depression vanished. That sermon he had heard a few years earlier came back to him. He thought of the Scripture:

"He who started a good work in you will carry it on to completion" (Philippians 1:6).

With confidence, Schuller called a church meeting. The associate minister and his allies were there as were the Schuller supporters. Schuller told them he came to Orange County to build one church, and he would not continue to pastor both congregations at separate locations. He offered three options: end the drive-in ministry, divide into two separate ministries, or merge the two churches into a drive-in/walk-in church. He told them he wanted the third choice, the unified church.

Next, Schuller faced a congregational meeting of committee members for a vote. It was there he rolled out the complete plan, including the all-glass sanctuary concept and the wall that opens to the parking lot. The skeptics wondered where the land and construction money would come from.

"I'm not concerned about money," he told them. "Our job is to create an expanding vision and have a dream that's great enough for God to work a miracle. God's job is to create that miracle—including whatever is needed to make it become a reality!"[9]

It took Dr. Wilfred Landrus, a Chapman College professor, to bring the ensuing chaotic and heated debate back to order with a motion to approve further study of integration and property acquisition.

Robert and Arvella Schuller shared a smile as the vote began. Robert Schuller quietly prayed. The motion carried: fifty-five to forty-eight.

Eventually, Schuller found ten acres—a plot of land that was perfect but not for sale. With prayer and faith that "God can move mountains," he visited the widow who owned the land, and she graciously agreed to sell. Surely, it was God's plan. But when it came time to sign the agreement, the widow said she had changed her mind. That quickly, Schuller was back at square one.

The ups and downs led Schuller to a place where he realized he was operating with his goals askew from what he had been professing. The words "I will build my church" struck him once again, and he was forced to admit to himself that he was building Schuller's church, not God's church. From that moment on, he gave himself over to God as the servant, and it was God, not Robert Schuller, who was in charge. At the next board meeting, the chairman's chair was left empty for the real "President of the Congregation and Chairman of the Board—Jesus Christ."[10]

Shortly thereafter, a real estate agent friend phoned Schuller about some land. It was ten acres of Orange orchard in the sticks three miles east of the stained glass chapel. The price was right.

At $66,000, it was half what the other property would have cost. Unknown to Schuller and the real estate agent, those sticks were about to be smack dab in the middle of a bustling Orange County at the confluence of several new freeways and just a few miles from Disneyland. The future-prized real estate in the county just fell in his lap at a bargain, and the real value of the location was not even imaginable at the time.

Schuller called it the brilliant leadership of Jesus Christ.

Skeptics saw the property as worthless, out in the middle of nowhere, and money was tight. But Warren and Rosie Gray believed. They gave the $2,000 required to open escrow. Schuller needed $18,000 more for the down payment and had just six months to meet that goal. While finding the money seemed next to impossible, a newspaper article cut the odds a little more. Reports of a new freeway rolling through the area had land prices skyrocketing. If Schuller failed to get the full amount, the property owner would double the price or more.

Six months later, on the day escrow was set to close, Schuller and his church were $3,000 short. With the clock ticking, the Grays, Rosie (who had already defied so many odds) and Warren, who was terminally ill with cancer, made another contribution for the balance.

Schuller wrote the $18,000 check, and the land belonged to the church. The joy of getting the land turned into the uncertainty of finding the $400 a month to pay the mortgage. That was quickly remedied when out of the blue the Sunday offering included a $100 check. That continued week after week. Schuller reached out to the family he did not know anything about and found that the family had begun attending church at the drive-in. Vern Dragt had had a stroke and was unable to work. His wife, Lavon, had to find a way to support him and the three kids. She found Tupperware and parlayed that into a successful business, among the most successful in the company's history. The $100 checks represented a grateful 10 percent tithe. The Dragt's $400 a month paid the mortgage.

And so, it went.

The *Hour of Power*

Architect Richard Shelly saw the sketches Schuller had in mind for construction at the new ten-acre site and immediately demurred—not because he did not like what Schuller wanted or some other disagreement, but because he believed there was another architect better suited for such a task as a glass building. He recommended Richard Neutra, a Los Angeles architect, renowned for glass structures. Neutra had a reputation for marrying design with nature and creating a harmony he called "biorealism."[1] He described it as "the inherent and inseparable relationship between man and nature."[2]

Neutra was already known the architecture world over and had been on the cover of *Time* magazine, so he was probably surprised at Schuller's approach when the pair first met in 1958. Schuller asked Neutra why he should hire him. When Schuller conveyed the story later, he did so with a tone of embarrassment. He wished he could have stopped the words as they were leaving his mouth. It did not seem to bother Neutra. It was the start of a long friendship that would last until Neutra's death in 1970. In that time, Neutra designed several ministry buildings. Unlike the stained glass chapel, none of the designs would have stained glass. It was a revelation that stunned Schuller. But the reason made Schuller even more certain he had found the right architect. Stained glass, to Neutra, ran contrary to biorealism.

For the next couple of years, smaller Neutra buildings went up according to budget. The first structures on that humble ten acres were the single-story large and small galleries that featured large sliding-glass doors or, more accurately, walls. The larger of the two was where Schuller held services. He used a platform to address those inside and those still preferring to listen from their cars. The glass doors looked across a reflecting pool toward the parking lot.

After three years of fundraising, it was time to build Schuller's first ever walk-in/drive-in church. Neutra drew up his design based on one that Schuller had crafted. It was dedicated November 6, 1961, as the Neutra Sanctuary and later renamed the Neutra Arboretum. It featured hundreds of individually framed panes of glass stacked and offset along the half-block-long walls. To the east, the parking lot had room for hundreds of cars. At a push of a button, Schuller released the motorized mechanism to pull back the 24' × 24' section of wall revealing his elevated pulpit to the congregation outside in the cars. At the same time, he could address the people inside. The exterior wall next to his elevated indoor/outdoor pulpit was a bright orange square—visible from a mile away, one could guess. It was the building's only shock of color. Inside, the room shimmered as sunlight reflected in the fountain pool that, like the windows, ran the length of the eastern façade. On opening day, the fountains, called the 12 Apostles, spouted, and there was no mistaking the scent of gardenia in the air. Dr. Norman Vincent Peale was the guest speaker for the dedication. Eventually, regular Sunday attendance reached two thousand.

A few years later, the Neutra-designed Tower of Hope was dedicated. It was designed by Richard Neutra and his son Dion. Because of its style and Eastern European influence, some circles in the architecture world believe it was more Dion Neutra than Richard. The elder Neutra was in his midseventies at the time. Later, a Neutra historian would downplay that theory. The building had thirteen stories and was the tallest building in Orange County, at least for a while—primarily due to the massive ninety-foot neon cross extending toward the heavens from the rooftop. At the top of the building was the chapel in the sky. With eight long pews, a tall cross, podium, and organ, it instantly became a unique and inspiring sanctuary with 360-degree views. Robert Schuller's office and study were on the twelfth floor. The twenty-four-hour suicide prevention hotline office was also relocated to the Tower of Hope.

The Neutra Sanctuary was filling up every Sunday, and times were very good for preaching the Gospel with the power of positive thinking—this despite the Vietnam War and much political unrest in the United States. It was the same for Billy Graham. There was a lot of hunger for the Word of God amid so much turmoil, and Graham filled stadiums around the country for his popular crusades.

When Graham set a date for Orange County's Angel Stadium, Robert Schuller served on a committee to help. That assignment had lasted a year, and the event did not disappoint. While visiting California, Graham saw what Schuller had built at the Garden Grove Community Church. He also noted that the Neutra Sanctuary was stunning enough to make a good picture on TV. But the production cost per year of $400,000 was enough to take Schuller's breath away. Graham suggested that Schuller let God decide. Schuller could make a onetime Sunday appeal for pledges equal to half the production budget. If the congregation liked the idea and pledged, it would be the sign Schuller needed to pursue a TV broadcast.

The *Hour of Power*, a name suggested by Graham, went on the air on February 8, 1970, at TV station KTLA. In five years, it was on stations in all fifty states. Schuller's oratory notwithstanding, guest speakers for the *Hour of Power* added variety. Norman Vincent Peale made several guest sermons, as did Billy Graham and Catholic bishop Fulton Sheen. The congregation began to burst at the seams. It was time to expand, whether Schuller wanted to or not. At least they had the land. More than thirty contiguous acres now belonged to the ministry. None of the ministry's progress, expanding campus, influence, and reach came easy. The next project, Schuller's crowning architectural achievement, made the rest pale in comparison.

By the mid-1970s, the Crystal Cathedral was a noble idea, but like many, it was harder won than Schuller had imagined. Despite early enthusiasm by the ministry's consistory, it was a process that began with fits and starts. The television audience improved fundraising for the ministry, but calls for support of a new sanctuary went poorly. The effort to lock down the right architect was even more difficult. Schuller had sunken into a midcareer crisis of sorts, and when the ministry abandoned plans for the new church, he was relieved—until he got another nudge.

The drawback of a Neutra-designed indoor/outdoor church was the elements. It was married to nature, iconic in its own right, but a little too close to nature for some, including the cold, heat, and rain, even in the perfect weather of Southern California. Unlike the drive-in, the Neutra Sanctuary at least protected the people inside. Those in cars had it okay too. But when the church was full and overflow seating was in folding chairs outside on the lawn, there was no escape from the weather when it had gone awry.

One Sunday morning, Schuller began his sermon with a chill in the air, followed by rain. He watched a couple sitting outside. When the cold and rain got to them, which was not long, they got up and left. Schuller decided that he must work to build a church that would always have space inside. But there was still no acceptable architect who could handle the outrageous request Schuller had in mind.

At the behest of his wife, Schuller read an article highlighting ten notable places in America that included the Fort Worth Water Gardens, designed by Philip Johnson. Arvella was right. Johnson was the kind of architect who would be able to complement Richard Neutra's biorealism because he had a thing for glass and landscape. Schuller flew to New York to meet Johnson.

Schuller explained to the renowned architect that he was looking to build a church to seat three thousand, and it had to be all glass while being married to nature. It had to fit in with Neutra's designs. Johnson, who had been interested until he heard the words *all glass*, questioned the wisdom of such a design in an earthquake zone. Johnson said it was impossible. In response, Schuller suggested Johnson could find a way if he would just go out and find some smart engineers. Johnson wanted to know the budget. Schuller said there was not one. His ministry had no money and would rely on a loan to pay for the Philip Johnson and Associates design. It was the design that had to inspire the congregation to donate, so a lot was riding on the decision. It would take a $200,000 loan, but would the donations really follow?

The first design, three weeks later, had a glass ceiling, but the walls were solid. Schuller sent him back to try again. Johnson's design was thoughtful, given the church setting, and he figured there was a need for privacy. But that was not what Schuller had in mind. What he wanted was a glass ceiling to express a limitlessness upward and glass walls so the congregation could see the outside world. Johnson was up for the challenge.

Later, Johnson flew to California, this time with a model. The shape and the functionality inspired Schuller to declare it must be built. But the cost, which seemed to be of no object at first, became very nearly the only object.

To get it started, Schuller and the ministry board prayed for God to lead them to a million-dollar donor. They did not realize at the time how much more they would need. The initial estimate for building the Crystal Cathedral came in at $7 million. Schuller knew that was going to make him the target of criticism. But he prayed and put it in God's hands. If it was His will, then Schuller would weather the storm.

At a time when he was struggling just to pay the design loan of $200,000, it seemed like a high hill to climb. He returned to the ministry consistory to discuss options. The bank would only lend $4 million. That was not even close. One member suggested a bond sale. But Schuller worried that would break the budget down the road. Turning that possible solution away meant raising the money himself.

Schuller eventually reached out to a well-known Orange County philanthropist, John Crean. A few days after declining to help because he just could not, Crean called Schuller and committed to providing the lead-off gift of $1 million. It was Maundy Thursday, the day before Good Friday. That donation came in the form of stock. Afterward, beaming with certainty that the Lord will provide, Schuller added a basement to the cathedral design. It added fifty-four thousand square feet of space and pushed the price tag to $10 million.

Schuller went on getting financial commitments everywhere he could. He put up memorial-naming options for each of the ten thousand panes of glass. At $500 each, it promised to equal five million dollars.

Schuller dodged another disaster when environmental regulations in California were set to change, barring construction of buildings with more than 50 percent glass walls. He squeaked in permit approval at the deadline. It was not the worst of his problems.

The personal tragedy of nearly losing his daughter in a motorcycle accident had put a new complicated strain on Schuller. Thirteen-year-old Carol Schuller was lucky to have survived, but she lost a leg. Even chronic optimism is a casualty when a reality like that weighs on a person. The recovery took months, but his daughter's optimistic view that God still had a plan for her life inspired Robert Schuller. Eventually, he accepted the situation and turned his focus to the pressing question of the Crystal Cathedral.

In an act that both baffles and intrigues, Schuller boarded a plane for Rome. The trip and his visit to the Vatican were not all that unusual for a man who was well traveled and had a proven affinity for classic cathedral architecture. Rather, it was the why and what he brought with him that became part of the cathedral's legacy. Schuller was determined to meet Pope John Paul II. Perhaps it was Possibility Thinking, or just ignorance of how difficult that would be, but he entered the Vatican with drawings of the Crystal Cathedral under his arm. As should have been expected, he was denied access. Or more accurately, he was actively thwarted. True to form, Schuller was undaunted, and there was more to that story, as a meeting was meant to be. The visit to the Vatican buoyed him forward as construction got underway for the Crystal Cathedral.

Schuller's Crystal Cathedral was completed and dedicated in 1980. It boasted twenty-eight hundred seats, and the organ, always important to Robert and Arvella Schuller on Sundays, was magnificent. The Hazel Wright Organ was designed to reach the congregants in their cars in the parking lot. Consider for a moment that "Hazel," the fifth largest organ in the world, may not have existed at all if the original plan had been followed. There was already an exceptional pipe organ in the original sanctuary. It was built by Padua, Italy's Ruffatti Brothers in 1970, and installed in the summer of 1977 with a great deal of pride. That was at a time when the Crystal Cathedral was in the planning stages. The all-glass cathedral, as it was imagined, would be a perfect home for the large five manual organ and its pipes. A manual represented a single keyboard, so when two keyboards were typical, five was very grand and exquisite. But would it be grand and exquisite enough, or more importantly, fill a space so much larger and with a ceiling 190-feet high?

The answer was apparently no.

It just so happened that a famed pipe organ known as the 1966 Aeolian-Skinner at the Philharmonic Hall in New York was set to be removed. The ministry bought it. But it was still not quite right until Arvella (the consummate music master of the ministry), master organist Virgil Fox, and Crystal Cathedral architect Philip Johnson finalized an ambitious plan to expand and modify the pipe organ to be built by Piero Ruffatti. The result was stunning. Envision the purchased Aeolian-Skinner organ's ninety-seven rows of staggered pipes called ranks, combined with the Ruffatti organ, and installed to a total of 197 ranks. Later modification would put that number at 270 ranks and sixteen thousand pipes. The smallest were the size of a whistle and the largest were thirty-two feet long. It was made possible by a longtime *Hour of Power* viewer in Chicago. Hazel Wright's $2 million gift was so generous that the organ received her name and a tribute. Piero Ruffatti was not done with what was the crowning jewel of the work of the Ruffatti Brothers, and neither were the craftsmen back in Padua. But that was decades to come down an unforeseen road.

Two massive ninety-foot sections of the glass façade opened to reveal the organ and the pulpit equipped to address those indoors and outdoors. It was all done at the push of a button by Schuller's hand. Soon, the Crystal Cathedral became synonymous with the *Hour of Power* international Sunday morning broadcast. Visitors from all over the world speaking dozens of languages visited the campus, bookstore, and the grand glass church daily. The ministry changed its name from Garden Grove Community Church to Crystal Cathedral Ministries, and in the decade that followed, donations skyrocketed. The cathedral, campus, reflecting pools, and statuary were remarkable, but Reverend Robert H. Schuller's positive Christian ministry was the cornerstone.

Immediately after the completion of the Crystal Cathedral, Schuller expanded again, this time into what he called the healing ministry. Donna and John Crean donated ninety-two acres of pristine real estate in San Juan Capistrano to Schuller for the purposes of building a retreat center. By 1989, Crystal Cathedral Ministries expanded it to 169 acres with the purchase of the neighboring Bathgate Ranch, which was 77 acres. The price was rumored to be $5 million, and the ministry reportedly considered a cemetery and a retirement home for the new acreage. The Creans had originally given the property to the Jesuits for a retreat center, but that plan fell through.

Schuller's oratory grew the ministry right from the start at the drive-in. His commanding presence and personal ability to communicate in person made him a force for fundraising. And fundraising was always necessary for achieving Schuller's goals. He was not fond of borrowing money and used his skills to generate the funds needed to expand with the goal of paying for it in full. Often, as it was with the stained glass chapel, it was at the last minute that the money came through—without a moment to spare.

Public-speaking appearances outside of the *Hour of Power* were very common for Schuller, but in the 1990s he relished a special opportunity to address the American Institutes of Architecture (AIA). Schuller's reputation with respect for architecture and his close friendship and work with Richard Neutra made him a popular choice, and it was a well-attended speech. Among those attendees who were very interested was the young design architect Jim Wirick from Pasadena, California. A few years earlier, when the Crystal Cathedral had first been built, he had made it a point to go to the campus and see the structural marvel. Wirick was impressed with Schuller, and he was not alone.

"He was talking to a lot of people who didn't have faith," Wirick recalled. "In the end, he got a standing ovation. Which, for architects, is not an easy thing to do."[3]

Schuller's relationship with the AIA would continue, including his time as the only non-architect to have ever sat on the AIA national board. Wirick was destined to become intimately familiar with Schuller and particularly Richard Neutra's buildings one day. By then there would be a lot more to look at on the sprawling campus.

The friendship between Philip Johnson and Robert Schuller only strengthened throughout the process of building the Crystal Cathedral. It was an unlikely closeness, given Johnson's very public identity as an avowed atheist and Schuller's international status as a Christian minister. The spiritual nature of the relationship and the softening of Johnson's heart became evident during a walk with Schuller after construction of the shimmering bell tower.

The plan for the bell tower carillon was to complete the vision Schuller had with the cathedral at the outset. It was the final touch and Johnson's last project for Schuller. Instead of glass it would be stainless steel, but at the same time it would complement the cathedral glass. It would reach 236 feet high, contain a set of 52 bronze bells, and house a small, circular meditation chapel at its base. As expected, Johnson's design delivered the harmony, brilliance, and innovation for which Schuller prayed.

On the morning of the dedication of the carillon, Philip Johnson saw the completed fourteen-story mirrored spire for the first time. It was during a walk with Schuller under a blue Orange County sky when Johnson was moved by the rising sun and trees and sky reflected around them. They walked together around the campus and through the garden as the sun climbed on the horizon. Every minute, the colors and light around them changed. The men were left without words as they stopped to view the spire. Schuller once wrote about the experience and described that Johnson's eyes became misty.

Later that morning, during the grand dedication ceremony, Johnson told the assembled crowd and the Hour of Power international television audience that he did not create the design alone.

"I have to confess," said Johnson. "Confess to the sin of arrogance. Cured this morning by an act of faith. My arrogance was that I thought I knew lots of things about how to build buildings and what they would look like when you built them. In designing the tower, I thought I knew about stainless steel. I thought I knew about the wonderous techniques that had never been used before. I thought I knew history. I thought I knew what the gothic spires of old stood for.... I thought I knew how to combine these things to create a great tower. I was wrong. I could not have done this, and I have to say it humbly, I don't ever feel humbly, but I do this morning."[4]

Johnson turned to Schuller and smiled.

"I got help, my friend," he continued and looked back at the crowd. His voice cracked. "I think you all know where that help came from. Thank you, Bob."[5]

Johnson biographers have noted that Johnson later dismissed the comments. But for Schuller, and many in the congregation, it was another sign of the hand of God working miracles and the Holy Spirit moving hearts.

Schuller then added the school building and the International Center for Possibility Thinking, which was commonly called the visitors' center, designed by Richard Meier. The new buildings completed the thirty-four-acre campus. The Memorial Gardens, sunken down below street level for peaceful isolation from the traffic on surrounding roads, rounded out Schuller's vision.

Reverend Robert H. Schuller lived to see his life's work and unprecedented evangelical success build a virtual empire on television, which spawned countless, though fierier and Pentecostal, imitators. He had written more than thirty books. Robert and Arvella had raised five children who had grown to work in the ministry. Sheila Schuller (Coleman), Robert A. Schuller, Jeanne Schuller (Dunn), Carol Schuller (Milner), and Gretchen Schuller (Penner) were born in that order.

Robert H. Schuller's renown for oratory and message of living a Christian life through positive thought and action led him to the speaker's circuit, where he made much of the money he and his wife lived on. In 2006, at eighty years old, health and time finally scuttled Schuller's boundless energy, and he retired from full-time ministry. He passed the keys to the Crystal Cathedral and the Head Pastor's gold medallion to his only son, Robert A. Schuller, who was in his early fifties. The transition did not go well, and whether it was a product of failed management by the younger Schuller or, as some reports suggested, a family feud, Robert A. Schuller was voted out, replaced by his older sister, Sheila Schuller Coleman.

To pinpoint exactly when the ministry began to unravel financially would take a close examination of the ministry's books, an interview with its accounting firm, and a careful study of the timeline. Barring the first two requirements, one must rely on news reports and public statements to craft a timeline.

By the time the ministry filed for bankruptcy in 2010, it had struggled financially for the better part of the previous four years, which put the beginning in 2006. There was a significant drop in revenues from the *Hour of Power*, and it started before the Great Recession. Financial mismanagement and continued spending on popular but expensive holiday pageants shouldered part of the blame. When there was more money going out than coming in and spending cuts and layoffs could not ease the flow of red ink, bankruptcy was only a matter of time.

Orange County bankruptcy attorney Craig Barbarosh told the *Orange County Register* at the time that Crystal Cathedral Ministry's troubles were not unique. "Churches and synagogues rely on membership fees and donations," he said. "With the tough economy, their cash flow has suffered significantly, leading to increased foreclosures and bankruptcy filings."[6]

The ministry started the year 2010 with an estimated $55 million budget deficit. The red ink spilled across the ministry's balance sheets faster than the budget knife could cut.

In a true sign of financial desperation, the ministry gave up the entire 169-acre retreat in San Juan Capistrano to pay its bills. Crystal Cathedral Ministries sold the property to Hobby Lobby Stores, which then leased it to Rick Warren's Saddleback Church. Hobby

Lobby donated the property to Warren's ministry the following year. Rancho Capistrano Retreat Center continued John Crean's original intent of the donation. He had grown fond of spiritual retreats for improved prayer and personal peace and wanted the land used for that purpose.

The recession, which spared little in the American economy, had taken its toll on Robert H. Schuller's legacy, and without the charismatic orator at the helm, church attendance dwindled. For quite some time, the real revenue stream for the church had been the *Hour of Power* TV program. But to save cash, the ministry ended its buys on seven stations. Revenue was reportedly down 27 percent since the recession began. By October of the same year, despite slashing payroll, cutting staff and cancelling plans for future major productions, Senior Pastor Sheila Schuller Coleman finally had to face the inevitable.

Acting on the guidance of the board and advice from lawyers, Crystal Cathedral Ministries filed for Chapter 11 bankruptcy. In the place where for decades the idea of proclaiming the Good News under the open sky was fulfilled every Sunday, the sky was gray and overcast. Schuller Coleman stood alongside brother-in-law and *Hour of Power* executive producer Jim Penner, in front of a microphone stand with mic-flags from the major local broadcast stations, to formally announce that court filings had been submitted.

"Budgets could not be cut fast enough to keep up with the unprecedented rapid decline in revenue due to the recession," she said. "Our ministry will continue as it has," she insisted.[7]

"We want to pay our vendors back," said Penner.[8]

The bankruptcy was a shock to Robert H. and Arvella Schuller, said grandson Bobby V. Schuller. "The way they heard about the bankruptcy was from the *LA Times*," said Schuller, "on their porch the next morning after it happened."[9]

A week later, the ousted pastor and son of the founder reacted to the announcement. He said he believed the ministry was sincere when it said it intended to pay creditors back in full.

"It's my prayer that they will be able to do that," said Robert A. Schuller. But he disagreed that it was entirely about the recession. He said a donation-driven ministry needed to change with the times. "The media has changed since the 1970s.... There needs to be a new financial model that has to be commercially based. Just like any for-profit network you see on television."[10] And that's what he said he was doing in his own new venture.

But Sheila Schuller Coleman focused on creditors for the reason the ministry filed Chapter 11. Court filings directly identified $7.5 million in unsecured creditors. That was on top of more than $30 million in mortgage. After six months of negotiation with a creditors group, several creditors filed a civil suit. Leading the legal efforts was a group owed payments related to the beloved but costly *Glory of Christmas*.

The national media, from the *Washington Post* to the *New York Times* and others, preferred to focus on the details that played up controversies and inner family turmoil. The collapse of the nationally recognized ministry made for good copy. In the ensuing months, stories in the *LA Times*, *OC Register*, and ABC7 News got picked up only if there was dirt to dish. Often relying on legitimate complaints and concerns by some disaffected longtime church members, there was plenty to feed circulation.

Around Orange County, the events of 2010 unfolded in a combination of rumor, heartbreak, and just plain grief over the thought that such a powerhouse could tumble in this way. Through the collapse, the aging frailty of Robert and Arvella Schuller became increasingly metaphorical as if the era was grinding to a halt with public spectacle and tragedy. There were prayers, too, and hopes for another miracle.

But the tapestry is woven from the back. The bleak picture conjured up images of condos replacing the Crystal Cathedral campus. Could something born out of the heartbreak of one small family and a sad end to a great ministry rise again to preserve the legacy of the Crystal Cathedral and become a place for Christ forever?

Chapman University

Orange County's marquee attraction, Disneyland theme park, held its grand opening as Reverend Robert H. Schuller gained his footing at the drive-in theater in the mid-1950s. At the same time, fifty miles northwest, plans were set to move a growing college from Los Angeles to a place more fitting of its name. Chapman University had its roots in the Northern California town of Woodland near Sacramento. It was founded in 1861 as Hesperian College by Disciples of Christ Christian Church. For the next few decades, the college moved around Northern California and changed its name to other variants containing the word *Christian* before finally landing in Los Angeles under the name California Christian College.

When the Great Depression choked the college's resources as it had for most everyone in America, Valencia orange magnate Charles C. Chapman funded its essentials to continue operations. Charles Chapman was the city of Fullerton's first mayor, but best known for building Orange County's citrus industry. His support was so important to the school that it repaid the debt by changing its name one last time, this time to Chapman College. Chapman died a decade later at age ninety-one.

The legacy of the name Chapman took on new meaning when, in 1957, Chapman College moved to the city of Orange, not far from where Schuller would one day build the Crystal Cathedral campus on Chapman Avenue. The name Chapman, already ubiquitous in Orange County, was destined to reach new heights with one of the region's most prestigious universities.

Dr. James L. Doti was a Chapman economics professor when he became the president of Chapman College in 1991. That was when it ceased being Chapman College and became Chapman University. Considering the drama that was to play out with the Crystal Cathedral, coincidentally one of Doti's first acts as president was to stop construction of an all-glass office building that had been a contentious project of his predecessor. It was seen as a grossly designed behemoth.

"A lot of CEOs or leaders of organizations lose sight of what their central job is," Doti said. "These fights and battles distract you—and you can't be distracted. The job is too important."[1]

Before moving to California, Doti had grown up in a suburb of Chicago, part of a middle-class family. His parents emigrated from Italy. Like so many immigrants of the time, neither of his parents had graduated from high school. His father sold shoes for a living. To that experience and sacrifice to come to America, the Doti house placed a high priority on education.

In high school, he enjoyed sports, and though he wasn't top tier, he lettered in tennis and played some baseball. It was a very different story when it came to numbers. Initially he wanted to be an accountant, but math led him to pursue an economics degree. Doti attended the University of Illinois on a scholarship for undergraduate studies, but it didn't pay for everything. To support himself, he worked at Brach's candy company in Chicago as a bookkeeper. A paper he wrote on sales forecasting for Brach's in his econometrics class landed him a promotion and an office. He went on to earn a doctorate in economics from the University of Chicago. He also earned a PhD in science.

Dr. James Doti took a teaching job at Chapman College in 1974 and moved to Orange County. The campus was three miles west of Schuller's growing ministry by way of Chapman Avenue. When Doti arrived, there was no Crystal Cathedral—only a keen understanding that the worldwide ministry of the *Hour of Power* was right next door and Robert H. Schuller had a lot of pull in town. It was also a fact that despite Christian roots, Chapman College had entirely transformed into a secular institution with only a historical association to the Christian faith.

Doti married Chapman College economics professor Lynn Pearson and later served as a dean before taking over as president. That job came at a time when Chapman was still a small decent school but without a formidable reputation, the kind that attracts the best and brightest students. Many Chapman students were unable to finish studies, and for those who did, it was more like a junior college. They would attend for two years and then get their degree at USC. The college prided itself on diversity and the willingness to accept anyone. Academic qualification among applicants was not a priority. The low graduation rate was in part due to that screening process. Doti set out for the school to remain a welcoming diverse campus, but also set out to increase academic requirements to enroll. It meant enrolling fewer students at first, but he expected that to change.

As a result of the university's lackluster status, and not a single graduate program, the university didn't attract motivated donors to grow the endowment needed to expand scholarships and expand the campus and its programs. In this, Doti excelled. In his first decade in the post, he raised $100 million and boosted the university's profile as well as prestige. Fundraising to support and grow the school was as important to Doti as a matter of necessity as it was for Robert H. Schuller's Crystal Cathedral Ministries and the Catholic Diocese of Orange. Between them tens of millions of dollars were raised in the greater Southern California region, often from Orange County and sometimes from the same philanthropic resources. The result was the expansion of educational opportunities, charities, and services for the distressed and needy, as well as a boon to construction companies. Eventually, at one hundred acres, there was no greater footprint of expansion than Chapman University.

One of the keys to expansion was the lucrative tool of building names. All over Chapman's campus the buildings bore the names of donors. At one point the cost of such an honor was a gift of $10 million or more. There were dozens of buildings. As the school's academic rankings climbed, so did the endowment. The school saw the edition of programs, from law to film, and the school's football program was brought back.

Doti's success was rewarded with a salary of $900,000 annually plus bonuses. His laudable achievements became evident early on in his tenure, and the buzz surrounding the college's emerging status reached Reverend Schuller. An invitation to lunch at the ministry's Tower of Hope soon followed. In Schuller's study, the marvelous twelfth-floor views were only dwarfed by the surreal nature of sitting across the table from a globally prominent community and religious leader. Doti was used to meeting people who had public personas. Schuller showed an interest in Doti's vision for Chapman

University and the possibilities of a collaboration one day between the school and the ministry.

"I got to know him," said Doti, who is not a religious person. "As Chapman grew and as the Crystal Cathedral grew, and then Horatio Alger, we would see each other from time to time." Doti and Schuller were members of the Horatio Alger Association of Distinguished Americans. It was an organization for people who had risen from humble beginnings to successful careers. "We were never particularly close, but there was mutual respect for each other. I certainly admired him and what he had done."[2]

The last meeting between Doti and Schuller took place not long after Doti and his wife donated a sculpture to the school. It had won a Lorenzo il Magnifico de Medici Medal in Italy. The Orange County artist was Nicholas Hernandez. The statue was placed at the entrance to the Hashinger Science Center on campus. The inscription was a quote from Carl Von Clausewitz, a Prussian general who penned what many regarded as the definitive book on warfare aptly named *On War*: "If the mind is to emerge unscathed from this relentless struggle with the unforeseen, two qualities are indispensable: first, an intellect that, even in the darkest hour, retains some glimmerings of the inner light which leads to truth; and second, the courage to follow this faint light wherever it may lead."[3]

Whether it was inner light, or a shimmering reflection off the Crystal Cathedral's eighteen-story spire, there was a tinge of Possibility Thinking when James Doti heard about the unfortunate circumstances surrounding the Crystal Cathedral Ministry's bankruptcy.

Chapman University was in the midst of transformation from a small liberal arts college to a strong comprehensive university, so the larger property transactions in Orange County were always of interest. Doti had been looking at ways to expand health sciences. Specifically, the university sought space for a pharmacy school, which was under development, and eventually a physician's assistant program and a medical school.

"All of that involves a lot of space, which we didn't have," said Doti. "I wouldn't be able to go to the board and say, 'Let's have a pharmacy school.' Where are you going to get the space?" He said that expansion on campus crowded out undergraduate studies, so "that's why I started looking at other potential sites."

What Doti had in mind was something like the campus of Keck Medicine of USC, which was a separate campus from the university proper.

"I thought if they can do it, we can do it," said Doti.

Then there was the Crystal Cathedral campus with all of its buildings and acreage, but buying it wasn't on his radar until he was approached by a friend.

Sherwood Oklejas (Oh-klee-us) was the father of a graduating Chapman University senior and had been a member of the Crystal Cathedral congregation since 1984. Robert H. Schuller performed the vows at his wedding.

"Probably the best thousand dollars that I ever spent," said Oklejas.[4]

He recalled what Schuller had told him. "You're really lucky that I'm your minister today because if ever anything goes wrong, you can come and see me, and I'll make it right."

Oklejas had noticed something had gone wrong. It was undeniable. The once great Crystal Cathedral Ministry had soured, finances had collapsed, and it had come down to bankruptcy. The problem was that the man who promised Oklejas he would "make it right" had struggled behind the scenes to even steady the ship as it began to sink.

Oklejas told Doti what was happening at the ministry. It was the first Doti had heard of the bankruptcy, which was only recently filed.

It did not shock James Doti. Despite his own well-established fundraising prowess, he knew the Great Recession had not done anyone any favors. The respected economist also understood that Robert H. Schuller's retirement from daily duties at the ministry, four years earlier, meant the loss of the face and voice of the ministry. Doti also noted how the ministry had slowly liquidated excess property assets, which was always a sign of trouble.

"I asked President Doti," said Oklejas, "if he would consider being involved with the Crystal Cathedral." He was alluding to the potential purchase or other financial support of the ministry.

"Oh really?" Doti recalled his response. He was no stranger to land acquisitions. Up to that point he had already shepherded the expansion of Chapman in the city of Orange from forty acres to seventy acres. He quickly made some calculations in his head. But one thing held him up.

"I did not want to be perceived as a vulture on the deal," Doti recalled of the conversation. "Difficult not to; in any bankruptcy court, that's what it ultimately ends up being. Trying to get a good deal and pick up the scraps of something that had failed."

The value of the Crystal Cathedral land alone was such that real estate speculators of every stripe immediately took note of the bankruptcy filing the moment news hit the papers. Bankruptcies were regularly mined for their fire-sale bargains. But there was risk, and when numbers reached a certain point, it was a game for the financially well-heeled alone. The way to survive in that group if one was not well-heeled was to be motivated by something other than profits and have access to the well-heeled who believed in the cause.

In bankruptcy court, Oklejas relayed the part of the conversation where Doti expressed his concerns. "He says, 'You can work on that yourself if you like, and I'll appoint a subcommittee to work with you. However, you must make sure that we aren't one of the vultures that is waiting for the bones to be picked. All the creditors must be paid, and the congregation has to go on. If you can do something along those lines, Chapman will do what they can.'"

Dr. Doti was practical. As he consulted and researched and jotted down notes, he concluded that the Crystal Cathedral itself might make a useful venue for the performing arts, but it was not a high priority. He was not sure if the university really needed it. It was a wild card of sorts.

"One thing I was hoping to do is we buy the campus," he said, "carve out the Crystal Cathedral, and sell it to the congregation in some long-term buyback." In hindsight, Doti admits he did not know just how weak the ministry was at the time and that its ability to buy back the church was virtually nonexistent. But it made sense to make it part of the offer. What Doti focused on was classroom and office space.

The Crystal Cathedral campus offered that possibility and at a price that was affordable—a bargain to be sure, but still a lot of money for the university. Oklejas told Doti that he figured the price was around $35 million, maybe as high as $40 million. Most of that was what was owed at the time to Farmers and Merchants Bank. Doti was intrigued. He knew about the architecture on that campus—notably, the Crystal Cathedral and the Neutra buildings. As a fan of architecture himself, Doti knew all about Richard Neutra. The school buildings and the welcome center offered immediate practical use. The cathedral itself might fill the need of a performing-arts center. If so, that one purchase would fulfill two important needs.

Doti recognized the practicality. From a strictly business financial sense, it passed the commonsense test. "It was like a million dollars an acre," said Doti. "We were buying land in Orange at two million dollars an acre."

But this was not a bankrupt real estate company downsizing; it was Robert H. Schuller's life's work. The Crystal Cathedral was known the world over, and in Orange County thousands claimed membership. It was an entrenched community treasure that could be a minefield for criticism if a purchase were mishandled.

Shortly after his conversation with Oklejas, Doti, who professes no religious faith, went to the Crystal Cathedral for Sunday services. He was curious and wanted to see what the university might be offering tens of millions of dollars to acquire. Doti admitted he could not make an expert's appraisal, but he could see the cathedral was in disrepair as were other buildings on campus.

It did not take long for news to get out that new bids had been submitted to the bankruptcy court by various parties. But Doti held off. He wanted first to talk to Schuller personally, to express his interest and explain how he may be able to work something out that would be mutually beneficial. A meeting was set at Schuller's home, and Doti went there with George Argyros, a billionaire real estate mogul who was a philanthropist and prominent community leader in the city of Orange. More importantly, he was a good friend of Schuller's and, like Doti, a fellow member of Horatio Alger. Arvella Schuller and some of the family members still involved in the ministry also joined the meeting but were silent throughout.

"We told [Dr. Schuller] why we thought Chapman would be a great partner with him and his congregation," Doti explained. "The congregation could continue using the church, but we wanted to own the property. We'll buy it."

Doti described Schuller as very gracious. He listened to the proposal and was interested.

"He certainly had great admiration for George [Argyros] and I hope he respected me."

Going into the meeting, Doti knew Schuller was no longer the formal leader of the Crystal Cathedral Ministries and not a voting member of the board, but as long as he was alive, he would have influence. It was also a courtesy to visit the founder of the ministry as a sign of respect and understanding that the campus meant more to the world than what had so far been treated like a real estate play. The difficult circumstances and Schuller's age began to show during the conversation. Doti had known Schuller at the peak of his success and popularity, so the contrast was striking.

"I felt that he was a little out of touch and that he didn't really understand the situation he was in," said Doti, the situation being the gravity of the bankruptcy and that the proceeds from a sale would go to the creditors.

"After I met with him, I didn't think that he'd be very useful or helpful to us, because I could see him losing any decision-making power in the family in that it would be going to a bankruptcy court." Doti accurately concluded that the family and ministry would play a role in court, but the decision would ultimately be left to a judge, as it was in most cases.

Soon afterward, there were two significant announcements. Crystal Cathedral Ministries declared its campus was not for sale and the bankruptcy court announced an open bidding process. The ministry was dead set on raising the needed cash through donations, but the court was not content to put the case on hold any longer. It had been eight months already, and the judge was losing patience. Chapman University formally submitted the offer paperwork to the bankruptcy court. The bid came in $11 million higher than what had been originally anticipated. The $46 million plan included a fifteen-year lease-back of the cemetery and a couple of campus buildings, including the Crystal Cathedral for $150,000 per month. The other open bids at the time included Hobby Lobby and Orange real estate firm Greenlaw Partners, which intended to build homes on the property.

In media reports, Doti said the property was a good fit because it was already configured like a campus and would be well suited for new veterinary and pharmaceutical programs. The added details about the lease were to show that Chapman wanted to help the ministry, not just take the property.

"They wanted to continue there," Doti explained. "That's why we thought Chapman would probably be a better partner for them to continue using the Crystal Cathedral."

Dr. Doti and Chapman University's reputation was such that, from the moment the offer paperwork was filed, Chapman became the top candidate to buy the campus. But it was also a signal to other potential buyers that the property would be sold, and it was no longer just a possibility.

This was only the first of several bids by Chapman, but it was also an open door to the Catholic Diocese of Orange. The bishop, Tod Brown, saw the entrance of Chapman University as elevating the auction of the Crystal Cathedral from hostile acquisition, or picking the bones of bankruptcy, to a legitimate opportunity to help the ministry and obtain a revered campus and church without causing a fracture in the local Christian community. Even so, it would take more than money to match Chapman's offer.

Bishop Tod Brown

Tod David Brown was born on November 15, 1936, in San Francisco, to George Wilson and Edna Anne Brown. He had just one sibling, his brother, Daniel Arthur. They were raised together in San Francisco and Monterey, but only Daniel would stay in the Bay Area, where he would marry his wife, Jeanne, and eventually provide the future clergyman Tod two nieces, one nephew, and six grandnephews to boast about. Tod felt the call to the priesthood at an early age. He had considered other paths, such as the legal field, social work, and teaching. But it was when he began to explore the possibility of becoming a medical doctor that he concluded, if he really wanted to help people, he would best serve them as a priest. Like Robert H. Schuller, Brown continued to do a lot of questioning during his formation, which led to a commitment to the ordained priestly ministry. He studied at Ryan Seminary in Fresno, St. John's Seminary in Camarillo, North American College, and Gregorian University in Rome, Italy. Through it all he earned several degrees, including a pair of master's degrees in biblical theology and education, which he earned back home at the University of San Francisco. In 1963, at twenty-six, Brown was ordained to the priesthood and assigned to the Diocese of Monterey-Fresno. Being a product of the California Coast, Brown was pleased when the Diocese of Monterey was re-established in 1967 and he was stationed at Saint Francis Xavier Parish in Seaside, on the Monterey Peninsula.

After his assignment to Monterey, he found no shortage of new opportunities. He would go on to serve in various roles, including parochial vicar, pastor, chairman of the Divine Worship Commission, chairman and member of the Presbyterial Council, member of the Vocation Committee, chairman of the Priests' Pension Committee, and director of education. He also served as chancellor, moderator of the curia, and vicar general.

In 1976, when the Diocese of Orange was founded, Father Tod Brown accompanied Bishop Harry A. Clinch of Monterey to the inauguration and installation of the first bishop of Orange, Bishop William R. Johnson. The move put Tod Brown historically at the foundation of the Diocese of Orange, which he would one day lead as bishop. But first, Brown was ordained bishop in 1989 to lead the Diocese of Boise, Idaho. While on the job there, one of his chief priorities was making the cathedral the center of Catholic life for the community. After more than nine years, Brown was appointed the third bishop of Orange by future Saint Pope John Paul II on June 30, 1998, succeeding Bishop Norman F. McFarland.

From its foundation to that year, the Diocese of Orange had grown from forty-four parishes and a Catholic population of 329,855, to fifty-three parishes and nearly 600,000 Catholics. It would double again to over a million by 2001.

Much of that growth came from an influx of Mexican and Vietnamese immigrants to Orange County. While Hispanic immigration north from Mexico and South America was a constant over generations, for the Vietnamese it came in a wave that began in the post-Vietnam War era, which saw an influx of refugees. Starting in 1975, more than fifty thousand Vietnamese arrived at Marine Corps Air Station El Toro in Orange County as part of *Operation New Arrival.* The aim was to evacuate and relocate those who had fought alongside the United States and their families. They were then shipped out to processing stations around the country to live temporarily in tent cities. Thousands ended up settling in Orange County, centered primarily in the city of Westminster. It eventually became home to the Little Saigon business district. More refugees who fled Vietnam by boat and raft eventually settled in the area because of natural associations and common language. The population of Vietnamese Catholics was about three thousand in 1975 and grew rapidly to tens of thousands by the time Bishop Brown arrived. As Brown oversaw the establishment of new parishes, he was also dealing with a growing need for Vietnamese-language Masses and priests.

Two of Bishop Brown's major accomplishments proved historic. One was born out of the Catholic Church's sex abuse scandal, and the other was to meet the rapidly growing needs of the ever-increasingly diverse diocese.

In 2004, Bishop Brown led the diocese through a difficult nego-tiation to settle allegations of Church clergy abuse that went back forty years and involved about thirty priests and a dozen Church employees. "Bishop Brown was instrumental in reaching a ground-breaking settlement with victims of clergy sexual abuse and instituted unprecedented reforms including the Covenant with the Faithful in 2004."[1] It was widely hailed as the most aggressive move yet by any Catholic diocese to come to terms with its past. That was one major accomplishment. The other was the unlikely christening of a suitable cathedral for the diocese, though it came about in a way no one could have predicted.

The settlement with abuse victims added a significant financial burden to the tarnished image of the Church, and Brown proved to be a practical leader in navigating both. Throughout his tenure as bishop, Brown watched Church financials closely, while regularly revisiting the plan announced a few years before to build a cathedral fitting for the nearly one million Catholics in the diocese. Holy Family Parish in Orange, which was the official cathedral of the diocese, was fine when the diocese had 325,000 Catholics, but inadequate since. The 850-seat capacity was hardly a third of what was needed. There had not been many years of economic stability, which made pursuit of a new sanctuary that much more difficult. Meanwhile, the major diocesan events—ordination of bishops, priests, and deacons—were moved to St. Columban in Garden Grove, which had a much larger seating capacity.

Brown had put diocese staff and volunteer laypeople together to work out details of what they hoped would one day be a true cathe-dral for the diocese on fifteen acres of purchased land in Santa Ana. Brown worked with the Segerstrom family to secure the land and a $500,000 gift from Henry and Elizabeth Sagerstrom to get the fund started. Brown would later choose the name Christ Our Sav-ior Cathedral, but it had not been decided when Brown made the announcement on June 10, 2001. Brown also announced the Dio-cese of Orange's first-ever capital campaign to raise $75 million.

"We hope this campaign will help us serve the least among us," the *LA Times* quoted Brown at the announcement that took place at Holy Family, "such as the poor, immigrants and those who live on the margins of our consumer culture—as Jesus would have us do."[2]

It was an ambitious plan with Brown saying he believed the money existed in Orange County to make the cathedral a reality. Brown hoped fundraising would take eighteen months and groundbreaking would happen within five years. But it took just three months for those plans to evaporate. September 11, 2001, changed everything with the terrorist attack on New York's World Trade Center.

Days later, on Sunday, the Diocese of Orange held an interfaith (ecumenical) church service for the country and the victims of 9/11. An ecumenical service is one that is interfaith and typically intended to bring together Jews, Muslims, and Christians of various denominations. Reverend Robert H. Schuller attended.

Like many Americans, Brown was already familiar with Schuller and his massively successful television ministry. Brown recalled that when he was bishop of Boise, Idaho, the *Hour of Power* program played at a local movie theater on Sundays. Within the first year of his appointment as bishop of the Diocese of Orange, Brown received an invitation from Schuller to visit the campus. Brown took him up on that offer, and they had lunch together before the tour of the campus.

"He was very cordial," said Brown, "and I was just kind of overwhelmed in a sense by the size and the quality of the facility."[3] Brown recalled that the tour happened just after construction of the campus Center for Possibility Thinking. He later received invitations to attend the Christmas and Easter pageants at the campus, which he accepted. The first time Schuller visited Brown's small cathedral at Holy Family was for the ecumenical service following 9/11.

The cathedral plan seemed to hit one delay after another, often the result of a downturn in the economy or news about clergy abuse, which naturally throttled back donations for the capital campaign. The most recent downturn was the Great Recession of 2008.

Several months before Crystal Cathedral Ministries filed for bankruptcy, in 2010, Bishop Brown was nearing retirement. His goal of building a cathedral, which he had always felt was what God had planned, was not going to happen. But if he were to raise the funds for a down payment and get it started, the cathedral that would one day be built would have been in part due to his own efforts and leadership. In that way, he would fulfill the plan that God so indelibly imprinted on his heart.

Brown turned to the Orange Catholic Foundation (OCF) to lead the capital campaign. It was, after all, part of the reason the OCF existed in the first place. It was created to act as a fundraising arm of the diocese to cover the costs of many Church activities. Part of that was supporting Brown's first cathedral capital campaign launched in 2001. Since then, the OCF had grown and branched out to be an all-encompassing fundraiser to support the diocese. At the time, OCF described itself on its website as "an autonomous pious foundation under canon law and incorporated as a tax-exempt independent charitable corporation under civil law."[4]

Its purpose was to help Catholics "leave a legacy of love and faith, uniquely aligned with their Catholic values and beliefs." In other words, it was a fundraising organization for Catholics to support the Church and its work. And it had been highly successful.

The chairman of the OCF, Jim Tecca, came from banking and ran Catholic health organizations. He was the first Catholic lay chairperson of Catholic Healthcare West, which eventually became Dignity Health. He was a self-described "numbers guy" and had the kind of expertise in such matters that was critical for any fundraising endeavor—particularly one involving tens of millions of dollars.

"He wanted to start a fifty-million-dollar campaign," said Tecca.[5]

Brown's commitment to achieving the goal of building a cathedral was well known. Tecca had heard many times that Brown wanted a large place for people to gather in Orange County, a center for Catholic life.

"He prayed about it," said Tecca, "and he wanted it to be a part of his legacy."

Tecca, like several others he worked with, did not know that a team inside the diocese had already begun plans to develop the diocese land in Santa Ana for what would be called Christ Our Savior Cathedral. So, the ball was already rolling in a sense when Brown laid out his plan before the OCF.

Diocese construction manager Joe Novoa had put in a lot of work. An architect had been selected and conceptual plans drawn up. There was a plan, a carefully considered plan, for the bishop to present. The only thing that worried the bishop was the cost projections.

With the economy still struggling through a recession, the idea of a $50 million campaign sent Jim Tecca's eyes rolling into the back of his head. Tecca, who had had a long and close relationship with Bishop Brown, understood his passion, but did not see how it was going to work.

"I honest to God thought, there's no way ," said Tecca. And he was not alone. The people most capable of animating a fundraiser and generating excitement to support the cause wanted to help Brown, but they agreed: the bishop's plan was not going to work. Tecca, joined by Tim Busch (an Orange County attorney and founder of the Busch Group) and Mike Hagan, went to visit the bishop at his home. Mike Hagan was Tecca's predecessor with the OCF and had a lot of experience.

"First of all, what are your pastors saying?"[6] said Hagan. "Are they gonna support this? Are they gonna get behind? This is one of the biggest things."

The plan was to lay out the reality of the situation and convince Brown to surrender hopes of raising $50 million. It was a team effort. The group was joined by Monsignor Michael Heher, vicar general of the diocese, the righthand man of the bishop.

"I think even the finance council and the like thought this wasn't really the right time to do it," said Monsignor Heher, who sat on the council at the time. "Just not a good time for fundraising."[7]

"The great thing about [Bishop Brown]," said Tecca, "was that he allowed all kinds of input. But we always knew who had the vote. There was no problem with Bishop Brown."

Over dinner they made their case against pursuing this capital campaign at that time, if ever. Tecca said it was not a simple process in any way, but they were allowed to speak their minds and be candid with their opinions, facts, and numbers.

"And he looked at us and essentially said, 'Good night,'" Tecca recalled. Brown was not angry, but he was not pleased with what he had heard. "He said, 'You don't understand the importance of a cathedral like I do and what if means to have the bishop's house to the people who are Catholics in such a large area.'" Tecca admittedly did not fully understand, and he fell back on what the research showed. "To raise money for a down payment, for a cathedral that research showed was a couple hundred million bucks. To do it in Orange County with just some plans. He said it would cost $130 million and we thought it was $180 million. And we were really concerned."

But Brown insisted.

"The bishop was so right on about his definition of what the need was," said Mike Hagan; "it was just that we didn't see the way of raising the money that needed to be raised from this ground-up deal. I don't think we could have turned on the people of the diocese."

"We left there with him looking me in the eye and saying, 'I disagree,'" said Jim Tecca.

It was an impasse. Logically, they did not know where to start. The silent phase of fundraising, which was what Tim Busch specialized in, would get the fundraising started as usual. But Mike Hagan and Jim Tecca would also have to be out there selling the idea and getting people excited about the plan.

"It wasn't in our hearts," insisted Tecca. "We couldn't figure it out."

Tecca believed it was not long after that meeting that the Holy Spirit inspired him to think that it was possible, and part of that was an early inkling that if the Crystal Cathedral was to be sold in a bankruptcy auction, there was a chance Catholics could preserve it as a place for worship. The bankruptcy was a prospect he did not look at with glee, but the possibilities were clear.

The news of the bankruptcy rocked Orange County and reached the diocese quickly. Bishop Brown read in the local newspaper that Reverend Robert H. Schuller's Crystal Cathedral Ministries had formally filed for Chapter 11 bankruptcy.

"I was saddened and shocked by that," said Brown. The merest hint of the idea of buying the Crystal Cathedral did not enter his mind. The ministry was thought of as a pillar of the community, and bankruptcy was such a major step. It all seemed so tragic. Brown understood how the Great Recession impacted church finances and noted the article pointed to massive debt as a key factor. Already it was well known that there were financial hardships as recently as January, when the ministry sold some unused property and announced layoffs. Bankruptcy had the feel of impending finality in some ways.

For seven months, there followed published stories as well as online and in-print op-eds and broadcasts about what happened to the once mighty "megachurch." Often, like the sometimes salacious and self-serving media reports, the focus was on the tabloidesque intrigues and inner turmoil of the Schuller family and ministry. But in late May 2011, there came a report of a bankruptcy exit plan that on the surface seemed to be a lifeline for the Crystal Cathedral.

Well before Chapman University got involved, court filings by Crystal Cathedral Ministries named a buyer. Newport Beach, California-based Greenlaw Partners had agreed to buy the entire campus for $46 million.

"The purpose of this plan is to generate funds to repay creditors without affecting the ability of the ministry to operate," said Marc Winthrop, the attorney representing Crystal Cathedral Ministries in bankruptcy court.[8]

"We are pleased that we are able to honor the debt that we have incurred and to honor the creditors who are due their payment," Pastor Sheila Schuller Coleman told the paper. "We are thankful to the vendors for their patience and we are so sorry for any pain that they have incurred. To pay them back 100 percent has always been a top priority and we are grateful to God for providing the resources to be able to do just that."[9]

There was more to the offer. Greenlaw's plan also included a proposal in which the ministry retained a guaranteed lease option for the Crystal Cathedral and other campus buildings with rent set at $212,000 a month. It appeared to be a potential win-win for the ministry since there was a further option, should fortunes change, to buy the property and its facilities back in four years for the bargain price of $30 million. That last part was almost dismissed outright, as the *Los Angeles Times* reported, "For the four months ending in April, the church's net loss was $1.14 million."[10] The *Times* also noted that some of the ministry's five-hundred-plus creditors may be left without full payment. Despite flaws, it could be approved by August 15. The downside in the details, which was soon to be clear, was how the proposal divided the property into five parts with apartments to be built on two of them.[11]

Tim Busch had read the same articles and followed developments more closely than many. He had extensive experience in real estate. It was, after all, the biggest news story in the county and related to land development and the greater Christian family of Orange County, of which he was an active participant. Busch had had a long relationship with the Diocese of Orange. He was behind the establishment of two Catholic schools. Together with his wife, Steph Busch, he co-founded the Magis Institute and was a member of the Orange County chapter of Legatus, an organization for Catholic CEOs and their spouses. He was a friend and advisor to Bishop Brown and supported Brown's Christ Our Savior Cathedral plan, although he knew realistically it was years off—maybe many years.

"There was no chance in the next quarter of a century that we were going to build a cathedral," said Busch.[12]

But Busch wanted a cathedral as much as Bishop Brown or anyone else in the diocese. He said as much when he met with Cardinal Mahony about the plan for a new cathedral in the Archdiocese of Los Angeles. "I'm not in your diocese, Cardinal, but I'm here because I want to build a cathedral in Orange someday." He was not a central figure in the building of what would one day be known as the Cathedral of Our Lady of the Angels, but he offered what advice he could. For Busch it was part of his continued philanthropy, but also a learning experience about what it took to build a cathedral. He learned enough to know it was a complex and expensive process.

It was not long after the report about the court filings and reorganization plan with the sale to Greenlaw Partners that Busch had a passing conversation about the general idea of buying the Crystal Cathedral campus. Greenlaw Partners was going to buy it, and the price seemed ridiculously low, so he did not think it was outrageously absurd, even while he saw it as highly implausible.

After a couple of months had passed and the bankruptcy story had faded from the headlines, Busch headed to the Diocese of Orange offices at Marywood to attend an executive board meeting. It was likely a regularly scheduled planning meeting for the ground-up cathedral plan for Christ Our Savior. Busch was not thinking much about the Crystal Cathedral; he was just listening to the board's discussions. Not a board member himself, Busch was a trusted advisor as a member of the laity. There were twelve to fourteen people present during discussions when Bishop Brown made an impromptu suggestion that Tim Busch had an idea.

"I had no plan to offer some grand idea or float some unusual concept," said Busch. It was out of the blue, and Busch knew that others were thinking it. The bankruptcy had been big news in Orange County. He did not claim the idea to be solely his own. But the direct prompt had him on autopilot and leaning forward as he told the committee what came to mind.

"We should buy the Crystal Cathedral," he said.

Monsignor Lawrence Baird, a board member, was the only one there, other than Tim Busch, who thought it was a good idea. He had read about the bankruptcy the day before. He also recalled bringing the subject of the bankruptcy up at that meeting. He said he wondered aloud about the possibility of buying the cathedral campus. Regardless of the order of the suggestions, the result was the same. The idea that others were just thinking was finally spoken aloud to the bishop.

Bishop Brown recalled what he heard from Busch and Baird. "They were saying, 'You must look at this because this is a possibility. We could acquire this and have everything we need and more at less expense.' All that's true," agreed Bishop Brown. It was hard to argue with the logic, but there was something about the suggestion that made him uncomfortable. "I wasn't keen on that idea, at first," he said.

There were two reasons for his cool reception to what seemed to Tim Busch and Monsignor Baird to be a once-in-a-lifetime scenario, even if unlikely to succeed. First, the Christ Our Savior Cathedral plan had been in the works for years and had moved into a new phase that was an architectural design and mock-up. Some money had been raised in the capital campaign and expenses had already been incurred. Second, and on the more emotional and spiritual level, Bishop Brown was afraid that it would seem as if Catholics were taking advantage of Crystal Cathedral Ministries when it was in trouble. It was an evangelical Protestant church but still a vibrant part of the wider Christian community in Orange County. Brown did not want to cause a rift that would have a lasting divisive impact.

"I was very concerned about the ecumenical ramifications of the whole situation," he said, and "in no way wanted to appear to be taking advantage of their financial crisis and gobbling up their property."

But bankruptcy proceedings had not yet settled anything, and it was evident that Crystal Cathedral Ministries was forced to liquidate property. The Greenlaw Partners plan was a lifeline; but Tim Busch was right: the dividing up of the property for development as apartments could end up leading to demolition of the rest of the campus. If the diocese offered a bid, probably something in the range of what the ministry needed to pay off all creditors, what could be wrong with that? At least it was a scenario that would keep the Crystal Cathedral a place of worship, and it filled a need for the diocese. That realization was enough for Bishop Brown to consider its feasibility, even if he did not want a lot of people knowing about it. So he called for a meeting with Maria Schinderle.

Maria Rullo Schinderle was well known around the diocese. She was a litigation attorney and general counsel for the Diocese of Orange. Along with her many other responsibilities, she had done some work she described as mostly on the periphery for the Christ Our Savior Cathedral plan up to that point.

The bishop told Schinderle that it looked like the cathedral ministry may be forced to liquidate assets as part of the bankruptcy. He said he trusted the advice he had received, and he said that some think the timing may be divine providence.

"I want you to start exploring this," said Bishop Brown. He was cautious. "This is a good opportunity to explore, but let's not be distracted from where we have already come on the Christ Our Savior Cathedral plan."

Brown gave Schinderle a list of a few names and told her to work with them to study the possibilities. He also assured her that when the time came, "the right thing to do would become known to us; it would be manifest." The names on the list included Rob Neal, Mike Hagan, Jim Tecca, and Tim Busch. Schinderle took the list and reached out to a friend.

Alan Martin was an attorney at the Finance and Bankruptcy Practice Group of Sheppard, Mullin, Richter, and Hampton, based in nearby Costa Mesa. The firm specialized in asset acquisition and disposition—and bankruptcy. Schinderle knew him as a great bankruptcy attorney and a good man. So, they got together, and Schinderle explained the situation. She made it clear: bankruptcy was out of her element.

"I don't know bankruptcy from Adam," Schinderle told Martin.[13] "We need your expertise. If we want to be the plan of reorganization and purchase this out of bankruptcy, we gotta have you." Martin agreed to join the team.

For Martin, it was an unusual request because of the timing. The bankruptcy proceeding had been going for the better part of a year, and the diocese was late to the process.

"It had to ramp up fairly quickly," said Martin.[14]

But it was also intriguing. "It was a fascinating situation, to me. It was an iconic property that was involved. Whether one had gone to one of the Crystal Cathedral services or not, just about anyone would know about that location or at least recognize it driving by. And I was also aware that there was a real need for the diocese." Martin, a Catholic in the diocese, immediately recognized that the campus provided a rare opportunity for the diocese to fill those needs.

As it turned out, the timing to enlist one of the top bankruptcy legal minds could not have been better. Two major news reports altered the equation established by Greenlaw Partners' proposal. One said that Robert H. Schuller was denying reports that he had been removed from the Crystal Cathedral Board. The other was about Chapman University's surprise bid of $46 million to compete for the Crystal Cathedral property with Greenlaw Partners.

On June 27, Chapman University's Board of Trustees had voted to authorize Chapman president James Doti to pursue the purchase of the Crystal Cathedral campus. Details, including the bid, were submitted to the court by the creditors' committee. The statement from the university explained the rationale.

"The offer is designed to address community concerns about the uncertainty of the Crystal Cathedral's present situation, as well as provide growth opportunities for Chapman University," read the statement. "The proposal would allow Crystal Cathedral Ministries to lease back the Cathedral and other property on the campus, with a purchase provision that could be exercised during the first four years of the lease."[15]

In the statement, Chapman president James Doti was quoted. He referred to Schuller's legacy in the community. "Dr. Schuller's life-long message of courage and ambition closely matches the characteristics that are so much a part of Chapman University," Doti said. "We are fortunate to be in a position where we can make this offer and are hopeful our proposal to the ministry and court will be accepted."

Chapman University had tremendous resources, was a known and respected part of the community, and had a charismatic, capable leader. James Doti and the university, more than the bid itself, automatically made Chapman's the most serious offer. Proof of the university's influence and confidence was that Doti did not feel the need to offer a higher bid than Greenlaw, just a better plan.

For the team at the Diocese of Orange there could not have been any greater reason to act. Doti's characterization of Schuller's "lifelong message of courage and ambition" may have been accurate, but did it really define Schuller's life's work and lasting message? It contrasted sharply with how the diocese saw Schuller's life and legacy as a Christian minister. If the Crystal Cathedral was going to continue to be a place for preaching the Gospel of Jesus Christ, the diocese would have to submit a bid.

When the situation was explained to Bishop Brown, he needed some time to think. He did not have long, but it was a big decision that would be made public the moment it happened. Tim Busch knew that Brown did not like the idea originally; the bishop had expressed his concerns about a possible rift in the Christian community. But diocese legal counsel Maria Schinderle never got the impression that Brown was cool to the idea; rather, she saw it as discerning and contemplative. The stakes were high spiritually and financially, and the bishop had to be aware of both. Despite the perception of his feelings, Bishop Brown admitted he did not want to wade into the controversial waters. He indeed was cool to the idea. But Schinderle was right where Brown's contemplative nature was involved. He was not going to make a rash decision that would result in hurt feelings.

Brown returned to his chief exploratory team members with a decision. Before anything was made public, before there was a formal offer, the diocese had to communicate the intent first with Crystal Cathedral Ministries and founder Robert H. Schuller. Representatives from Chapman University had had a meeting with Robert Schuller and some board members. Tim Busch and the team wondered, if the ministry had a meeting with Chapman, why not afford the same courtesy to the diocese?

Tim Busch penned a letter to a legal representative with Crystal Cathedral Ministries. He had hoped for a response soon and maybe a small miracle.

He got one.

Meeting Dr. Robert H. Schuller

The letter that requested the meeting from Tim Busch's office to the attorney for Crystal Cathedral Ministries went by U.S. mail. Even when sent in the same county as its destination—or closer, the same city—it was not colloquially referred to as snail mail for nothing. So, what happened while Tim Busch was having lunch at the Pacific Club in Newport Beach with a well-known priest from the Eternal Word Television Network (EWTN), the next day, was mind boggling.

Father Robert Spitzer was a Catholic Jesuit priest, doctor of philosophy, and host of *Father Spitzer's Universe* on EWTN. Spitzer recalled lunch when Tim Busch got a voicemail from Robert H. Schuller.

"It was the miraculous luncheon," said Spitzer.[1]

Spitzer was blind, so it was about what he heard when Busch said he had to check the message. Spitzer noticed a curiosity, even some urgency, in Busch's tone. Busch listened to the message and set his phone down.

"After the call, I said, 'Who was that?'" recalled Spitzer. "'He said what?' After that [Tim Busch's] heart just turned on."

Busch told Spitzer that the attorney for the ministry had handed Dr. Schuller the letter.

"He said he was very interested in talking to the diocese about purchasing the cathedral," said Busch. "He wants to meet. He was very excited."[2]

With the bankruptcy proceedings and rules for the lawyers being what they were, rather than calling Schuller directly, Busch called the attorney for the ministry, Marc Winthrop, to arrange the meeting. To Spitzer it was the day when the work to buy the campus began in earnest. But was that moment miraculous, and did it say anything about the work of the Holy Spirit?

"Everyone was thinking about this," said Spitzer, "and then there was this call out of nowhere." The call certainly was unexpected at that moment and gave Tim Busch the sense that just maybe it was meant to be—a foundation of hope.

There was something reassuring about going to a meeting in the Tower of Hope, especially a meeting that was so frontloaded with high uncertainty and anticipation. Inside there were a pair of large glass-backed elevators. Bishop Brown and Tim Busch were in the elevator, as was diocese general counsel Maria Schinderle. Schinderle was not fazed by the pressure. She was too busy making the case in her mind, the way she prepared for trial. Also riding up was the bankruptcy expert she had recruited, Alan Martin.

"It was a beautiful sunny day," Martin recalled. "The sun seemed to glimmer off the Crystal Cathedral and the Tower of Hope."[3]

There was a lot of hope to go around as the group took the elevator up. The other person in the elevator was an escort from the Crystal Cathedral Ministries who had pushed the button for the top floor, one floor above Schuller's office where the Chapel in the Sky was located. When the elevator doors opened, they stepped out quietly into the rear of the chapel. There was a small service underway, and they watched for a moment, marveling at how true to the name the Chapel in the Sky really was. It may have been tempting to say a prayer before the meeting. It is not known if any took advantage of the opportunity before stepping back into the elevator.

There was hope that Dr. Robert Schuller would be as interested in talking as he sounded in his voicemail message to Tim Busch—hope that what the diocese had to offer would be enough, hope that there was enough time for the bankruptcy court to allow serious consideration of the plan. As the elevator approached the office floor, they had to wonder also what hopes Reverend Schuller held for the ministry he founded and the Crystal Cathedral. That was where Bishop Brown's mind hovered.

Brown was not feeling particularly reassured, but instead admittedly nervous. He was a man devoutly committed to trusting God's will, but he was also intensely aware of Schuller's vulnerability. It pained the bishop to think about how Schuller must feel. So, he had not had much to say on the ride over to the cathedral campus. Brown had confidence, though, in the people going to the meeting with him, including Tim Busch, who saw the meeting as monumental.

"The bishop was kind of downplaying it," said Busch, "but I said to him this is going to be one of the most important meetings you're ever going to have in your entire life. It's history making."

To prepare for what diocese general counsel Maria Schinderle called a "pivotal meeting," the team had done its work.[4] Over several days they culled from a batch of ideas a few ways the offer might work. There were phone calls, research, meetings, and casual conversations that had led to a general plan short of a formal offer. The stakes were high, and the potential to offend Dr. Schuller existed. It was imperative to think about all those people who had much to gain, but also to the many with much to lose. The list was long.

The price was in most respects the easiest to settle on, because the diocese only had so much money and Bishop Brown wanted to be conservative. They were set to tell Schuller it would be in the range of $50 million, but competitive with the Chapman University offer.

Among the toughest was what to include that might help the Crystal Cathedral Ministry live on doing its work for the congregation and the community.

"We knew this was a congregation that was hurting," said Maria Schinderle. "They were going to lose their home."

It went beyond the loss for the Schullers' and for the *Hour of Power* TV program. It was about people whose hearts were breaking through the whole process. And what about the homeless who were fed every single day from the campus kitchen? Or the twenty-four-hour crisis line operating out of the Tower of Hope? There was ongoing missionary work happening at the campus. Those concerns drove much of the discussion and thought led by Bishop Brown. Schinderle said they were dealing with a decision that would impact jobs, worship space, and people's faith.

"We had to find a soft landing for the congregation," said Schinderle. "We had to ease what they were going through."

When the team from the diocese worked through the ideas, they concluded that what the diocese needed in an offer was an alternative space, someplace the ministry could go. But it had to be move-in ready and have space for a school. There was space near the Crystal Cathedral, just a few blocks away. It was a church and a school, with parish office space and virtually everything the ministry needed. But that was not an easy solution. St. Callistus Parish, part of the Diocese of Orange, had its own congregation. It had its own families, charitable works, and schoolchildren to be concerned about. That plan would displace two congregations instead of one. It was a hard decision. But if the diocese were to buy the cathedral campus, St. Callistus had to go. It was not possible to have two parishes within a couple of blocks of each other.

The more they discussed how and why that would work, the more it began to make sense. The chief reason St. Callistus would make a good home for the continuation of the Crystal Cathedral Ministries was that there were two soft landings. St. Callistus parishioners and Crystal Cathedral students would trade spaces. Both congregations would make a hard change, but it was a positive outcome. And to make it easier for the ministry, the lease rate would be nothing the first year and remain small over a ten-year term.

It did not end there. Bishop Brown had to consider the reaction of more than a million Catholics, some of whom would not like the plan at all. The plan going in was to make it clear, no matter what, that the Catholic Church intended to preserve the Crystal Cathedral as a place of worship for the decades, if not centuries, to come. It was not a symbolic gesture just to reassure, but a recognition of the status of the campus as a historical and meaningful part of the broader community.

Dr. Schuller's office was a bright open space that took up the entire floor. That was not to say that it was huge. The Tower of Hope was tall, but its footprint was on the small side. There was a complete 360-degree view, creating a sweeping panorama of Orange County. Naturally, it married with the outdoors. Wall-to-wall ceiling lights balanced out the light-blue carpet to create harmony with the view. The windows facing north garnered a view of the top of the eighteen-story, stainless-steel spire, as it shimmered over the top of the Crystal Cathedral. East, the view went on for miles. It was not the tallest building in the county anymore, but the views were nothing to complain about. Schuller had positioned a desk facing that direction, backed by built-in, dark-stained wood cabinets and shelves. The desk was adorned with a crystal cross and a leather-bound Bible. A large, light-color, patterned sectional couch backed up against the east windows extending to the north-east corner. It had a glass-topped coffee table. Along the north-facing windows was a conference table with seating for eight in cushioned office chairs. It was a lot to take in, but there was plenty of time to do so. Schuller was late—two hours late.

It turned out, Schuller's wife had suffered a medical emergency the night before, and Schuller was up with her most of the night in the emergency room. When he walked in, there was relief all around and a great deal of sympathy for what delayed him. They sat down at the conference table for lunch. He was at one end, and immediately to his left was Bishop Brown. Maria Schinderle was next to Brown; the others, Tim Busch and Alan Martin, took the next seats over. On the other side of Schuller was his youngest daughter, Carole Schuller Milner.

The nervousness of seeing Dr. Schuller for the first time in person was more a buildup in the mind. The reality was he had a very calming demeanor.

"He's not a person who makes you nervous when you're in his presence," said Schinderle. "He was warm, welcoming, and thoughtful."

He shook Bishop Brown's hand and, along with standard greetings, added that he had always thought of Brown as his bishop. The Reformed Church of America did not have the kind of leadership structure that called for a cathedra or bishop, and Schuller would go on to reiterate those words in other settings. But at the time it was a surprise to some in the room.

"That's a very strange concept," said Tim Busch, "when you think you're walking into a non-Catholic environment. All of a sudden, the televangelist is calling him 'his bishop.' He was not Catholic, not under his jurisdiction, but in [Schuller's] mind he was."

The net effect was to set the team from the diocese at ease. Bankruptcy attorney Alan Martin said it was palpable.

"There seemed to be a real chemistry there," said Martin, "between folks at Crystal Cathedral Ministries on one hand and the diocese on the other." More specifically, Martin pointed to the chemistry between Dr. Schuller and Bishop Brown. Both men were at ease with each other, which was helpful because Schuller had just experienced a long, exhausting night. Schuller, as it turned out, was still ready to discuss what the diocese had in mind.

"It was our opportunity to show our cards," said Schinderle. "That we were in the market for a church. For central place. For worship, for culture, for education, for exercise of our faith."

She had been full of confidence and energy from the outset when Schuller so kindly stated that he had always considered Brown to be his bishop.

"I thought, no matter what gets thrown in our way," she said, "no matter what offers Chapman makes, no matter what offers anybody else makes, I really think this is meant to be."

Then Schuller turned to Schinderle and smiled.

"What would you dream," Schuller asked, "if you knew your dream could come true?"[5]

It was a familiar question for those who knew him, but it was surreal for Schinderle to be asked that question right there, face-to-face.

"Well, Reverend Schuller," Schinderle said without hesitation, "I would dream that we could purchase the Crystal Cathedral and make it a church for all time. I think Chapman has other plans for its use."

"Why should I choose the Diocese of Orange as the buyer?" he asked.

Bishop Brown responded, "We will always be a place of worship and a place of faith, and a place of Christian ministry, and a place of God's light and Christ's light."[6]

Schinderle marveled at the sincerity of the moment as she watched two men, both leaders, humble servants, communicating with each other.

The meeting lasted two hours. On the way out, the earlier hope had become optimism that it was meant to be. Alan Martin, on the other hand, had the bankruptcy court on his mind. The chemistry, sincerity, and mutual goodwill were welcomed, but the court proceedings might not be impacted in the least.

"It was a positive situation," said Martin. "It was good to have had the meeting. At the same time, I did not walk away and say, 'Wow, this is all going to come together.' There were a lot of other wheels in motion. It was far from given," he added, "that it was going to result in a sale to the Church."

"Dr. Schuller was still hopeful that the financial matters could be resolved," said Bishop Brown. "So, he didn't say yes or no at that luncheon, but he was sympathetic."

The diocese announced a bid and reorganization acquisition plan on Friday, July 22, a mere month after Alan Martin joined the team. The all-cash offer topped the other leading bids by $4 million and carried incentives to aid Crystal Cathedral Ministries postbankruptcy. The diocese said it would pay $50 million due within thirty days of approval by the court and include a three-year leaseback plan for some of the campus buildings. The proposal included a letter from two major bank-lending institutions that a loan could be secured. The diocese would not be able to raise that money in the time required. Perhaps most important for the continued operation of Crystal Cathedral Ministries was the offer of a new church and a school.

There was no confusion about the bishop's feelings regarding a cathedral, nor of his feelings about the plight of Schuller's ministry. He did not take the decision to enter the bidding process lightly.

"There was a lot of prayer and consultation," he said, "you know about whether to do this or not. I mean, not everybody was in favor of this; I had my critics of course. Getting into such a financial obligation, etcetera, do we need a cathedral?—though I announced years before we needed a cathedral."

It was a serious decision and haste could have meant disaster. But now, because of the court's schedule, time was not on the side of the diocese and Brown's team. It had to be done quickly and with extraordinary care.

An Informed Decision

The value of the Crystal Cathedral and its campus was evident right from the announcement of the Chapter 11 bankruptcy. Then the ministry announced an optimistic reorganization plan that appeared to include an agreement to sell to Greenlaw Partners, which wanted to develop the land. Jim Tecca, Tim Busch, and others with expertise in large real estate transactions were not surprised that developers such as Greenlaw were looking for a deal in what would amount to a fire sale. It was a deal so good, it could only happen if the bankrupt party were forced by the court to sell. As a land play, it was on the radar of developers and others across the region. At an estimated $34 million floated in some media reports, it was a steal. Although, sensible figures put the final price at closer to $50 million. The questions were, how high would it go, and what would happen to the property after the sale? The bankruptcy court's obligation was to require the debtor to take the highest and best bid and to get the maximum amount of money to pay creditors, in full if possible. The highest estimates suggested that figure was between $50 million and $60 million.

After rejecting the idea of buying the Crystal Cathedral, Bishop Brown was finally moved to act on the opportunity many months after the initial bankruptcy, the inevitable sale, and the clear writing on the wall. The construction manager for the diocese, who had been working on the Christ Our Savior Cathedral plan, Joe Novoa, set out to hire a firm for a feasibility study. This would include cost projections for rehabilitation and campus maintenance. The inspections of the roofs and major structures would also serve as due diligence for drafting a bid document. It was information Maria Schinderle needed to put together a serious plan for what that purchase would look like.

Bishop Brown remained concerned about causing a rift in the local Christian community. Ecumenism was not a sudden notion for Brown; it was a longtime commitment. He once headed the Committee on Ecumenical and Interreligious Affairs of the United

States Conference of Catholic Bishops. So, it was deeply important to Brown that the diocese act in good faith. With some bids suggesting demolition and others leading to a wholesale change of the campus, it appeared that some of the risk of a rift was mitigated. Some of the bishop's closest advisors also understood that the city of Garden Grove would not be too excited about approving apartments on what had become one of the county's most recognizable features. Ensuring the property's continued service as a Christian church seemed right all around.

"I don't think the city of Garden Grove would have ever approved apartments there," Schinderle said.[1] Demolition would be unthinkable. "Not for gold architect award-winning buildings, oh my gosh."

Despite Bishop Brown's desire that a Catholic cathedral worthy of one of the largest dioceses in the country would come to fruition, there had never been any overwhelming support for entering the bidding process. But there were meetings, emails, and discussions that were enough to lay out the pros and cons. First, the expense of building a cathedral in modern dollars was mind boggling.

"The problem is building cathedrals is prohibitively expensive per foot," said developer Rob Neal.[2] "Whereas we might talk about, in my case, industrial buildings, cost of construction could be sixty to ninety dollars a foot. The cost of a cathedral could be fourteen hundred, sixteen hundred, nineteen hundred, two thousand dollars a foot."

There was recent history to draw from locally. The Archdiocese of Los Angeles, of which Orange had been a part, had been trying for years to rebuild its cathedral that was damaged by the Northridge earthquake. The historic Cathedral of St. Vibiana opened in 1876 and had served the diocese for nearly a century. But at 4:31 a.m. on January 17, 1994, the ground shook on a hidden fault in the San Fernando Valley. The 6.7 earthquake sent rolling waves of deadly destruction across concentric circles over thirty miles. Even at the outer edge of that radius, it shook hard enough at St. Vibiana's that the cathedral's eighty-five-foot bell tower cracked. The building was condemned out of fear that the next seismic event could cause the tower to collapse onto the sanctuary.

The inspection report released almost two years later said the cathedral "experienced a relatively low level of ground shaking during the Northridge quake, but the cracking to unreinforced masonry walls is extensive and penetrates the entire wall thickness."[3] The conclusion was that underneath what was still standing was little more than rubble that couldn't support the weakened walls. With an investment of $20 million the diocese could rebuild, but it would be, for all practical purposes, a whole new building—the old building replaced by a replica.

Cardinal Roger Mahony, who had been at the head of the diocese for a decade, took the report as proof that his plan for a new cathedral was the more pragmatic move. He had been pursuing an uphill effort to build a more fitting cathedral representing the largest Catholic diocese in the United States for about $40 million. The report on St. Vibiana forced the next step. At the very start of the effort to build from the ground up, the estimate jumped to $50 million and eventually climbed to $100 million.

The diocese purchased just fewer than six acres at another location in the heart of downtown LA for $10 million and commissioned Spanish Pritzker Architecture Prize–winning professor José Rafael Moneo to design the cathedral. When Our Lady of the Angels opened in 2002, it was the third largest cathedral in the world and the first new cathedral in the United States in twenty-five years. The cost? Two hundred million dollars.

What the Our Lady of the Angels project had going for it was both the obvious need to replace the condemned cathedral and Cardinal Mahony, who, despite later criticism, was a charismatic and effective fundraiser. The remarkable and unusual structure represented Mahony's hope for a center of Catholic life in the diocese, and it was proof that it was possible to build a new cathedral from the ground up.

In the Orange diocese, nearly a decade later, the Christ Our Savior cathedral land was slightly larger at about fifteen acres, which had been purchased from the Segerstrom family. Even so, estimated construction costs in 2010 dollars still reached $130 million to $250 million. Unfortunately, the first-ever capital campaign in the diocese suffered from several setbacks including 9/11 and the Great Recession, and while not impossible, the goal would take a substantial time to reach.

Meanwhile, Bishop Brown's Christ Our Savior Cathedral Committee, tapped to consider design plans and make other progress on the Santa Ana cathedral, was at work. And they too were troubled by the ambitious nature of the funding requirements.

"We were deep into that process," said Berni Neal, a Christ Our Savior Cathedral Committee member. "Our biggest concern was it would take thirty to fifty years to raise [the money] little by little to see a complete campus built."[4]

"Most people considered it to be a pipe dream," said Berni's husband, developer Rob Neal. Still, Rob and Berni, along with many others, were asked to work on it for the diocese. They did, even if it was just the beginning of something that might not be finished in their lifetimes.

The most glaring figure was $250 million, the top-end estimate, of what it would cost to build Christ Our Savior Cathedral. That was the sanctuary alone. There was no pastoral office, no school, no ancillary buildings, and certainly no room for expansion.

"That was what I told the bishop," said Tim Busch, as he made the case in discussions and to the decision-makers at the diocese.[5] "Guys," he recalled telling them, "we're paying fifty-seven million for this place. The land is worth one hundred million dollars." Fifty-seven million dollars for thirty-five acres, which was more than double the Segerstrom land. And the buildings were already there, even if they had to be rehabbed. The ministry's Welcoming Center, just one of the campus's major structures, had cost $52 million when it was built, and the whole campus would cost just slightly more than that.

"All-in, we're somewhere around a hundred and thirty million dollars," Bush insisted. "Even if it's ten million more or less, it's still a better deal than two hundred fifty million."

The "all-in" was what it would cost to buy the cathedral campus including extensive renovations. The bishop's team was asked to make all considerations. If the diocese was going to make a bid, it would do it with eyes wide open. So, it was aptly noted in diocese construction manager Joe Novoa's feasibility study and due diligence that the property had fallen into disrepair because of budget cuts. Much of the space had gone unused for quite some time. The inescapable reality was that the Neutra Tower of Hope, which was built in 1968, did not meet California earthquake code, so it was going to be a costly project just to do the retrofit. All the cathedral glass, along with the glass of the Neutra Arboretum, would be an ongoing annual expense that must be factored into future diocese budgets. With Bishop Brown set to retire, the ongoing burden would be left to someone else. That was why Church leadership away from the diocese worried about saddling the next bishop with the responsibility. And the renovation was not just about shoring up and washing windows; it was about taking a church designed as a sound stage and turning it into a Catholic cathedral.

Tim Busch sat down with a friend who was vehemently opposed to the diocese buying the Crystal Cathedral. This friend wanted a traditional church. He had worked on the original cathedral plan to build from the ground up. His chief complaint was how out of step with tradition it was.

"From a procession point of view, it's not long cruciform, so you can't process in from the back," said the friend.

"We can still process in. It's not going to be long." With traditional Catholic churches, built with a cruciform floor plan, processions were long and dramatic. The Crystal Cathedral was not cruciform. But Busch tried to convince the friend it was possible. "Can't we construct it so it's liturgically respectful of our faith?"

But the friend remained convinced that the purchase was never going to happen. It was the way many conversations went that made it clear the matter was as personally complex as it was complicated to achieve—the renovation, more than just the repair. For Busch and those trying to make it happen, it became a matter of cataloguing the pros and cons and weighing the results. The location, which was viewed as providential when Robert Schuller acquired the land, had proven to be even more so as the community expanded over the years. Now it was at the heart of Orange County.

"This property is in the center of the county," argued Tim Busch. That was no small advantage. It was far more accessible than the Santa Ana property where Christ Our Savior would be erected, particularly for the Asian and Latino communities, which are primarily located in the northern part of the county.

Regardless of the benefits, the purchase would require the approval of the Vatican, which prohibited purchases over $10 million, and, at the time, the waiver request from the Diocese of Orange had already been declined.

Before filing a bid, bankruptcy attorney Alan Martin and diocese general counsel Maria Schinderle went to the Ronald Reagan

Federal Building and Courthouse in Santa Ana, where the case was being adjudicated. The courtroom was crammed with spectators and lawyers representing bidders, creditors, and Crystal Cathedral aka the debtors, among others.

Judge Robert Kwan, who had presided over the lengthy process for nearly ten months already, saw Alan Martin approach the podium microphone to introduce himself. Maria Schinderle heard the judge immediately recognize and greet him.

"The judge said, 'It's good to see you,'" recalled Schinderle.

Martin and Judge Kwan were familiar with each other from years of work in bankruptcy. Any judge working on the complexities of a bankruptcy that involved the liquidation of real property relied not only on his own knowledge of the law, but also on the skill and expertise of the lawyers involved. Negotiations and meeting goals often depended on the lawyers putting together cogent plans in careful collaboration. Alan Martin knew going in that Judge Kwan was presiding, and any appreciation for the knowledge and skill Martin brought into the courtroom was reciprocal.

"Judge Kwan is a very experienced, well-respected judge," said Martin.[6] "I think universally."

And Kwan was patient, as he had exhibited for months on end, though the case was not going to last forever. Even under pressure, Kwan was not expected to cut corners or leave details unexplored.

Martin formally introduced himself and Schinderle and told the court why they were present.

"At that point, we were just asking the court to have an opportunity to submit a bid," said Martin.

Judge Kwan agreed to welcome the diocese into the process. But being permitted to submit an offer and having a realistic chance at succeeding were not the same. The diocese planned to enter the bidding at $50 million. The existing Chapman offer was said to be $46 million. It was commonly accepted that Chapman had the financial power to outbid the diocese as soon as the diocese filed with the court. After the first hearing, the realistic assessment by Alan Martin was that since bidding had not met the 100 percent payback of the creditors, the court was obligated to sell to the highest bidder. Which, as of the end of that hearing, was Chapman's $46 million bid.

"That was a concern to us," said Alan Martin, "because in theory, there might have been a final auction even prior to us having the opportunity to submit a bid to get into the conversation."

This is where the hard work the representatives of the Diocese of Orange had put in from the moment Bishop Brown greenlit the effort to pursue the bid paid off. They had established plans to join the nearby St. Callistus Parish and school with the cathedral campus. Closing St. Callistus made sense for several reasons, not the least of which was the parish moving to the Crystal Cathedral campus meant that the campus would be active from the start with thousands of families attending Mass on the weekends. The diocese would move its offices from the Marywood property to the Crystal Cathedral campus. Proceeds from the sale of the two properties would be critical. But more immediately, the diocese had aligned with local banks to borrow the funds that made the bid possible. Alan Martin's assessment was accurate, and had it taken an extended period of time to put bid details and financing together, a final auction could have happened in quick order. Given the court's growing impatience, it was likely.

Instead, the diocese filed its formal bid of $50 million just days after the hearing. Chapman countered by amending its original offer and increased its bid to $50 million. The result was the pronouncement in the media that a bidding war had erupted. The judge then fulfilled his obligations to seek maximum relief for the creditors and moved swiftly toward a final decision. In negotiations that took place inside and outside the courtroom, bid details changed and dollar amounts increased. Chapman University ended up giving three separate offers. The details provided leaseback discounts and potential buyback opportunities that were so generous, they could not be matched by the diocese. Chapman's bids only slightly edged increases from the diocese. But the Chapman offer included net operational savings in real dollars for the Crystal Cathedral Ministries equal to tens of millions beyond the final auction sale price. It was a costly long-term commitment, but a bold move.

On paper, the Chapman offer was the better offer for Crystal Cathedral Ministries to stay in the Crystal Cathedral, and if it could raise money down the road, they could possibly buy the cathedral and some buildings back. The offer caused divisions in the Crystal

Cathedral boardroom. One faction wanted to sell to Chapman, hoping beyond hope that they would be saving the Crystal Cathedral for their own use. The other side argued that there was no way to raise the money, and eventually they would be forced to move. Selling to the Diocese of Orange was the only way to ensure that the cathedral would always be a place of worship.

Following a deadline imposed by the court, the board announced in late October 2011, a year since the original bankruptcy filing, that it had endorsed the Chapman offer. But it was a reluctant endorsement, according to church leadership, and one board member who voted in favor of the diocese in a separate vote was sure it was not the final word. However, from a legal perspective, the bankruptcy court and the creditors' committee now agreed that Chapman was the preferred buyer. Judge Kwan set a date to confirm Chapman as the buyer.

The diocese was not ready to quit, and some at the highest levels of the Crystal Cathedral Ministries had grown more certain every day that endorsing the Chapman offer had been a grave mistake.

The Bids

With only days separating them from the judge's hard deadline of Monday, June 14, 2011, the team from the Diocese of Orange tried to come up with the best new terms, if any, and be prepared. It had one last document to file. The diocese and Chapman had the same dilemma: file bid modifications, after hours if necessary, over the weekend, or do nothing and hope the bids hold.

Chapman had been consistently lower in the cash offer than the diocese until it raised its bid to $51.5 million, which at the time matched the diocese. Its edge was the university's leaseback and buy-back generosity, which was so robust and meaningful for continued ministry operations at the cathedral and budget savings that it had the look of a winning strategy. The diocese was forced to find more money and boosted its offer to $55,400,000 all cash, a week earlier. It was $4 million more than its previous bid. It was a significant threshold for the creditors and improved the hand of the diocese. The change guaranteed creditors would be paid in full on the effective date.

The diocese's offer allowed Crystal Cathedral Ministries to retain the rights to lease the campus, excluding the family life center and Memorial Gardens, for three years. At $100,000 rent, it was $50,000 less than the Chapman plan. They could also lease the school for two years at $10,000 per month, a further $55,000 savings over the Chapman offer. Then there was the alternate worship space. The diocese was the only offer that put up for long-term lease a church, parish hall, offices, and a school altogether at one location. The first year at what was then St. Callistus would be rent-free. The total lease term would be ten years.

Another key provision was that the diocese would maintain the Memorial Gardens as an interfaith cemetery and would cover the costs of moving remains if families chose to do so. There had been such threats. There would be refunds to any families who had already reserved space but would choose to cancel as a result of the sale of the campus.

Responding to specific requests from Crystal Cathedral Ministries, the diocese offered the following:

- The organ would be carefully maintained and used at all Masses.
- Dr. Schuller's office in the Tower of Hope would be preserved in its current state for his personal use as long as he so chose.

U.S. Bank and Farmers and Merchants Bank were committed to consideration of the fully secured $54,500,000 loan.

But Monday loomed, and the diocese looked at the math. It was a competitive bid if not for the millions in promised savings and the potential buyback of some buildings in the Chapman offer. Bishop Brown had drawn the line, and the diocese was all in with a loan to underwrite the purchase at nearly $55 million. Diocese advisor Tim Busch urged the bishop to go to $57.5 million. Bishop Brown shook his head, but after careful consideration relented. He told Busch that if he wanted to raise the bid, he would have to raise the money himself. It could take weeks if not months to raise it under normal circumstances, even with Tim Busch's experience. He was looking at just days. But he was committed and so were a few others. *If it were meant to be, it would*, he thought.

Tim Busch and his wife, Steph, stepped up, with a half million dollars of their own money to get it started. Rob and Bernie Neal matched it with $500,000, and the John L. Curci Foundation gave $1 million. To get close to the $2.5 million, Jim and Susan Tecca gave $50,000, and Rand and Rosemary Sperry added the final $12,500. If push came to shove, Busch was sure he could raise more, but he later said in his heart that he felt the diocese had hit the right number. Before the weekend was over, the diocese filed a bid modification with the bankruptcy court for $57.5 million. But this was a race that was about more than money.

On Monday morning, as 9:00 a.m. approached, the gallery seats were filled to the point of standing room only. It was a problem for the court. The judge asked any attorneys seated in the gallery to move to the jury box or a bench to make room.

"Those of you who are standing, could you sit down, in the back?" said Judge Kwan. "Members of the public, if you're standing, there are seats. Would you please sit down? It's very uncomfortable having to stand up."[1] He was determined to make sure the public had the seats to observe proceedings. He was also intent on confirming Chapman University as the preferred buyer. It had taken a year to get to this point, and designation of a preferred buyer was paramount to finally reaching a conclusion to this lengthy bankruptcy. Judge Kwan was not new to this process.

Judge Robert N. Kwan had been an assistant U.S. attorney in Los Angeles for the Central District of California for nearly two decades before his appointment to the bankruptcy court in 2007. He was the deputy chief of the Tax Division, where he was a civil and criminal tax litigator. He received his law degree from Yale and his juris doctorate from the University of California Hastings College of the Law. He also obtained a master of laws in taxation. He had plenty of experience and was familiar with many of the major bankruptcy lawyers, including Alan Martin, who appeared for the diocese.

The first order of business was to recognize the bid increase by the diocese, and it was approved at $57.5 million. The creditors' committee, which is the group of organizations and people owed money, represented by Nanette Sanders, agreed that a bid at that level put the diocese offer on equal footing. But going into the morning's proceedings, Chapman University was the preferred buyer. Since the judge appeared to be intent on certifying the sale that day, it was an important position to be in. That was why the question came up early. It was to be a certification hearing.

"I mean there is a possibility that the Chapman offer could be modified here today," insisted Nanette Sanders for the creditors. "I just want to understand whether there's a firm stance that one buyer is preferred by the Schuller parties over the other."

"Yes," said Carl Grumer, representing Robert and Arvella Schuller. "If the money were the same, then we would be agreeable to the same understanding."

It was not a revelation that Chapman remained formally the preferred buyer, and in the gallery among the few representatives from the Diocese of Orange, there remained a sense of optimism despite the odds. Alan Martin, who was an optimist by nature but also the diocese's bankruptcy expert, knew the odds as well as anyone.

"My sense was," said Martin looking back, "that it was more likely than not that they would have been confirmed that day."[2] Martin waited for his opportunities to contribute. Micki Schinderle and Tim Busch could only watch to see where the proceedings headed and hope the bid increase would give the diocese a boost. But the judge had a lot to get through.

Thomas Polis, the attorney for Robert A. Schuller and his wife, Donna, said there had been a contract between his clients and the ministry that dated back to late 2008. That was when Robert A. Schuller was replaced as pastor. "There was a document that provided how much both Robert A. and Donna would be paid." He said it was a fixed amount.

"It's black and white," said Polis. "It's not sort of fuzzy like the intellectual property claims."

He was referring to intellectual property and other claims filed by Dr. Robert H. Schuller, Arvella Schuller, Carole Milner, and Timothy Milner.

"It's not fuzzy," said the judge flatly.

"Well, it's a written document," said Polis.

"The committee would obviously dispute that characterization," said Nanette Sanders. "We think it's very fuzzy."

"Yeah," agreed the judge. "I think it's probably not best to characterize the claims."

This was the bulk of the day's work, trying to make these insider claims less fuzzy. To figure it out exactly would take a claims-estimation proceeding, which was not going to happen if it required further delay. There were Robert A. Schuller's unpaid contract claims, the claim by Robert H. Schuller about an annuity that amounted to a retirement of $300,000 per year for the rest of his life, and intellectual-property claims from Dr. Schuller and a daughter. Whatever the final figure was, the claims at least were in the millions.

There was also testimony about the ministry's sources of income. It was stated that 70 percent of the revenues were tied to the *Hour of Power* broadcasts. Other revenue included the Memorial Gardens and a small amount of income from the bookstore. The store on campus had since closed and no longer was bringing in revenue.

While this was going on, numerous conversations were happening among legal counsels and clients , either by electronics, hushed conversation, or talks outside the courtroom. The court recessed by request for about ten minutes for some of those conversations to consolidate. There was no predicting what happened when court reconvened.

During the break there were developments and two important participants had not returned, which was not lost on Judge Kwan. Chapman's attorney Jeffrey Broker and the creditors' committee attorney Nanette Sanders were steps outside the courtroom in an attorney conference room. They were aware of their tardiness, but they had to talk. Judge Kwan let them confer and gave them a few extra minutes. When another attorney volunteered to go to the conference room and nudge them a bit, the judge agreed. It was enough out of the ordinary to feel like a dramatic pause with most left wondering what was happening.

The most experienced bankruptcy attorneys there, including Alan Martin, saw the delay as business as usual for bankruptcy court.

"That's very standard," said Martin, in a later interview. "Typically, judges are willing to allow that and entertain that and it keeps the process moving. In theory, he's going to improve offers." What Martin was thinking, at that moment, was that the diocese position, based on the new bid, was gaining momentum.

But he was not aware how what came next was going to alter the direction of the case. In that way, he was not much different than the typical spectator. Only a few knew where the delay was headed. In minutes, Broker and Sanders returned.

"Judge Kwan, Jeffrey Broker on behalf of Chapman University," he reintroduced himself as was customary after a break. "The university has presented to the debtor and committee an alternative proposal relating to purchase of the Crystal Cathedral property." Suddenly onlookers in the gallery were leaning forward and giving each other curious looks. Broker said the committee for the creditors was reviewing it with financial experts and the Crystal Cathedral Ministry's attorney was discussing it with board members. They needed some time. The judge granted another fifteen-minute recess.

In the hallway, just feet away from the attorney room, diocese lawyer Maria Schinderle had a lump in her throat as she saw the attorneys for Chapman enter and close the door.

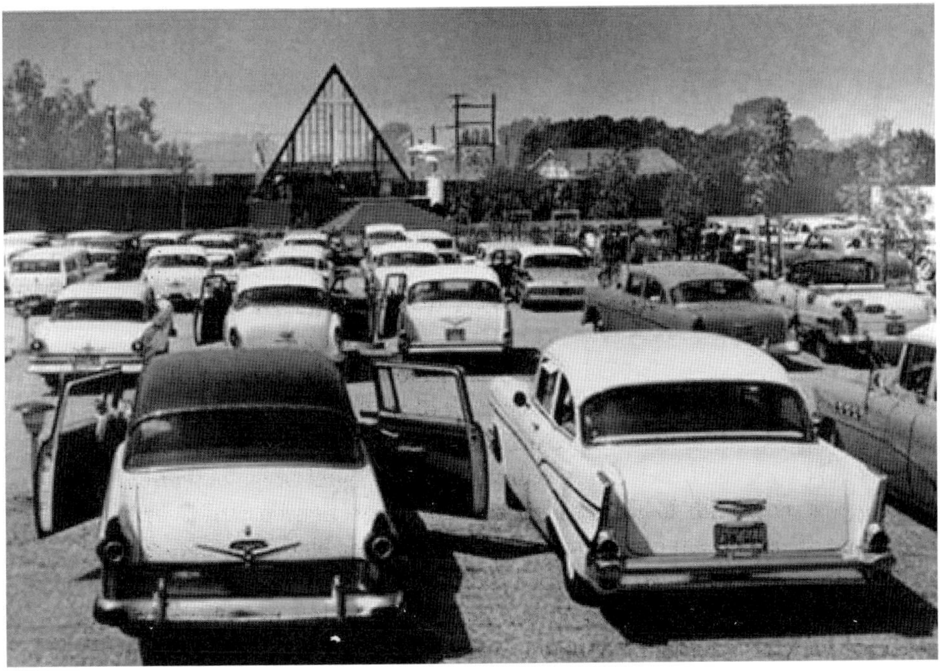

Source: Los Angeles Times

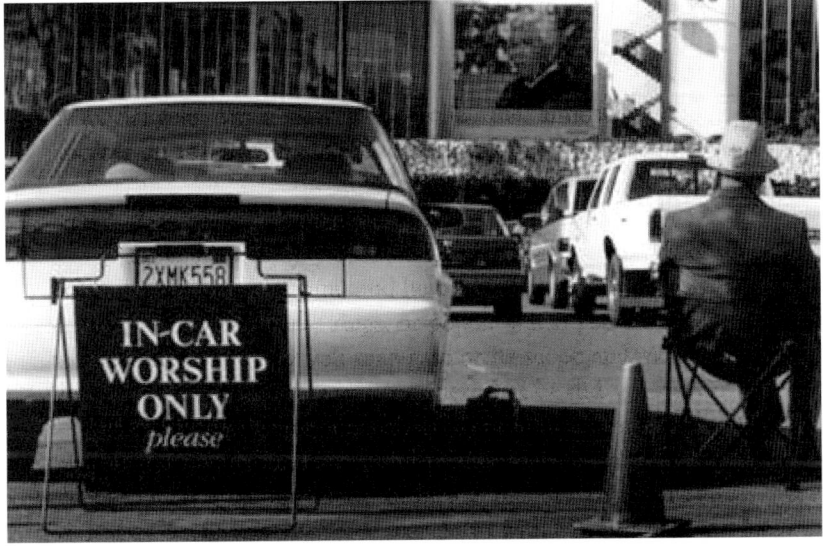

In June 1957, the Rev. Robert H. Schuller held his Garden Grove Community Church service at the Orange Drive-In. The church had no permanent building and rented the drive-in each Sunday.

2XMK558
IN-CAR
WORSHIP
ONLY
please

Source: Gail Fisher, Los Angeles Times

At the Rev. Robert H. Schuller's drive-in church in Garden Grove, designed by Richard Neutra, parishioners could view the service from cars on a giant video screen.

Ruby Rinker and Dr. Robert Schuller

Pope John Paul II and Dr. Robert Schuller

Source: Courtesy Berni Neal

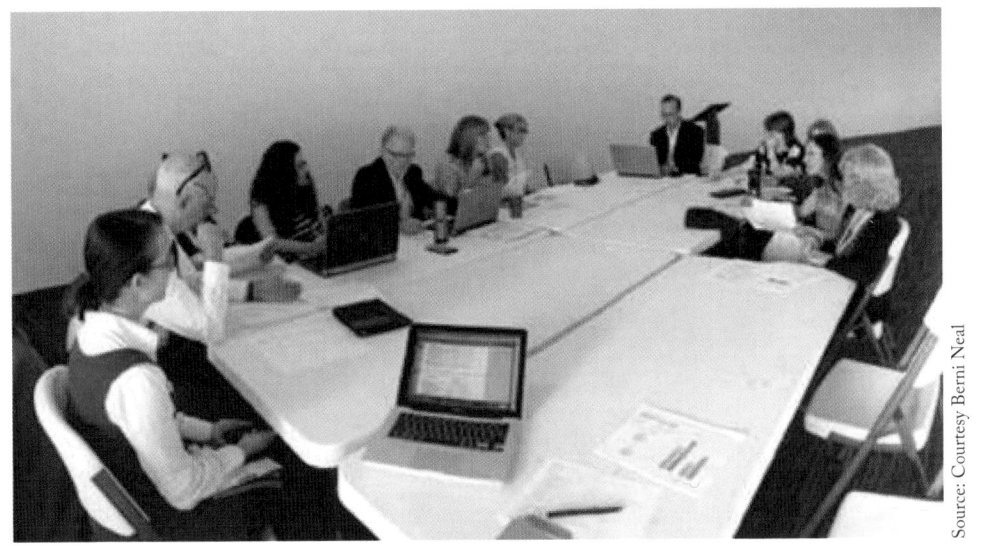

Construction meeting for Christ Cathedral

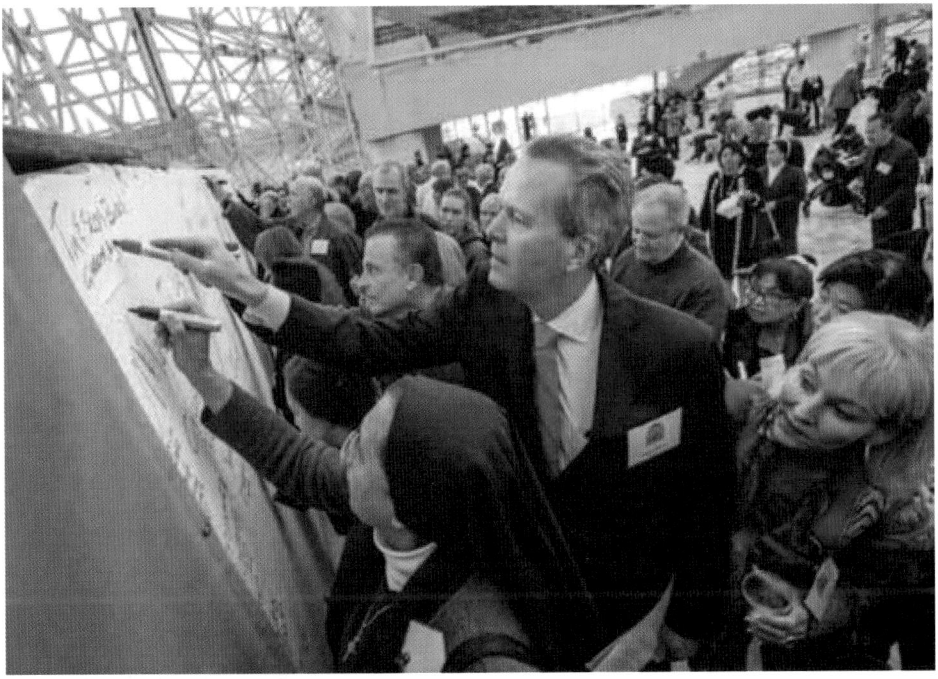

Photo by Paul Rodriguez, Orange County Register/SCNG

Catholic diocese kicks off $72 million Christ Cathedral remodel

Construction meeting
for Christ Cathedral

Construction meeting for Christ Cathedral

Construction meeting for Christ Cathedral

Construction meeting
for Christ Cathedral

Pope Benedict XVI and Bishop Tod Brown

Christ Cathedral

"I can remember thinking, 'How can they come up with this at this late date?'" She knew the diocese had limited funds. She pulled Tim Busch aside.[3]

"Tim, we're going to lose this," she said. "Do you think we could offer more money?" She was serious with a hint of desperation. She later recalled what she was thinking at that moment. "I don't want to be the gal who loses this for another five million dollars. You're gonna lose the whole thing," she said.

"No, we're not," he said.[4]

"How do you know?"

"I know."

Tim Busch could not explain his confidence to Schinderle, but as he sat there, he felt a voice in his ear say, *No more.* It was a leap of faith.

Schinderle felt like it was another one of those moments when she lapsed in her own trust in God. She recalled that she repeatedly learned during the process that when she wanted to be in control, things went off the rails. "The only time I got misdirected in this," said Schinderle, "if I ever did, during this whole thing, was when I got in the way of the Holy Spirit." She pointed out that Bishop Brown was an example of leaving it up to God.

"So, that's basically what we did," she said.

It was hard to do when they also knew, if it were going to be about the highest bidder, Chapman could go to $65 million and keep going if it wanted.

After recess, the court came to order. Broker returned to the podium with a man most people in the room recognized.

"With me at the podium is President James Doti," said Broker, "president of Chapman University, and he wanted to make some comments before I went into discussing a second alternative for the debtor to consider in this case."

Judge Kwan granted the request, and Doti, who was no stranger to public speaking, was gracious and confident in thanking the court for the opportunity.

"It's become more obvious that the Crystal Cathedral is a central and special part of this county," said Doti. "It's really become a global beacon for the inspired vision and incredible generosity of the Crystal Cathedral congregation over the last fifty-five years.

In our bid, we are giving the church as much as we can, we felt, to remain on the campus and occupying the buildings and facilities critical to the continuation of this important ministry." Doti went on to point out that John Crean, a Newport Beach philanthropist and namesake of the shimmering eighteen-story stainless-steel carillon steeple, was one of his closest friends. Crean was buried in the Memorial Gardens.

"I received a letter from his daughter on behalf of the family, saying that they would disinter his remains if this were to go to the Catholic Church, and they were hoping that we would do everything we can as a university to give the Crystal Cathedral the opportunity to continue its important work."

In media reports, the Protestant cemetery possibly changing hands to the Catholic Church was part of the story, but there was not unanimous agreement about whether it was a good or bad thing should it transpire. A lot more about that issue was destined to be addressed at another time. The Crean family letter to Doti clearly identified where they fell on the issue. Doti invoked Crean's name and circumstance skillfully because it was a matter that seemed personal and resonated with some in the gallery. Those heads nodded in agreement. Doti said the Crystal Cathedral's mission was symbiotic with the Crystal Cathedral itself, and it was built using the finances of church supporters. But it was also a matter of the future of Chapman University; he said the purchase would aid "future academic interests," and the cathedral campus would be a place to potentially expand the health-sciences campus so that the university could one day become a medical and/or pharmaceutical school. To that end, and the financial viability of the Crystal Cathedral Ministries, Doti insisted that the new proposal was necessary.

The energy in the room had shifted. The contingent of those in the audience focused on retaining the Crystal Cathedral began to buzz as Chapman seemed on their side and now on offense. James Doti turned the details of the offer over to the attorney Jeffrey Broker. It might have been a bit of a letdown to hear Broker first mention the subject so intensely referenced already: the reserve of six, or so, million dollars to cover claims by the Schuller family. But then he explained how the new offer would work. For the audience, the key changes flowed like a sporting event escalating in excitement.

Broker pointed out that the cash bid would remain unchanged, with net proceeds working out to $54.5 million, a point that raised eyebrows since the highest bid remained with the diocese. The two-year lease for the Crystal Cathedral Academy for $65,000 a month also would not change, and the university would use the white four-story campus structure as the health-sciences facility.

But then it got interesting.

"It's my understanding that an emergency meeting of the board of Crystal Cathedral Ministries is in the process of being called," he said. Another surprise, and a major wild card. "There's a minimum of forty-eight hours' notice, and the expectation is that they can meet and discuss what I'm about to put out on the table midweek and be able to tell the court and everyone else whether there's interest in pursuing this second possible way to go."

It was a stunning development in a courtroom fully expecting a confirmation of Chapman University as the preferred buyer that day. The judge could not have been clearer about his intentions to hear the motion to confirm. But that was now in doubt.

What was on the table?

Broker identified the "core buildings" as the Crystal Cathedral, the original sanctuary called the Neutra Arboretum, the Memorial Gardens, the Crean Tower aka carillon steeple, and the thirteen-story office building Tower of Hope.

- The Memorial Gardens would be subject to a fifteen-year lease at one dollar per month.
- The ministry would be able to utilize the Crystal Cathedral on Sundays and at other times based upon mutual agreement with the university.
- The lease option for the Neutra Arboretum, for everyday use, would go from fifteen to thirty years at one dollar per month.
- The buyback option would change from a five-year "repurchase option" to a fifteen-year right of first refusal after six months' notice.
- The Welcoming Center, as originally planned, would immediately be taken over by the university.
- There would be a cap on the reserve for the unsecured claims at $2 million, a provision that eliminated the contentious plan

note. This meant that the Schullers and ministry as debtor would resolve the matter at a later time limited by the cash in reserve.

"In other words," Broker added, "only in the event that the university decided to sell would a right of first refusal come into effect."

It meant the buyback under this, now the third Chapman proposal, was off the table unless Chapman chose to sell. It was this point more than anything else that sent representatives of the Crystal Cathedral scrambling. Whether Broker and his client Chapman University knew it or not at the time, the new offer with its more generous provisions raised questions about the buyback. It was the provision that supporters of the Chapman offer at Crystal Cathedral Ministries had clung to as their ticket forward. Chapman knew its status as preferred buyer held sway, and as the hearing continued, it was obvious they still wanted to see confirmation happen that day.

"Your Honor, just briefly," James Doti added, "I just wanted to relate that I've come to know members of the congregation these last few weeks and have come to understand and appreciate their resolve, their commitment, their passion for continuing its very important ministry. There's a maxim, 'When there's a will there's a way.' I have come to realize there's certainly a will. And I'm pleased that Chapman University, we believe, is offering a way."

Throughout the rollout of the new option and comments afterward, there had been a rising volume from the gallery that ebbed and flowed between awe and, confusion, disappointment, and exhilaration. It had gotten so loud the judge had enough.

"Okay. I'm going to—just hold on," said Judge Kwan. "I'm going to ask members of the audience to tone it down. This isn't a competitive event. I realize that emotions are running a little high, but I think we need to be respectful. So, I'm not going to ask you— you know, I know you may feel some emotion inside, but I ask, as a matter of respect for all parties concerned, if you could restrain yourself. It's not a football game or—this is a very serious situation for all concerned. There's a lot at stake, and I'm asking members of the audience to control your emotions. We are a court of law and we need to be respectful. Thank you."

When calm had returned, the attorney for the ministry, Marc Winthrop, confirmed what some suspected and others dreaded. After conferring with some members of the Crystal Cathedral Board, it turned out the proposal included an element that needed to be evaluated by the board.

"That is the loss of the right to repurchase," said Winthrop, "which would be replaced with a right of first refusal." While the proposal appeared to be thoughtful and constructive according to Winthrop, he felt *right of purchase* and *right of refusal* had two very different meanings. "Right of first refusal is only available if the property is to be sold. Therefore, the ministry would have no control over that."

To answer the question as to whether that is acceptable to the board would require a continuance of the hearing. Another halt in proceedings, just the suggestion that the board could meet no sooner than forty-eight hours, was a jolt. Winthrop was among those reluctant to even ask for a continuance. It was supposed to be decision day. But the bylaws required the forty-eight-hour notice for a meeting, and that was Wednesday afternoon. Taking that quickly into account, Judge Kwan saw a stop sign rapidly approaching.

"You're asking for a continuance, right?"

"I'm just informing—it's not my—"

"You're not asking for a continuance of the hearing for the court's ruling?"

"I don't even have the authority to do that from the board. But all I can do is advise the court that this alternative is one that cannot be accepted by the board without a board meeting."

"Do they want to entertain this proposal? By necessity, they'd have to ask for a continuance. So, if you don't know, then the court would be inclined to just continue with the hearing. Who is asking—no one is asking for a continuance?"

The creditors attorney Nanette Sanders did not request a continuance either, but she supported the idea of allowing the board time to consider the proposal, whatever that looked like. Her point went back again to the question of the unsecured debt. The new proposal created a $2 million fund for the Schullers' outstanding claims.

"In many respects," she said, "this is a very elegant solution to the dilemma that has now been laid out before the court today." She went as far as to call it an opportunity for the Schullers to play the hero, "to stand before the court and say, 'Yes, our focus is this ministry and its ability to survive, and we're willing to accept that reserve.' We have $1.8 million and we have $2 million on the table as a reserve for insider claims."

Exactly what the Schullers were willing to accept and the precise amount the various insiders intended to claim had been the big unanswered questions for most of the hearing—that is, until the new Chapman proposal was introduced. As the court was forced to consider a continuance, the pathway went right through the core of those questions.

Carl Grumer—the attorney for Robert H. and Arvella Schuller, Robert Harold, and the Milners—ran through circular arguments with the judge. During that time, Judge Kwan was able to bring the questions a little more into focus. But halfway in, Crystal Cathedral attorney Marc Winthrop interrupted.

"Your Honor," said Winthrop, "on further reflection, after consulting with the members of the board who are in attendance here, I do feel that I would need to ask for a continuance." He emphasized that it was a brief continuance, so the board could consider the proposal. "There are certainly some very attractive aspects, and as I indicated, there's an aspect that would result in the ultimate loss of the cathedral."

The attorney for the creditors' committee opposed on the grounds that the outstanding unsecured debt questions remained unanswered. The judge agreed and allowed some testimony to figure out outstanding questions about Crystal Cathedral Ministries' contractual obligations to pay Robert H. and Arvella Schuller what amounts to a retirement. Other questions related to intellectual-property rights, both for the *Hour of Power* TV program and for the many books Schuller had written. The effort was aimed at figuring out if the reserve was to be more or less than $6 million. Did the combined claims at the length of the payouts make sense including the terms? Some payments to Robert H. Schuller and his wife would go on until their deaths. In their eighties at the time, life expectancy was a question. Would they live long enough, beyond the century mark, to deplete the requested reserve?

At one point, the subject of the ministry's credit worthiness, its solvency going forward, and its ability to fund its ongoing obligations postbankruptcy came up. If any responsibility for paying debts to the Schullers remained, would it be they who would assume the risk? Testimony showed that the ministry's plunging donations had leveled off since Reverend Sheila Schuller Coleman took over.

"You don't think the ministry is going to make it?" Judge Kwan asked Carl Grumer.

"I don't know. Years ago, we would have thought the ministry would have been doing fine now. It's not. That's why we're here. We're talking about the reality here. And the fact is, if you had asked five years ago, I'm sure everybody—Dr. Schuller would have felt the ministry was going to go on as it was forever. But that's not what's happening, so we have to look at the reality. We have to look at what has happened and try to calculate what might happen."

At stake here was a bankruptcy sale pushing $60 million, not to mention the human toll on the ministry, the congregation, and the Schullers. So, the time and detail spent on the subject of unsecured debt wasn't trivial. In bankruptcy, unsecured debt was the last debt paid, and often not paid at all. The goal of the court was to get 100 percent of the secured debts paid. But this level of detail provided a glaring example of why it took a year to get to this point. When the parties came to some agreement on what the questions were surrounding certain numbers, the judge finally decided to conclude for the day.

"Okay. Thursday at one-thirty," he said. "So, the board can decide which of the Chapman proposals, if any, they wish to designate as preferred." But he knew it was also a chance for the board to consider the revised offer from the diocese. "This will give the board time to consider this."

Both offers, he said, were feasible.

As the courtroom cleared there were somber emotions about yet another delay. Although it seemed the door was open a crack for the diocese, the diocese team did not necessarily agree.

"I don't think it'll happen," said Tim Busch, as he headed out the door. Later, he felt a tinge of shame for his lack of faith. But he recalled saying, "It will take a miracle."

Diocese bankruptcy lead Alan Martin had a different take. "While it would appear on its face that it was going to be an offer that was more favorable to Chapman, at that juncture, time was our ally."

Martin believed that, with time, the board might consider the Chapman proposal but also consider, with the help of the rapport the diocese had built, the diocese's motives as well as its bid.

But just as the board was to vote, Chapman University dropped an eleventh-hour bid, which seemed insurmountable.

The Board Votes

It was late morning in Palm Beach, Florida, when there came an unexpected doorbell ring at a home on the exclusive Millionaire's Row. The pink-stucco mansion with the terracotta roof was secretly up for sale, and Ruby Rinker would have known in advance if the visitor had something to do with the sale. Though the sale was important, it was not what occupied her mind at the moment; she knew that was not the reason for the ring. The sale was on the back burner. What she was thinking about was the imminent board vote, now hours away. If that was not enough to make her day feel a little off kilter, the Crystal Cathedral Ministries Board member had visitors—quite by mistake, really.

Standing there at her door were two men easily not mistaken for door-to-door salesmen, though not entirely different from Halloween party guests. But it was not Halloween. That passed weeks ago. The two men wore brown robes—more accurately, brown monastic tunics commonly worn by monks. Their attire was complete with the Cincture of Chastity, the leather belt monks tied over their tunics at the waist. All things considered, it was still a surprise that they were indeed Carmelite monks from Wyoming, and they were at the wrong address. A happy mistake.

Ruby Rinker invited the young men in anyway, to sit down and have a cup of coffee. During the conversation, she learned they were from Wyoming and they enjoyed coffee. They enjoyed it so much, roasting beans was how they supported the monastery. Their beans and brews were available online at Mystic Monk Coffee. With all that was going on, it was a welcome distraction. The board meeting teleconference, the one that would change everything, neared. It took everything she had to keep her mind on something else.

The vote had remained at the front of her mind since she was alerted to the announcement Tuesday morning, underscored by her conversation with her old friend Tuesday night. Robert H. Schuller

105

was known to call her on occasion as late as eleven o'clock at night Florida time, to discuss this or that dilemma, and they would talk about solutions. For Ruby Rinker, those conversations usually ended with her suggesting the obvious. She would tell him to pray and the answer would come. This time, however, it was Ruby Rinker calling Schuller. She would never know a more difficult time for Schuller and the church. Now the board situation was in uncharted territory. She knew the preacher neared the end of the ministry he had built, and there was not going to be another vote after this one. She wanted to know straight from him how he planned to vote.

He told her.

Rinker's call to Schuller was hardly the only one that day. There were many, and not just for the board of the Crystal Cathedral.

When Bishop Tod Brown got his phone call, he had just returned home to Orange County after a long trip to Baltimore, Maryland. He had attended the four-day annual meeting of the U.S. Conference of Catholic Bishops (USCCB), which had just concluded. The conference happened at the same time every year. As a result, Brown's birthday landed in the middle of the gathering of bishops. As it happened, he just marked his seventy-fifth birthday. It was a significant anniversary, since it was the one at which bishops were required by canon law to submit their resignation and retire. There had been a lot of questions from peers and other leadership in attendance about the Crystal Cathedral.

"I just told them I didn't think we were going to get the cathedral because Chapman made a bigger offer and we couldn't increase our offer," Brown explained.[1]

On the phone, diocese advisor and friend Tim Busch was in a less than optimistic mood. There were so many times that what he had witnessed seemed the work of the Holy Spirit, and that feeling remained. Still, while he prayed about it, that did not make it God's will. Monday's bankruptcy hearing that should have certified Chapman University as the buyer had ended with a surprise delay. Chapman upped its offer yet again. The dollar amount was the same, but the long-term concessions to the Crystal Cathedral Ministries, including rent of one dollar per month for three decades, seemed insurmountable for any competing bid. In tangible benefit to the ministry, this aspect of the deal alone added tens of millions of dollars in concessions that the diocese could not match. A phone call or a brief meeting was usually how Bishop Brown found out about developments in bankruptcy court. He had not attended any of the hearings, mostly to avoid being a distraction and to tend to other obligations. It was not important for him to be there anyway, he reasoned. So, he had to be updated when there were developments.

Tim Busch told him what had happened Monday—all about how Chapman University again modified its offer and university president Doti addressed the court after a break, and how the judge decided to give the Crystal Cathedral Ministries time to have its board vote on choosing between the two Chapman offers. The forty-eight-hour reprieve from certification seemed to provide an opportunity for the board to also consider the offer from the diocese. But there was more to tell Bishop Brown.

Who knows how Busch would have really felt, and how the conversation with the bishop would have gone, if not for the news that Chapman University submitted a new bid of $59 million at around 2:30 in the afternoon, just as the board was preparing for a final vote? The new bid, which could not be matched by the diocese, seemed like the final blow. If approved, it would leave Crystal Cathedral Ministries more than a $7 million surplus, topping the diocese by over a million dollars. And that was on top of the already lucrative long-term concessions offered by Chapman.

"We're not going to get the cathedral tomorrow," a somber Busch told the Bishop.[2] It went against his instincts to say it, but he was also trying his best to be professionally objective. "They've outbid us. We can't go any higher." Brown's response was not lengthy, and Busch was certain Brown was comfortable in leaving it up to God.

It was true Tim Busch was feeling the pressure getting to him. He was not the only one. There was media attention and criticism from all sides, right from the start. It had never eased up, but only got worse. The circle of people who believed the cathedral purchase was the right and pragmatic move was small at the beginning, and it was not always clear who really believed and who just said they believed. By the first court date, there were numerous people with daily involvement to make it happen, but it was an up-and-down ride. Many were left unsure, and isolated, leaning on faith to move them forward. Tim Busch did not give up easily. He was used to working hard toward a goal despite obstacles. But this was some-thing so unique and surreal, he would have to be superhuman not to suffer from doubt and disillusionment. For his part, he did not show it on his face.

"I've never seen a guy move into action like Tim Busch," said Father Robert Spitzer of *Father Spitzer's Universe* on EWTN.[3] As mentioned previously, Spitzer was with Busch when Busch got his first call from Dr. Robert H. Schuller.

"It was the miraculous luncheon," Spitzer had said.

But was it? Was any of what had happened since, and all the work of so many people, the work of the Holy Spirit? No matter how the board vote turned out, Crystal Cathedral Ministries was going to lose much of what Schuller had built. What about that work and that of his congregation?

If the work of the Holy Spirit were at play throughout this pro-cess, the court proceedings, the rush to secure financial backing, and finally in the days leading up to the Crystal Cathedral's vote, how could they have known? How could Tim Busch and others know for sure?

"You can't know definitively, through empirical knowledge," offered Spitzer. "But you certainly can through the eyes of faith that enough clues are present." Spitzer said it was about looking at those clues to see the guiding hand of providence at work.

"When doors suddenly open," he said, "and things begin to sweep in, things begin to work, you can start assembling some of the clues."

Spitzer said he could not count the bankruptcy of the Crystal Cathedral Ministries as a blessing for the church. Looking back on it, he said it was "a terribly bleak moment" in Schuller's life.

"He was a man of real faith," said Spitzer. But the bankruptcy happened; the property was set to be sold. "We either step into the breach and think about the possibilities at that moment or not. And I think Tim Busch was an instrument at that moment for stepping into the breach."

There was no opportunity like it before, and likely never again. The campus had all the buildings the diocese needed, with a great potential in the cathedral, a school with room to grow, a pastoral center, and so much more. It could continue as a destination for tourists around the world, Catholics and non-Catholics, preserving and building upon what Schuller spent his life building up from a ten-acre orchard. For the diocese, the opportunity offered it all at a price that made it that much more a moment like none before.

Tim Busch finished his call with Bishop Brown thinking about all the work that had been put into the effort to acquire the Crystal Cathedral by Maria Schinderle, Alan Martin, Bishop Brown, and the whole team of lay experts and the diocese. The work of the instruments at the diocese was all but over. Some of the people who were instrumental and supportive of the effort had faded into the background and were unavailable. It was a lonely feeling.

"I was scared," said Busch.

He did not know for sure what everyone else was thinking, but he felt alone, as if there was not anyone left but the bishop who really believed. He did not want to lose that sense of providence, but that call to the bishop felt final. There certainly was nothing left he or anyone at the diocese could do.

The bleak period for Schuller's ministry neared a close, as the board vote loomed on that winter day in 2011.

"The Holy Spirit is not going to do it for us," said Father Spitzer. "The Holy Spirit always needs instruments. He can inspire those instruments. He can make things happen through those instruments."

From Schuller's voicemail to Tim Busch at lunch, to the end of Monday's long bankruptcy hearing and the court's decision to allow forty-eight hours for a Crystal Cathedral Board vote, there were many instruments, including Rob and Berni Neal, Rand Sperry, Joe Navoa, Jim Tecca, and a last-minute financial boost from the John L. Curci Foundation. Many others played their parts large and small as the instruments. None was more important than the others. They had done what they could for the diocese, putting together offers, securing bank credit, conducting due diligence on the campus, and cutting through Catholic Church red tape. And they did it in a couple of months, which was no small miracle in itself. It was all they could do, and the diocese had reached its bidding limits. All that was left was the board vote, and its main purpose was to decide between two Chapman offers, one that had just been boosted to outbid the diocese. It seemed like an easy decision. At least, that was what nearly everyone assumed.

When it came to the final board decision on the future of the Crystal Cathedral, if God's hand guided, it was Robert H. Schuller who was the ultimate instrument. As it had begun, it would end.

Most people by the age of seventy-nine would have been eager to pass the reigns of the family business off to a son or daughter. In 2006, Crystal Cathedral Ministries was turned over to Robert A. Schuller, who had been groomed for the role for much of his life. But it was short-lived. A rift developed early on between father and son over who had the final say for the ministry's major decisions. At least, the younger Schuller believed it had more to do with his father's inability to fully relinquish control.

Crystal Cathedral Ministries was a massive operation with a budget rivaling many businesses in Orange County at about $72 million. At the time, there were five hundred employees and thirty-five hundred volunteers for the new senior pastor to manage. It became apparent quickly that there was more than just tension between father and son. The board of directors watched as *Hour of Power* viewership and finances fell. It placed much of that blame on Robert A. Schuller. The new senior pastor saw the board as antagonistic. He worried that since some board members were paid employees of the church, it was a conflict of interest. Some accounts suggested his own family members on the board felt threatened that they too would be removed, including the founder. Robert A. Schuller has said he sought to re-create the board as a more independent body.

In 2008, the board, led by his father, rejected Robert A. Schuller's bid to expand the board, and he later resigned as senior pastor. The situation did not improve with his father, and a month later, the younger Schuller was dismissed by the senior Schuller from the *Hour of Power* program. Robert H. Schuller blamed a "lack of shared vision."[4]

Not long after, Sheila Schuller Coleman, the eldest daughter, was named pastor, but in a shared role with her father, Robert H. Schuller. The elder Schuller, now eighty-two, had returned to a prominent role at the church, buoyed by the desire of the board of directors to boost revenues. It was a role he had announced, and hoped, he would fulfill for a period of three years. The ministry was desperate for a rescue with a reported drop in ratings for the *Hour of*

Power of 50 percent and the reluctant liquidation of excess property assets to pay its bills. The shared leadership arrangement lasted just one year.

Schuller announced his full retirement after fifty-five years in July 2010. In that year working with his daughter, revenues reportedly dipped from $30 million to $22 million—a staggering number when just four years earlier the ministry had an annual budget of $72 million. Debt was piling up.

The slide continued for the ministry and for the *Hour of Power*, the primary source of revenue, and allegations of board member conflicts of interest continued. It could only be classified as a power struggle, a struggle for control of the Crystal Cathedral. Pastor Schuller Coleman had also taken the ministry in a new direction with a Gospel choir and a more Pentecostal message. It had caused divisions within the congregation.

Robert H. Schuller held little influence; he was tired and aged, but he and Arvella remained voting board members. The announcement that Crystal Cathedral Ministries had been forced to file for Chapter 11 bankruptcy in October 2010 could not have been a bigger sign of Robert H. Schuller's powerlessness, but there was one more blow to come. By June the following year, the bankruptcy court was calling the shots and the sale of the Crystal Cathedral seemed inevitable. Schuller mustered up the strength to take calls and meetings about what might be done with the campus and ministry after a sale. Pastor Sheila Schuller Coleman tried in vain to rally parishioners to give, coming up well short of any chance to save the ministry.

Later that month of June 2011, the Crystal Cathedral Board convened a meeting for a vote for removal of Reverend Schuller from the board. One account by Robert A. Schuller said his mother, Arvella, was there and voted no. Carol Schuller Milner later said neither her mother nor father were at the board meeting. Either way the result was the same. Robert H. Schuller, founder of Crystal Cathedral Ministries, was voted off the board as a voting member and moved to a ceremonial nonvoting position of chairman emeritus.

The move by the board of the ministry he founded was a blow. Sheila Schuller Coleman's hold on power was precarious at best, and the congregation was in turmoil. And a petition drive, by some congregants, was launched that aimed to "take the church back."

"It is time to rise up and take our church back," it stated.[5] "This means: no family members, no paid staff, no paid contractors."

The ministry's assets faced liquidation in court, and disintegration under its own roof. The Schuller family, still fractured, put on a good face with its traditionally optimistic attitude publicly. Robert H. Schuller never addressed the subject publicly about how he really handled this particular dark moment in his life, but he was known to wait on God and to have faith that "he who began a good work in you will bring it to completion" (Philippians 1:6).

The tapestry is woven from the back.

Before he had formally retired, he recognized that the ministry's board was in trouble. He had reached out to his longtime friend Ruby Rinker in Palm Beach, who had been a board member years before. He told her the board was in disarray. There was infighting, suspicion, and not many people wanted to sit on a dysfunctional board. He needed people he could trust and asked her if she would return to the board. He did not know for how long. Ruby Rinker accepted the offer.

When the board moved to vote Schuller out a year later, Rinker voted no. She could not believe what was happening. She was prepared, if it happened, to vote again to reinstate him. Schuller worked behind the scenes to make it happen while dealing with inquiries and bankruptcy proceedings. Chapman University's offer was submitted just days after Schuller had been ousted from the board. Even without a vote, serious potential buyers wanted his approval.

In late July, just one month after removing him, the Crystal Cathedral Board held another vote. This time, Robert H. Schuller was reinstated as a voting member, and two members who had voted to remove him were forced out.

The board expanded from five members to nine.

"It was a very stressful time for the board," said Rinker. "Nobody knew how stressful."[6]

Bankruptcy court proceedings would eventually narrow the focus to two serious buyers and come to a head with a forty-eight-hour break, so that the board could make a choice. When court recessed on that mid-November Monday, the choices were clear, and all that was left was for the nine members of the Crystal Cathedral Board to debate, discuss, and decide.

It was in that moment of forty-eight hours that Ruby Rinker's placement on the board nearly two years earlier, Schuller's reinstatement, and the sudden reorganization of the Crystal Cathedral Board only a month earlier revealed their purpose.

One offer was $57.5 million, and at the last minute, the other offer grew to $59 million.

Despite the higher bid by Chapman University, the board turned to the question of the offer from the diocese. Ruby Rinker sat in her Florida home on a teleconference to attend the Crystal Cathedral Board meeting. The question was not whether the Chapman offer would be acceptable, but instead, under the given written bid proposal and commitments as submitted to the court, and to the board, should the board approve the sale to the Diocese of Orange?

Rinker knew the answer. She knew it before the question was asked. It was cemented in her mind when someone supporting the Chapman offer called her and suggested what a wonderful performing-arts venue the Crystal Cathedral would make. She was incredulous.

"I felt it should remain a church," she said. "I never felt like it was going to be sold to Chapman."

There were nine sitting board members.

The vote was five to four in favor of selling to the Diocese of Orange.

Early the next morning, Tim Busch got a call from Crystal Cathedral Board member Dr. Diane Highum. They had gotten acquainted and developed a rapport sitting in court next to each other for several of the hearings.

"We voted," said Highum.[7] "The Holy Spirit's alive in Orange County. You're going to get the cathedral today." She told Busch the bylaws required that the resources of the Crystal Cathedral be dedicated to the preaching of the Gospel of Jesus Christ. "Chapman University," she explained, "is not about preaching Jesus Christ."

Tim Busch broke down—the strain of the countless hours and effort that had mounted, released in a single unbelievable moment. He called Steph, his wife, and released some of that pent-up emotion. His next call was to Bishop Brown. Not long after, his phone rang again. It was Maria Schinderle, who had just heard the news from the bishop. Good timing. Busch had a request.

"I want Bishop to be there today," he said.[8]

"I have reserves of [him] being there, just my reserves, and us being turned down," Schinderle cautioned over concerns about how it might look.

"Don't worry; I'll pick Bishop up and I will drive him there myself."

"As long as he's with you, or somebody."

The five votes in favor of selling to the diocese were Robert and Arvella Schuller, Diane Highum, James Dawson, and Ruby Rinker. A bittersweet result, but a relief for the majority. It was a hard-fought vote amid what Rinker recalled was some very nasty opposition to a possible sale to Catholics. There were hurt feelings, and Rinker was among those feeling very sad about the criticism.

Rinker later underscored just how difficult it was to vote to sell the church Schuller had built. She held no ill will toward Chapman University. Jim Doti and the college had the best of intentions. But she could never shake the words from that caller who mentioned a performing-arts center. It had been suggested by Chapman as a possible use for the Crystal Cathedral. Rinker imagined some of the more risqué programming that would inevitably be held there, and she did not think it was appropriate for a church. Her vote was a vote for keeping the Crystal Cathedral a place of Christian worship. It came down to why it was built in the first place. Rinker said the congregation and people around the world built the church. Immeasurable love and commitment went into the effort to grow the ministry over more than five decades. It was so deeply heartbreaking to give it up that, nearly ten years later, many remained devastated. Rinker and the Schullers knew there was no way the ministry could raise the money to buy the buildings back, and the future of their beloved cathedral would be bleak at best. What good would it have served if not as a church? For the board it was the toughest of decisions in the face of harsh criticism. But Ruby Rinker said it was the only sound and logical decision.

The move by the board would stun the bankruptcy judge and nearly everyone who entered the federal court building in downtown Los Angeles the next day.

And it still was far from over.

The Lower Bid?

Just before one o'clock, Maria Schinderle walked into the courthouse and into the security line just behind a woman who was a member of the Chapman University legal team. Schinderle's phone chimed the arrival of a text message, so she looked. It was from an attorney for Crystal Cathedral Ministries.

It simply read, "Congratulations."[1]

Crystal Cathedral Ministries had issued a formal press release announcing the results of the board's vote and the news that it had chosen to sell the cathedral and campus to the diocese. The news was riding the power of digital information around the world. For Schinderle the moment of hesitant disbelief was interrupted when an attorney from Chapman turned around to face her and said, "Congratulations." To Schinderle, the walk the rest of the way to the courtroom was a blur. It was unbelievable and yet totally believable.

If it came to fruition, it would be quite the birthday surprise for Bishop Brown, who had just turned seventy-five two days earlier and was set to send his canon law–required resignation letter for retirement. The age is significant for being the age of retirement for bishops. Suddenly, Maria Schinderle was glad Tim Busch had asked to have Bishop Brown join them in court. But it was far from settled, and a marathon session would cast all assumptions aside.

Inside the courtroom the audience took their seats as the court came to order.

"I'll take appearances," said Judge Kwan, through a somewhat low and scratchy throat. He was not trying to be dramatic.[2] He was just suffering from a chest cold. He apologized in advance for any use of lozenges that became distracting or bothered any of the participants.

"Good afternoon, your Honor. Alan Martin," Martin introduced himself, "on behalf of the Roman Catholic Bishop of Orange," he said. "Maria Schinderle, the general counsel of the RCBO, is also here as well."

The lawyers and representatives from the other parties involved stated their names, including Jeffrey Broker with Chapman, who said university president James Doti was also present. Representing Robert H. Schuller was Carl Grumer. The ministry was represented by Marc Winthrop. Representatives from the Ad Hoc Congregants Committee and Farmers and Merchants Bank of Long Beach and Nanette Sanders with the Committee of Unsecured Creditors were among several others present.

Judge Kwan explained that the reason for the hearing was to allow the debtor's board to consider an alternative proposal that had been submitted by Chapman University. But there was also the critical matter of the results of the Crystal Cathedral's board meeting and recommendations. It was not known at what point Kwan became aware of the board's vote, but his next statement was unusual at the very least.

"The Court will take further testimony and receive evidence, if necessary, regarding the confirmation," said Judge Kwan. *An evidentiary hearing?* There was a smattering of murmurs in the audience.

Schinderle sat near Tim Busch and Bishop Brown. "It was something I'd never seen before in a bankruptcy hearing. It's usually a done deal by that time. The creditors have all agreed, everybody's agreed, and you bring it in, and the judge signs off on it and says fine." But Judge Kwan was concerned about a proposed sale that would have the debtor taking a lower bid. In other words, despite the clear endorsement from the board, which chose the proposal from the diocese, it was not going to be that easy.

"I think it's important that I allow this opportunity for people," said Judge Kwan, "parties in interest, to be heard because I think it will help me make the best decision that I can make. I'm expecting that I will make a decision today, and I'm optimistic."

Barring any unforeseen complication, one way or another, a decision was imminent. The court had previously declared that the offers from the diocese and Chapman were both "feasible and capable of confirmation." It had also understood that the Chapman offer was the preferred offer. But at the previous hearing, the court left it up to the board of Crystal Cathedral Ministries to make the decision. That was what happened and presumably should have ended the discussion.

"The board deliberated yesterday evening," said Crystal Cathedral attorney Marc Winthrop, "on the selection of a buyer after receiving enhanced bids as described on Monday and a further enhanced bid that came in yesterday from Chapman University. After very, very serious debate and deliberation, a great deal of thought, and appreciating the generosity of both offers, the board of directors of Crystal Cathedral Ministries voted to designate RCBO as the buyer of the campus. And that is the decision of the board."

"One of the things that the Court considers is that the money on the table is less than the alternative offer," Judge Kwan pointed out. "The debtor and the committee will offer evidence to show that this is an exercise of good business judgment and it's a sound business decision."

Winthrop was put on the spot. Not only did the judge want to hear evidence that it was sound business judgement, but he also wanted it right there and then. He was not going to delay the hearing again. Winthrop protested.

"Ultimately, your Honor, you are attempting to put the court in the position of telling a ministry, a non-profit corporation, that you should take a deal that gives you a little more money rather than one that gives you a little less money."

"If you're asking the Court, 'just accept that this is our decision' without evidence, then I'm not accepting that," Judge Kwan responded.

Before that could happen, Jeffrey Broker with Chapman modified the recently modified offer, to further adjust lease terms. "We didn't know until ten minutes to one o'clock today that the previous position of Chapman as preferred buyer was no longer the case." The offer from Chapman, on the table, had been $25,000 per month with escalating rent of 10 percent a year for ten years. "I've been advised and instructed by my client to change that lease calculation and lease term as follows: The rent shall be $1 per month for those properties for ten years." Then the following ten years, it would go to $25,000, escalating 10 percent annually. The total lease term option would be twenty years.

The bankruptcy proceedings and changing bids up to that point had been characterized by some in the media as a bidding war. It was more complex than competing bids. It was competing terms. For one side, that process had reached its end. Chapman was willing to go further. When faced with Chapman's extremely generous lease terms and duration alone, the diocese was unable to counter in any meaningful way.

This was hardly more evident to attendees in the audience than it was to Tim Busch and Maria Schinderle. They had entered the building with the news that the board had chosen the diocese offer. Suddenly, the deal seemed to be slipping away. Since the hearing started, Schinderle was repeatedly looking down at her phone. News alerts popped up at an increasingly rapid pace. News of what was happening in the courtroom was spreading around the state, country, and globe. It was unreal, but why should the hearing be any less of a rollercoaster than everything else that had happened up to that point? It seemed just moments since she had gotten the text of congratulations about the board vote. But then the judge took the unusual step of calling for an evidentiary hearing, and Chapman again boosted its terms.

Judge Kwan opened comments to anyone in the room interested in making a statement. He had accepted the recommendation and confirmed with the attorney for the unsecured creditors. The group's attorney agreed that the Catholic diocese's offer of $57.5 million more than covered all creditors and was a sound business decision for the creditors. But was it a sound business decision for Crystal Cathedral Ministries? The judge was interested in hearing any and all comments.

"Here we are three and a half days later from the hearing on Monday," said Thomas Link, representing the Ad Hoc Congregants Committee. "The Chapman offer was increased on Monday and the Chapman offer was increased yesterday. It would be a very negative action to allow a shell game to be played with the Crystal Cathedral and its acreage." Link pointed out that the process had become a moving target where at one point the price was the most important element and then it was the board's choice that was most important. "So if there is a possibility that the current board is engaging in a kind of scorched earth policy, then perhaps the Court might consider going forward on the basis of the least disruptive buyer in terms of the congregants who, I would remind the Court, have spent hundreds of millions of dollars over the past 55 years."

Link offered an alternative to what he saw as a board that was constantly switching preferred buyers. "The highest offer, to my understanding, is the Chapman offer. And the Chapman offer is approximately a million and a half dollars more than the Bishop's offer. So, if the Court's criterion is highest bidder, that would be Chapman." He said the offer from the diocese defied logic because the Chapman offer had increased twice. "We love our Roman Catholic brothers and sisters," added Link. "We'd like to proceed on a positive basis and not say anything negative about the goals of the Roman Catholic Church."

Judge Kwan listened and continued to invite counsel for the other parties to address the court. Kwan made it clear. What he wanted was proof that the decision by the board, to take a lower offer from the diocese, was a sound business decision. Link and the Ad Hoc Committee clearly preferred the Chapman offer. Chapman University also argued that the board's vote was illogical.

"There was a board meeting yesterday, and we were not advised until about 10 minutes to one o'clock today of the results," said Jeffrey Broker representing Chapman. "I would ask the court, how fair is that? Broker insisted it was not about sour grapes. "I think that what this is is disappointment in the process that we all embarked on here." He said the university acted in good faith and noted that Crystal Cathedral Ministries and the creditors' committee had previously designated Chapman as the preferred buyer. The board may have said both offers were acceptable previously, but it had still said Chapman was preferred. "And we filed with the Court late yesterday a copy of this revised letter of intent that not only had a proposal B but had a third proposal at $59,000,000. I think that at the end of the day, this court has said previously that it would do what's not only in the best interests of creditors but in the best interests of the congregation. And they're here and they'll tell you what they feel."

Even the nonlawyers in the room were invited to address the court. Jim Dawson was a voting Crystal Cathedral Ministries board member who said he'd been put on the board only recently as the board's newest member.

"I just want to advise the court and all of the people sitting here in the audience today that this was a heart-wrenching decision for myself and for all the board members, to have to vote to sell our beloved church." Dawson said he had been a member of the church with his wife for forty years. "The board has legal and fiduciary responsibilities to watch over the ministry and the assets. The board, as it stands today, is nine members. It only has three members of the board that were on the board when the financial problems arose, and that includes the two senior Schullers who are still on the board." He continued. "It's our understanding that we had a decision to make. We were charged by the Court on Monday to make a decision between the two offers. The thing that has come to my attention, being a new member, is—I've just been supplied with some information such as the bylaws and so forth. And I noted in the bylaws in the dedication of assets section that it states that all ministry assets are irrevocably dedicated for religious purposes. And I believe that's something that you can't ignore since it is legally in the bylaws and that is the intent of the creators of the bylaws of the Crystal Cathedral Ministries."

For Lillian Forry it was not her first cathedral bankruptcy hearing, just her first opportunity to be heard. The eighty-three-year-old had been involved right from the start. Her concern was not Robert Schuller's legacy, the glass sanctuary, or money. What Forry focused on was her husband. Harry Sterling Forry was not in the courtroom, but his presence loomed as a symbol of so many others. His remains were in the campus's Memorial Gardens in a wall crypt marked with his name. Alongside, Lillian Forry's own plaque carefully etched with her name awaited that faithful day. Until then, she would be the vanguard in the fight to protect the sacred ground. The Forrys had never attended the Crystal Cathedral services. They were an earlier generation of congregants when Lillian drove her husband to the in-car worship services at the drive-in.

No, it was not about money or the cathedral, but about what would happen to the Memorial Gardens. When Forry first heard about the passé Greenlaw Partner offer, her heart sank out of fear that there would one day be apartments built up against the Memorial Gardens' border where that would be their view.

"The church is not like it was when Reverend Schuller was in it. Things have changed. Even my friends that used to listen to the *Hour of Power*, now they turn it off halfway because it has changed. They've forgotten to put what Reverend Schuller originally had in there. And also, a cemetery is sacred ground. What is the university going to do there without a church being there? The Catholic Diocese has said that it will be interfaith and that I may have my own minister there. I won't have to have a Catholic priest; is that right, sir?" She asked, looking toward Bishop Brown, who nodded in agreement. "So, I'm remaining there if the Catholic Church gets it, because I know it will be taken care of and honored."

Lillian Forry also wanted to know what had happened to an endowment fund for the cemetery that was intended for the care and upkeep of the garden and memorials.

"It's still there," insisted cathedral attorney Marc Winthrop.

"It's still there? The money has not been taken?" asked Forry.

"The endowment fund for the cemetery is intact."

It did not entirely assuage her concerns, but she sat down.

Several congregants addressed the court. Each expressed some form of hope that the Chapman offer, because of its buyback provisions, could still be chosen. If it was a plan that would keep the congregation in their home church, they favored it.

"This is a church that we all love as congregants," said James Kirkland. "And the congregation—yes, this almost has me in tears, because this church was built for people worldwide, somewhere they could go to worship, somewhere where they could listen and have the word of God at their hands. They put in everything they could to make this church work as a working church. I love the Chapman deal, and I love these great people at Chapman because they came to try and save us as the congregation."

Others were deeply critical of Robert H. Schuller and his family.

"As attorney Mr. Grumer suggested the other day," said Robert Ekno, "that we should take care of Dr. Schuller with six-and-a-half million dollars because he has been the leader of this ... the thing he should be doing is going down with the ship if the ship's going down. You know, it was him and his disciples on the board that have decided to funnel away all this money."

Ninety-two-year-old John Simpson said he was a member of the congregation for fifty years and his wife was buried in the cemetery. He volunteered as a tour guide at the Crystal Cathedral. "I have a vested interest," he said, "and proven financial support that allows the Crystal Cathedral to continue its ministry in the iconic location. I pray that you will decide on the Chapman University offer. And if the Catholics take the church over, we'll lose the *Hour of Power* and the Meals on Mondays for the homeless and different projects like that we have initiated here."

Anne Marie Crain said she worked with the New Hope Crisis Hotline as a counselor for fifteen years. She said it was her heart's desire to continue to serve the twenty-four-hour hotline. "Please do not allow us to be evicted from our home church. I believe we, as a congregation, have a vested interest and proven financial support that allows the Crystal Cathedral to continue its ministry at the iconic location."

Pastor James Richard complained that the congregation had not been consulted on the bankruptcy decision making. "We see the Chapman plan as a God-given plan for us to be able to stay there. Is it the perfect plan in the world? Of course not, because we have to give up certain things. But it allows us to continue as a Protestant church on the very premises that we have worked so hard for over the years."

"My mother's been crying for days," said Carol Schuller Milner. "My parents care deeply. They've given their lives to this. They gave their lives to do what they did." Schuller Milner, the second youngest daughter of Robert and Arvella, was the only family member to speak at the evidentiary hearing. It had to hurt to sit and listen to the stinging criticism by some congregants along with the reality that the bankruptcy was going to change everything. "I understand it looks like—and it came across the other day, like it was all about money, but it wasn't. It was about this place remaining a place of worship. And when the Tower of Hope was built, my father said, may this be a light in this county that never goes out."

Schuller Milner said that she and her parents were early advocates for the Chapman University offer as they had deep respect for Chapman and the performing arts, but the reality was the fundamental change for the use of the property. "I think what really hit some of the board members was the uncertainty of the future of this campus as a place of worship." The congregation would have to move eventually. At least with the diocese, "the Catholic Church would keep the grounds sacred." She praised the diocese for going out of its way to accommodate the Schullers' concerns. "Immediately, when they found out about the concerns about the memorial gardens, offering to make it an interdenominational cemetery, the

Chapel in the Sky an interdenominational place of prayer—they just went on and on. Everything they could do to accommodate, they tried to do. And realizing that the Catholic Church has maintained sacred grounds and they tend to last centuries—and we believe that there is a very real physical testimony to the campus that we don't want to see lost."

Chapman University president Jim Doti spoke up to address Lillian Forry's worries about the cemetery. "I'm sure you and your beloved husband have nothing to worry about with respect to either the Catholic Church or Chapman University. The Catholic Church has a long record of honorably treating and dealing with the remains of loved ones. Chapman University has a columbarium on our campus, so we have experience as well. So, no matter what happens, Ms. Forry, you have nothing to worry about at all."

"Oh, I think I do," Forry replied from her seat.

"There's a letter," Doti addressed the court, "that was released just early this afternoon from part of the Crystal Cathedral Ministries board. It began with the following statement. 'While we continue to believe and pray for the miracle that will deliver the Crystal Cathedral campus, our board has voted to select the Diocese of Orange County.' Your Honor, our original proposal, which was lower than the Catholic Church in terms of the acquisition price, at the same time it gave the Crystal Cathedral fifteen years—a fifteen-year lease but more importantly a five-year period in which to buy the Crystal Cathedral Ministries back. So, if there were hopes for a miracle, the only way for that miracle to occur would be to accept that original offer that was presented by Chapman University."

Susan Dawson, board member Jim Dawson's wife, said her mother is buried at the cemetery and her father who was ninety-two would be buried there. She was confident that the Catholic Church had the means and the experience to care for the grounds. "They will honor and respect the grounds. They will honor and respect our Lord Jesus Christ." She added that she was not afraid to move to a new location. "The Crystal Cathedral will go on. The members ... will love wherever they go, because we are a community. We are a community of loving believers."

In the audience, Susan Dawson's kind words seemed to be in the minority. The lengthy hearing had Bishop Brown restless. "Tim, what's going to happen?" he asked. "Why are they going on so long?"[3]

"What the court is trying to do is, it is so unbelievable what is happening here, that the judge is trying to make a factual case," Busch explained. "He wants to validate that the board voted five to four. Because it's too close and it doesn't make any rational sense what happened here."

The court went into a fifteen-minute recess so Winthrop and Crystal Cathedral Ministries could make the case that, despite the higher bid of $59 million and $1 rent, the RCBO vote was still sound judgment.

The Hope for Sound Judgment

No one expected the hearing to last hours or that it would take on such a contentious air. Clearly it had been a long time just to get to this point. Bishop Brown of the diocese was sitting with attorney Tim Busch and marveled at Judge Kwan's focus.

"Neither one of us knew where he was going, what the Judge was going to do," said Bishop Brown.[1] "I mean, he let anybody and everybody in that courtroom speak up if he or she wanted too."

A year since the first bankruptcy filing and the original offer by Greenlaw Partners, that offer came and went and the ministry dug deep into its fundraising resources to gather the contributions that would lift it out of financial straits. That effort was only briefly alluded to in court, and no result was ever given other than the conclusion that was to return to bankruptcy court. It had become painfully clear that the Crystal Cathedral and the other iconic buildings had to be sold along with all of the property's acreage. The emotional toll on the Schullers, the ministry, and the congregation was laid bare in open court. It had at times been uncomfortable to hear the harsh criticism of ministry management and the Schullers. As one speaker pointed out, the family was largely absent.

"Do you look around this courtroom anywhere and see one of the leaders of the Crystal Cathedral in here?"[2] asked Robert Ekno. "Do you see Dr. Schuller, his daughters, any of the pastors? You see one. You see one. Do you see the leadership?"

Chapman University president Jim Doti was among those who could not escape the feeling of sadness as it played out as members of the congregation like Ekno pleaded with the judge.

"It was sad to see that," said Dr. Doti in a later interview. "It wasn't a very happy experience, quite frankly."[3]

Of course, the Schullers had been at some of the other hearings. Robert H. Schuller testified at one early hearing. He and his wife had been a critical part of the board vote that named the diocese as the

125

preferred buyer. Upending the entire direction of the proceedings, as frustrating as it was for those surprised by the board vote, was due to Schuller's direct involvement and leadership. Still, why the board voted the way it had, at the last minute, remained a mystery to some people in the courtroom, particularly Judge Kwan, who was charged with making the decision and confirming the buyer. His determined effort to get it right meant hearing directly from the members of the congregation who were present. Many were critical of the Schullers. That was not surprising, considering it was the congregation's home, their church, that they feared was disintegrating before their eyes. They did not know how hard the board's decision was and the logic behind it. Some of the congregants still believed the Chapman offer was the one that kept them in their space, or at least in the Crystal Cathedral. But for how long and at what cost?

Judge Kwan said it had become an auction of sorts and made it clear he was bothered by the late word of the board's choice. But he did not need to bring it up himself. The lawyer for Chapman made it the focus of his objections.

"Up until 12:50 today, Chapman University believed that it was the preferred purchaser," said Chapman's attorney Jeffrey Broker. He pointed out that the provisions applicable to the plan/purchase options directly state the time limitations. According to the record, the committee must designate a purchaser/sales proposal that had been selected by the debtor and the committee no later than fourteen days prior to the confirmation hearing. Since this was the confirmation hearing, and the board vote selecting the diocese as the buyer happened in the previous twenty-four hours, it was Broker's intent to show that decision not only violated the spirit of the agreement, but failed to meet the agreement to the letter.

"Your Honor, this is really important because it goes to the concept of good faith, bottom line," Broker argued.

Central to Chapman's claim was the previous agreements and written statements to the court that the debtor, Crystal Cathedral Ministries, submitted. One such statement in support of the Chapman offer pointed out that "the buildings and structures on the Crystal Cathedral campus are inextricably intertwined with the Debtor's spiritual mission and religious identify [sic]. The relocation of the Debtor's operation out of the Crystal Cathedral campus would adversely affect the Debtor's religious identify [*sic*] and therefore its ability to raise the funds necessary to carry out its spiritual and charitable mission."

"They've done a 180 on that, and it's not fair," said Broker. "They filed this on October 31st." He called it inappropriate to permit Crystal Cathedral Ministries to change its mind. "After the plan clearly stated and the parties relied—at least Chapman relied on the fact that it was chosen as the buyer and in reliance on that, it tried to make it better."

"Well, I agree with you," said Judge Kwan. "The way that your client was notified was shabby, and it's an embarrassment to this whole process that your client was notified of the decision a half hour before the hearing. The board meeting was conducted and concluded last night. And I don't see how the debtor—where the debtor and its board and its representatives didn't notify your client of its decision."

"I think my client deserved better," said Broker. "I could have taken it if I had an email, text, phone call. I've known Mr. Winthrop for many years. I've known Ms. Sanders for many years. They were under orders not to divulge what happened. And they will confirm that that's what they agreed to and they would not tell me." Broker acknowledged the attorneys could not divulge information if their clients instructed them not to. "Again, after the 9th, Chapman was the preferred buyer. Then ten minutes to 1:00, I'm showed a press release on an iPad that says it's now the Diocese. I mean, that's wrong."

"The last thing the ministry wanted to be was unseemly," said Winthrop. "However, we did make a decision which, as everyone will note—or has noted—was perhaps somewhat unexpected." Winthrop said the board acted in complete good faith. The struggle was when and how to make the important announcement public. It was going to be a shock to some, many in the congregation, and the news would travel fast. The announcement needed careful planning, and the wording required respectful calculations.

"It was very important that the announcement of this be made appropriately to the world," Winthrop insisted, "including the congregation and everyone else, other than by a phone call saying 'I'm sorry, you know, we've decided to go in a different direction here.'"

Winthrop said the moment the ministry issued the release, he shared it and it came together in such a way that it got out of control, but it was not bad faith. It was sound business judgment. The board took multiple factors into account.

"I understand on the merits," said Judge Kwan. "But you have basically a course of conduct here in terms of negotiation. And everyone in the world knew that the debtor's board was meeting last night, and they made a decision." He added, "They could have announced it."

It did not bode well for the Crystal Cathedral Board, and Judge Kwan's opinion was that it was "unseemly" and "unfair." Despite that, the offers were modified and changed so recently, it came down to whether the delayed announcement was relevant despite being a major last-minute change.

"We've had revised offers," said Judge Kwan, "and there was a revised offer that was made over the weekend, right, by the RCBO?"

"Correct."

"And that apparently has been entertained by your client. We've had revised offers—"

"We got a revised at 2:30—between 2:30 and 3:00 yesterday afternoon hours before we were convening the board meeting. So, you know, this is just—"

"I'm not going to back down from my observation that I really think it's unfortunate, given the course of conduct and the fact that Chapman has tried to meet the offers, that they worked closely with your client in developing the plan proposal and then they get kind of left at the altar like that."

Judge Kwan saw it as unfortunate, but ultimately a matter of "agree to disagree." It was not going to change a lot. There had been offers and counteroffers inside the fourteen-day window, up to and including Chapman's revised offer that day in open court. To enforce that provision would have meant to go back to Chapman's original offer, which came in below a level that would pay back creditors in full. A more pressing matter was the ministry bylaw that the board used as justification for voting in favor of the diocese—a bylaw that was codified long before bankruptcy was on the horizon. The Crystal Cathedral campus was to remain a place of worship.

"We've tried to enhance the offer," said Broker on behalf of Chapman. "The Court can order the charter to be modified in order to permit this transaction because they've sold real estate before. If there was a prohibition, it should have been put out there six months ago before people incurred expense." Broker brought up the Green-law Partners offer that almost had its day in court. "They're not a church. And they were going to sell to them for $46 million." He said if the bylaw was going to be a problem, Crystal Cathedral Ministries should have put it in disclosures that the sale would only be for religious institutions. "It's inappropriate to come up with this at the last minute. So, I would urge your Honor to deny confirmation with the proviso that the debtor has a choice to accept Chapman 1, Chapman 2, or Chapman 3 or they can go back, and the chips will fall where they may. That's what I think the appropriate result is here. Chapman didn't create this problem, and it is unseemly."

"I think much more is being made of that by Mr. Broker than was made by the witnesses," said Winthrop. "The witnesses said they were influenced by that, but I asked the specific question: If the bylaw hadn't been there, would your decision have been the same? And the answer was 'Yes, my decision would have been the same.' So, it was a factor, but it wasn't the determining factor. So, we could get rid of that bylaw right now. That wouldn't change the board's determination. It wasn't like, oh, we have to do this, so we're compelled to do this."

One of those witnesses was Dr. Diane Highum, a voting member of the International Board of Directors for Crystal Cathedral Ministries. She was one of three board members who represented the Crystal Cathedral Consistory. Like many in court she had a lot at stake in the outcome—maybe more so, as a longtime deacon and elder. She had been a member of the church for fourteen years, most of the time deeply involved with the Crystal Cathedral. Her seventeen-year-old daughter was attending the school on campus, and her husband was buried in the Memorial Gardens.

Highum was one of the recent additions to the board of directors. She was part of the sweeping board reorganization that also saw Robert H. Schuller and his wife, Arvella, restored to the board as voting members. That shake-up had happened in late July, and she was surprised that she had been called to the witness stand to be sworn in. Marc Winthrop needed the testimony to "prove up" the board's vote, that it was a sound business decision.

The testimony focused on the bylaw and to what degree it was a factor in the final vote for her and therefore for the board. Highum said she was an academic person, and she wanted to be informed, so she read the bylaws but did not necessarily dwell on the single bylaw about maintaining the property for religious purposes.

"There was also discussion of the thousands of people that have contributed through the years to the building of that ministry," said Highum, "the dedication of all of those assets basically to the greater glory of God, that the donations were received in that respect and were committed to that purpose, and that the cathedral particularly was thought to—that we had an obligation to maintain it as a worship space."

What it came down to in her mind was the Crystal Cathedral sanctuary more than the disposition of the other buildings. The board favored the Chapman offer primarily because of the buyback that would have kept the ministry in its iconic church and offered the chance to perhaps buy it back one day. They did not want to leave a place they loved. The offer to repurchase was attractive for that reason. But when the offers changed, and it appeared the buyback was off the table, with the bylaw and other factors, the offer from the diocese made the most sense. She concluded the Catholics "would be good stewards of the property and ... are part of the Body of Christ."

When pressed by the judge, Highum insisted the bylaw in question was only a part of her decision-making process.

"The loss of the cathedral was the concern that you had," said Judge Kwan.

"No one really wanted to separate the properties, but it was the actual loss of the cathedral which we felt absolutely had to be dedicated to a worship space."

Jeffrey Broker for Chapman was unconvinced that the board's decision was sound and logical. He correctly noted that one of the three viable Chapman offers still included the buyback option. When he had a chance to ask Diane Highum follow-up questions, he focused on this point.

"Chapman 1 has not been taken off the table," said Broker.

"No, it's not been taken off the table. But in spite of our very good financial advice, there has been concern among various board members—because we've seen a decline in attendance, and we've seen declines in revenue that are all unknown. And when we looked at that, when we were choosing last night, one of the concerns was, if we are not able to raise the money for the buyback and we are not able to maintain the lease payments, if we had, you know, defaulted on the lease payments, the congregation would have been—I don't want to say out on the streets—but would have been without a worship space altogether." At least under the diocese offer there was the promise of a long-term worship space, even though it was not going to be the cathedral or even on the same campus.

"If the bylaw did not exist," asked Marc Winthrop, "would your decision have changed last night?"

"No. And it is the issue of the donations and the thousands, perhaps millions of people that have dedicated money to the church for the building of that campus and primarily to the greater glory of God. And my personal opinion would have been that it should be maintained under a religious organization."

"So. the answer would then be—"

"Without the bylaw, I would have still."

"Still voted as you did?"

"Uh-huh."

Chapman produced its own witness, one with an even longer track record at Crystal Cathedral Ministries. Mike Nason was once the chief spokesperson for the Crystal Cathedral Ministries and executive producer of the *Hour of Power*. In his twenty-five years in the job, he was known for helping expand the television ministry from 18 stations to 146 nationwide. He resigned in 1988 during financial struggles afflicting many televangelists of the time. Although there had been budget cuts to deal with the donation shortfalls, Nason had said his resignation had to do with personal reasons. He remained a member of the church, however, and served for a time on the board of directors, so his inside knowledge seemed relevant to Chapman attorney Jeffrey Broker.

"What would the effect be if they closed it down, on the campus?" asked Broker. "Closed down the *Hour of Power* on campus?"

"No," the judge clarified. "If they moved the *Hour of Power* to a different production facility."

"It would cease," Nason replied.

"It would cease, in your view?" The judge continued to help guide the conversation. "How do you know that?"

"Well, I think when you're intimately involved in something for a number of years as I was and the cathedral itself is the face of the television [*sic*], I think that people would no longer associate *Hour of Power* because of the loss of the cathedral."

But to the more important point about the religious purpose bylaw, Chapman's attorney continued to make the case that the bylaw had only been brought up at the eleventh hour as an excuse. Broker asked Nason about his experience as a board member years before at a time the ministry had sold a building across Chapman Avenue from the cathedral.

"Do you recall there being any special reference to a bylaw that prohibited the sale of that property to Kaiser Permanente?" asked Broker.

"No."

"Did the ministry own a warehouse that it sold to a real estate developer during the time that you were on the board of directors?"

"Yes."

"Was that real estate developer a religious organization?"

"Not to my knowledge."

"And do you recall what they did to that property?"

"I think they bulldozed it, and I think they built apartment buildings."

Crystal Cathedral Ministries had multiple properties in the area that had been sold off over time when money was tight. Sometimes that money helped build or expand the Crystal Cathedral campus. The point was that the bylaw in question hadn't seemed very relevant in the past. Nason's testimony seemed to bear that out, but he also admitted he didn't know if the bylaws had changed in the years since he'd left the board.

It had been grueling, like the machinations of a criminal trial with all the requisite objections, case law references, and repetitive clarifications that came about at a snail's pace. When the judge closed evidence, it felt like the end was near. There were three major questions to be answered in final arguments. The court had to decide whether sound business purpose existed using the following factors according to Judge Kwan. "One, sound business reason, two, fair and reasonable price, three, adequate notice of the sale, and four, good faith." Had the debtor, Crystal Cathedral Ministries, met its burden of proof? The creditors' committee's attorney Nanette Sanders was the first to make what amounts to her case.

Sanders said that the court had laid out options A and B at a status conference a week before. Option A, the debtor cooperates and picks the buyer. Option B, the debtor doesn't cooperate, and the committee picks the buyer. A simple choice. Since the options gave the responsibility to the board and the purchase price of the diocese plan paid the creditors, the decision had to be considered reasonable.

"Was there a sound business reason?" asked Sanders rhetorically. "The debtor believes there was. Is the price fair and reasonable? No one can argue that this particular price will provide for payment to creditors in full. That would appear to meet that standard."

But the court was clearly concerned about some aspects about how that decision happened, whether it was reasonable or not. Why at the last minute? But to Sanders it had all played out over five months, publicly and with all parties and potential buyers represented.

"The other element being, is this a good faith transaction?" said Sanders. "There's no evidence to indicate it is anything but. All parties have been represented by counsel. The proposals have been negotiated and renegotiated—and perhaps renegotiated. But at this juncture, the debtor believes it has chosen the best alternative." Anderson said it was the decision by the creditors' committee early on not to decide the ministry's future. "And unfortunately, people will be unhappy regardless of the choice that's made. But the debtor has articulated its reasons."

The creditors' committee was certain that the decision by the board met the four criteria Judge Kwan outlined. But the onus was on Crystal Cathedral Ministries to show it had proved the burden was met. Attorney Marc Winthrop said the sound business reason was tied to the fact that the campus must be sold to pay creditors regardless of the buyer. The result of the sale would be the creditors would receive 100 percent of what they are owed. The price was fair and reasonable.

"When you take in the totality of all of the circumstances," said Winthrop, "not only the price, which is fifty-seven-and-a-half million dollars, but all of the other attributes that have been testified to in terms of leaseback and alternative space, then this is a very fair and reasonable transaction."

Judge Kwan gave him a pass on arguing the "adequate notice" for reasons stated previously by the creditors' committee.

Winthrop was also certain, and the court agreed, that since there was no prior relationship between the diocese and Crystal Cathedral Ministries, along with general circumstances, good faith also existed. But Winthrop also wanted to address, on a more personal note, members of the congregation who fretted about the future.

"The fact that we have more favorable offers that inure to the benefit of the debtor and the creditors," said Judge Kwan, "I think indicates that there was adequate notice to affected parties."

"It should also be mentioned," said Winthrop, "because it has come up so often in the comments of the congregants who have appeared here today, that the board is obviously very cognizant of the survival of this ministry. And the idea of 'Don't take away our church,' that's the last thing the board wants to do. The board wants to ensure the ongoing viability of this church. This church has existed at various stages in its life anywhere from the roof of a concession stand in a drive-in theater to a small 150-seat chapel, which is known now as the arboretum. And this is—when the ministry relocated it will still be a ministry, a positive ministry and has every intention of continuing its many excellent programs." He added, "No one is more committed to continuing to minister to the homeless community than our current senior pastor, Sheila Coleman. So, I'm a bit baffled in a way and disappointed that people don't realize that it's the ministry we're talking about here that will continue somewhere else after a period of three years but will still continue and do the many good things that were described by the congregants. The programs will all continue. They just won't be at the same place. And we do believe in the importance [of the] iconic nature of the Crystal Cathedral structure."

The diocese supported Winthrop and Sanders and what had already been said, but also addressed worries about what would happen next.

"These proposals really address concerns, both financially and what I'll also call spiritually," said Alan Martin for the Diocese of Orange. "Financially, we moved our offer from what was originally roughly $50 million and then up from there, some of it being earmarked, to now all cash, $57.5 million, to a level we thought gave them sufficient surplus to go forward for the ministries and their mission at the appropriate location. But we also listened to a lot of their other spiritual concerns about maintaining and respectfully continuing their ministry wherever that might be." He said the plan was fair and reasonable, financially as well as spiritually.

Carl Grumer, representing the Schullers, hadn't said much up to this point but added, "Dr. and Mrs. Schuller, with great respect for both Chapman and the RCBO, they'll vocally support the RCBO offer largely because it will keep the ministry—it will keep the property dedicated to religious purposes, which is what it was for in the first place. This does not mean an end to the ministry itself. The ministry is not a building. It's not a series of buildings." He said the buildings were important, but ministry was not defined by the buildings. "We're just talking about real estate ultimately. It's important real estate. It's iconic real estate, and it's very important to everybody. But it is not the ministry."

Grumer noted Dr. Schuller's "Possibility Thinking" and the slogan 'When faced with a mountain, I will not quit.' Whether or not this is even a mountain," he said, "whether it's a move down the street, whatever it is, it's a challenge. There's no question. But that doesn't mean we're going to quit. And this ministry will continue."

But many in the room from the congregation were unconvinced. One unidentified man said from the back of the room, "We feel we are being thrown under the bus for the Schullers to get what they want."

"We are being evicted," said Anne Marie Crain. "We have practiced the Protestant faith for a long, long time at the Crystal Cathedral. We've not only worshipped there, but we've served our community. Please allow us to do that."

Throughout the day, anyone who wanted to have a say seemed to have that opportunity. Representatives from the diocese, the bishop and others, just listened as they left the talking up to the diocese's attorney, Alan Martin. True to Martin's description of Judge Kwan, the judge did not appear to be skipping anything in coming to a decision he knew would have tremendous ramifications for many people, and he seemed to realize that there were going to be people who would be upset by the decision. It was the moment the bankruptcy court had long sought, and what looked to be the end of the uncertainty Chapter 11 bankruptcy had inserted into countless lives at the ministry and certainly for the Schullers.

The hearing lasted about five or six hours, and in the closing minutes, Judge Kwan laid out his justification. He said there was sound business reason for the sale and adequate notice. The price was fair and reasonable. The sale was in good faith, though he pointed out his previous reservations about the timing.

"Good faith was also shown," said Judge Kwan, "that the board deliberated on the proposal and articulated by the board members their sound business reasons for choosing this buyer as opposed to the other buyer, based on the concerns that the board members had raised and which the Court heard during the testimony in this case. So, the Court will grant the motion of the committee and the debtor to select the Roman Catholic Bishop of Orange as the buyer."

Leaving federal court, the parties walked into a scrum of reporters. Dr. Doti, said Chapman, had accepted the judge's decision.

"I think they were expecting us to say we were going to appeal," said Doti. "We could have and dragged this out in the courts." But by that time, Doti had mulled over many eventualities that had him feeling the pressure of the situation. He had begun to question the $59 million and to question what it would take to work with the Schullers and the congregation to not let them down.

"I was beginning to get a little gun shy," said Doti. "I said to [the reporters], 'The decision's been made. I believe this is for the best and we're not going to appeal the decision.'"

The deal was done. Or so everyone thought.

The Thanksgiving holiday was a week after the evidentiary hearing. There should have been more to be thankful for, at least in the households of Tim Busch and of the many people who went all in to secure the purchase of the cathedral. But while Busch did his best to put on a positive face, the news he had received could only mean one thing. The purchase of the Crystal Cathedral by the Diocese of Orange was to be voided by Vatican intervention. To Busch's shock and dismay, the Vatican refused to approve the purchase because it was over $10 million and it had to go through the Congregation of Clergy.

"They said you can't buy it." Busch recalled the finality of that declaration.[4] "Because it was so late in the episcopacy of Bishop Brown and they didn't want to saddle a new bishop with the burden." Without a nihil obstat, which is Latin for approval, the diocese lacked the legal authority to buy the cathedral campus, which meant the deal was void.

The diocesan staff who were against the purchase of the Crystal Cathedral knew that the Diocese did not have the nihil obstat, so Busch was afraid they would leak it to the press and Chapman University would return to court to argue that the diocese did not have legal authority from the Vatican to purchase the property since it cost over $10 million.

Chapman would be back in court to demand proof the diocese had the authority to make the purchase. Having none, there would be no argument to give the court and the deal would be lost. Busch was on the phone trying to talk to anyone who would listen as close to the pope as he could get, including Cardinals Dolan and Law, who were at the Vatican at the time.

If by some miracle there was a quick reversal, the other problem was it would have to go through the Apostolic Nuncio's office, but Italian archbishop Pietro Sambi, the Vatican nuncio to the United States at the time, had died earlier that year on July 27. There was no nuncio to make that review. The Vatican traditionally relied on the input of the nuncio of the country involved to make big decisions.

Bishop Brown wrote a letter in response to the decision and explained the situation. He called several supportive cardinals to make a personal appeal.

"My advisors and the people who were supportive of this project," said Brown, "would never understand how this kind of opportunity could be passed up without someone in Rome who could make some decision about what was so clearly the right decision thing to do at this time in Orange County."

Despite the lack of a nuncio, there was at least one person in that office trying to coordinate the review to help.

"I was panicked," said Tim Busch.

The following Monday, Busch was traveling home with his wife. The long weekend left him dejected and just about ready to admit there was not anything anyone could do at the late date to fix what would logically follow. But his wife could see the gears in his mind continuing to grind away at the problem.

"What are you going to do?" his wife asked.[5]

"Get on a plane and go to Rome," he declared, as crazy as that sounded. "I can't get this done over the phone. If we're going to lose it, I'm going to give it my all."

Back in town, on the 55 freeway, Busch's phone buzzed. The caller was Monsignor Cook, of the diocesan office of canon law. He explained it was his second call that morning.

"We received a fax from the Vatican this morning, at about one a.m. our time," said Cook. That would have been about ten o'clock in the morning in Rome. "I'll read it to you. It's very short."

"Alright," Busch squeezed out. His mind raced.

"Your Excellency," read Cook, "this congregation has received your letter of the [*sic*] 12 October, 2011 with its appended documentation, together with your request for reconsideration of 2 November, 2011. The Nihil Obstat is hereby granted to your request."[6]

The letter was signed and faxed on the same day.

"The Vatican doesn't get anything done in three days," Busch said. "It can take months or even years."

It was the second time in a very short period that Busch ended a phone call in tears, convinced of the intercession of the Holy Spirit to make all things work to achieve God's goals.

"There's no way it was natural. This was God's intervention," he said.

One of those blessings, and what Bishop Brown described as a turning in the nihl obstat roadblock, was an unsolicited phone call he received from Cardinal Timothy Dolan. He was president of the United States Conference of Catholic Bishops and in Rome. "He offered to write a letter in support," said Brown, "and I readily approved."

Tim Busch did not know about the call, just like most people involved. And Bishop Brown did not know what would come of it.

"Anyway, God's goodness came through on that," said Bishop Brown.

There were numerous calls to Bishop Brown of varying levels of importance from urgent to casual, from immediate business to a note for future reference, but a decade later he would only be able to list a few. One of those was from Rick Warren. He was a well-known Baptist evangelical Christian pastor and author who was head of Saddleback Church, which had taken over Crystal Cathedral Ministries' massive San Juan Capistrano retreat in August 2011. Warren called Bishop Brown personally to congratulate him on acquiring the Crystal Cathedral and said he had told Schuller he should sell to the Diocese of Orange. Given the interfaith ramifications of the acquisition, Brown said the call was "further affirmation of the purchase."

Bishop Brown was grateful to God for the blessing to the diocese. Blessing as it was, it was not free and would require years of commitment from Catholics and non-Catholics and fundraising. The first order of business was to decide exactly what to do next, or at least to make a game plan. Rob Neal had always been instrumental throughout the short but epic phase of acquiring the cathedral. He was an experienced advisor in acquisitions, but also a strong supporter and booster of the effort. He was also a man of faith and someone who, when decision time came, happily with his wife, Berni, donated a lot of his own money to help reach the final winning bid. It was Bishop Brown's job to lead the diocese into this new phase, and when he needed a man to run the restoration and a newly formed corporation, he leaned on Neal and Neal's life's work as a restoration manager and a builder.

The Way Forward

From Capistrano Beach, California, Robert Neal was managing partner of Hager Pacific Properties and the firm's leader of acquisitions and renovations. The private real estate investment firm had nearly $2 billion in property assets. He was part of multiple Catholic organizations, including Catholic Relief Services, the Becket Fund, Catholic Leadership Institute, the Pacific Club, and the Magis Institute of Reason and Faith. He shared membership in the Papal Foundation with his long-time wife, Bernarda "Berni" A. Neal.

Berni was on the board of the Orange Catholic Foundation, which would carry much of the load for fundraising. She would bring her own enthusiasm and volunteer countless hours of her time to the restoration and more. She had already been an active force in the diocese on multiple levels, including Bishop Brown's efforts to build a cathedral long before Crystal Cathedral Ministries went bankrupt. To list more of the organizations and committees Berni Neal either ran or participated in would still not do justice to the amount of work she had done for the diocese and Catholic Charities. Rob and Berni Neal were already dedicated to the task at hand and rarely if ever said no. Rob Neal was a natural choice to oversee renovations, and, as his work before, he did it without compensation. But he also had to operate a company with billions in assets.

No sooner had the drama over the nihil obstat ended, Rob Neal called Bob Theirgartner and expressed his intentions to juggle those two major responsibilities.

"I knew he'd need help," said Theirgartner.[1] So, the CEO of Davis Partners, a construction management and development company, offered to assist. He correctly predicted at the time that the project was going to take years and it needed reliable relationships that worked together well. Theirgartner and Neal were already good friends who regularly worked together and socialized. Theirgartner's addition to the team helped to ensure a culture of friendly cooperation going forward.

Friday, February 3, 2012, the sale closed escrow, and within a month, Maria Schinderle and Tim Busch had created a pair of nonprofit religious corporations: one to manage the property and the other that held ownership of the property, both under the control of the bishop of the Diocese of Orange. It was a way to establish organization and manage costs as well as direct fundraising dollars. It was Christ Catholic Cathedral Corporation that now owned the property and was responsible for restoration.

Psalm 37 says, "Take delight in the Lord, and he will give you the desires of your heart" (37:4). An old saying responds, "Be careful what you wish for; you might just get it." It was safe to say, a few months after the close of escrow, there were those in the diocese basking in much delight that God had seen fit to entrust the Crystal Cathedral to the diocese and its 1.2 million Catholics. At the same time, there was a sizable portion of those very same people who opposed the acquisition of the campus and just expected a disaster, considering the cathedral ultimately unworthy of the dignity of God. That included dozens of parish priests and others in the diocese who were bewildered by the whole process. For this group, the words of comic actor Oliver Hardy could suffice: "Well, here's another fine mess you've gotten me into." But one summer day changed the hearts of those who wondered aloud, "Why?" And it only took a five-minute speech.

The diocese was only beginning to occupy small spaces on the campus, and Father Smith had the only dedicated office in the Tower of Hope. On extremely rare occasions, Reverend Schuller could be found in his office. The diocese promised he would continue to have that office for as long as he lived. Bishop Brown extended an invitation to Schuller to speak to an assembly of priests from across the more than sixty parishes. When he accepted, the priests received invites to join in the rare opportunity. For most it would be the first time they had ever seen him in person. It was a first for Schuller too.

The priests packed the auditorium downstairs in the visitors' center, also known as the Meier Building. The theater setting was not much different than attending a movie. There was a stage and curtains. The priests arrived and made themselves comfortable. What they did not see was Schuller arriving.

Several people were backstage with Schuller, including the diocese's legal advisor and fundraiser Tim Busch, who thought Schuller was nervous about addressing the priests. He suggested Schuller tell the priests what Schuller had told Busch on a previous occasion.

"About the church of Peter," Busch recalled, "about the bishop, and about [Schuller's] legacy."[2]

To restoration manager Rob Neal, Schuller looked like he was not feeling well. He looked so weak and frail to Neal that, instead of Schuller walking onto the stage at the Freed Theater, Neal helped him to the back of the theater and seated him in a chair behind the curtain.

"My God, how is this gonna work?" he thought.[3] "We've invited everybody. We have 150 priests. The bishop's there."

Neal gave Schuller some water and then walked off the stage.

Schuller sat alone while the introduction was made on the other side of the curtain. The curtain went up, and Reverend Robert Schuller faced the crowd, seated Lincoln-esque in a dark suit and tie. Rob Neal was among those wondering how Schuller could manage to stand, and perhaps he would address the audience seated.

But to the surprise of virtually everyone there, Schuller leaned forward, slowly lifted his body from the chair, and strode up to the podium. It was draped with a red cloth, at the front of the stage. He reached up with his left hand and bent the adjustable microphone stand upward toward his mouth.

"This is my first invitation to speak to my Mother Church," said Schuller with a soft voice. "Thank you."[4]

Schuller was candid and opened up about having special teachers in his sixty years in architecture. But also, he spoke about a secret agenda he had early on to make sure the Crystal Cathedral and campus would not be inherited by his successor or by his own denomination.

"It was my plan to, hopefully, see to it that the title and ownership of my life's work in land and buildings would be under the control of the Roman Catholic Church. So, that's why I'm so honored to see you today. To tell you that and to thank you for taking it." Schuller's broad smile grew. "Well, you didn't just take it; you paid for it."

The room erupted with laughter and applause.

"[The Crystal Cathedral's] recognition as a piece of art and architecture is global. I trust it to you; it's yours."

Schuller's words included a list of great potential for what could be done with the property and buildings at that central location, in Orange County, California, United States of America. But in typical Schuller style he went further ...

"I don't think anyone in here, this group, is thinking big enough!" he said. "This could be a global place for dynamic energy to be generated. And that's what the church needs today and tomorrow. Dynamic creative energy. And if it can be found anywhere, it's gotta be in you! You are the church! I know that! Respect that! Honor that! I thank you for taking charge of a physical facility that can be used for the glory of God and to honor the name of our Lord and Savior. I love him, and I know you do too."

Schuller received a standing ovation. When the audience settled down again, he returned to the podium to recognize Bishop Tod Brown, who he said was a friend and mentor.

"This is the Mother Church; you're the bishop. Anytime you have advice for me, criticism, constructive or whatever, my ears open to you, because I respect you."

Bishop Brown was moved, and he knew the critics, skeptics, and those concerned who were either still on the fence about the purchase or seemed behind locked doors were swayed. It was a remarkable day. Afterward, Brown's rector and episcopal vicar for Christ Cathedral, Father Christopher Smith, had a personal encounter with Reverend Schuller that struck Smith as something he would never forget.

Smith recalled Schuller's words. "He said, 'Father Christopher, I built the cathedral for Christ. I always wanted the cathedral to be for Christ, and I know with the Roman Catholic Church it will be a place for Christ forever.'"[5]

"A place for Christ forever"—Schuller's words would grow to be part of the life of the cathedral restoration going forward.

"It was a very beautiful statement of trust that we would always keep this as a sacred place for Christ," said Smith.

Bishop Brown called the event a turning point for those who worried about the wisdom of taking over the Crystal Cathedral and worried about how much it was going to cost the diocese. It was the end of a long saga, and as that chapter closed, the diocese needed a unified focus to turn the page. In that respect, Schuller's address to the priests was a motivational speech to move forward boldly and think big. So that is what they did.

The finality for Crystal Cathedral Ministries (CCM) was bittersweet. It was a sorrowful end to a very audacious run of worldwide evangelization, but the last six years were filled with so much angst and turmoil, moving on was also a relief in many ways. It poured out a wave of mixed emotions across the CCM campus for the staff and those who had survived the cutbacks and year-long bankruptcy. But their new guests who were preparing to take over did not sense much animosity.

"They were remarkably gracious," said Rob Neal, who was set to lead the restoration of the campus.

It could have been uncomfortable for those who showed up to begin the task of transition, but the workers with the ministry and the leadership welcomed Neal and cooperated. One person they had become familiar with on campus, because of his involvement in pre-purchase inspections, was Joe Novoa. He was the longtime construction manager for the diocese.

"He did a lot," said Monsignor Michael Heher. "People would listen to him because he would know how things should be done. Kudos to him."[6]

Though Bishop Brown had turned seventy-five and was set to retire, he remained as leader of the diocese. A replacement had not yet been named. "Our God is a God of surprises," Brown said, and "certainly the biggest surprise I've ever received from God is the Crystal Cathedral."[7]

The June ordination of Catholic priests held at St. Columban Catholic Church in Garden Grove was the backdrop to a major announcement by Bishop Tod Brown. The Vatican had approved the name for the new cathedral. No one expected the diocese to continue calling the glass sanctuary the Crystal Cathedral. Not only was it impractical; it was not possible. The Catholic Church had strict guidelines about names for churches. But Bishop Brown wanted the name to in some way call Dr. Schuller to mind. Brown sent out an invitation for anyone in the diocese to support any name or names of their own liking and had only one requirement. The final name had to be Christological.

The name change proposal was sent to the Congregation of Bishops in Rome in anticipation of the close of escrow. A curia would decide. Defined as departments or ministries that assist the pope with governance, a curia could be small for a diocese and get larger. Further up the chain of authority there were patriarchal curias, and finally the Roman Curia at the top. The Congregation of Bishops was the curia in Rome that had the duty of considering all Catholic names. Brown's priority in deciding on the name was to "ensure a clear Christological reference."[8] He invoked Robert H. Schuller in the process.

"We hold Reverend Schuller and his ministry in the highest esteem," Brown told the seventeen hundred in attendance.[9] "It was important that any change of name for the cathedral itself be respectful of its spiritual legacy while accommodating our needs to clearly define this important facility as a Catholic center of worship."

It was Father Christopher H. Smith who was given the honor of standing at the ambo to announce the name to the packed church. The Crystal Cathedral would be henceforth known as Christ Cathedral. Bishop Brown appointed Smith episcopal vicar and rector of Christ Cathedral in March, just after the campus sale had closed escrow. Bishop Brown paid Smith a personal visit to Smith's office at Marywood Center. Smith had been vicar for priests for the Diocese of Orange and had just completed his first six-year term and signed on for a second. Brown asked Smith if he would be willing to serve as vicar and rector of the new cathedral, which at the time had not yet been named.

"Well, I said, what would that entail?"

Bishop Brown, having no better frame of reference for such an unprecedented circumstance, was honest. "I don't know," Brown replied.

Smith recalled telling the bishop, "Well, it sounds like a good assignment to me. I guess together with the Holy Spirit we'll figure this out."

The job did not formally begin until July 1, but since his appointment he had learned that he would lead all major administrative activities at the cathedral campus, including renovation and restoration of the cathedral and other buildings. Smith could not help but think of how unlikely it was that he was chosen for the task and made the announcement of the name. It was a moment that only a few months earlier would not have entered his mind.

Smith easily recalled growing up in Orange County with his grandparents, living just around the corner from the only drive-in theater in town. He was six years old when he first stood among the eucalyptus trees and watched Reverend Robert H. Schuller dazzle from his rooftop podium and listened to the sermons that blared from the drive-in speakers hanging from car windows.

Father Smith would have been pleased to know Rob Neal had already asked Bob Theirgartner to work up a Request for Proposal (RFP) that could be sent out to potential liturgical design consultants. It was a critical starting point, and it was going to take a while to find the right candidate, but they had hoped to get it done by the end of the year. A selection committee was organized with Smith, Neal, Theirgartner, Monsignor Arthur Holquin, Lisa Truex, and Kory Kramer.

Father Christopher Smith quickly formed a task force just for the purposes of preparing to move the parish at St. Callistus to the cathedral campus. It was made up of Smith, Father Tuyen Nguyen, and members of the parish pastoral council. Susan Stoneburner, an architect, led the effort and would see it through to its conclusion. It seemed at every turn there was a new committee or board forming. Often, key people from the clergy or the laity sat on multiple boards, committees, and subcommittees at the same time. They were typically headed up by laypeople like Stoneburner volunteering their time.

The financials had to be watched. There would be money coming in from fundraising and there would be money spent on restoration. Irvine, California, CPA Robert Randolph "Randy" Redwitz volunteered to do some financial analysis for the diocese and the Board of Directors of the Christ Catholic Cathedral Corporation. His role would expand greatly over time until he was tracking the facility's budgets and accounting for money raised and money spent as the CFO of the corporation.

The work of the liturgical consultant was going to take five years. The committee did not want it to take years to find one. The committees and administrators looking to recruit were never guaranteed that the search for designers, architects, contractors, and consultants would lead to the right people, particularly in the time frame in which they were required to choose. Still, they seemed to find the perfect people. It was a process, and it had to be done with faith and discernment. Another such find was Brother Woeger, who provided the earliest look at what Christ Cathedral could become.

Brother William J. Woeger, F.S.C., director of the Office for Divine Worship for the Archdiocese of Omaha, was one of three finalists in the application process for liturgical design consultant on the cathedral renovation. With more than three decades of experience, he worked on projects around the country, including the Cathedral of Christ the Light in Oakland, California. The job called for a vast knowledge and interest in church design but also art. A 2008 report on new work that Woeger started with the Diocese of Oakland said the job required a "sleuth mode."

"Brother Woeger goes into his artistic sleuth mode," the staff writer wrote, "becoming the tracker of beautiful paintings and statues that already exist. He also becomes a seeker of artists, carpenters, and crafts people who can create one-of-a-kind crucifixes, Stations of the Cross, statues, altar screens, tabernacles, candlesticks, and paintings."[10]

The committee had many goals in its search for a candidate, including those kinds of qualifications, but there was a more personal aspect, again, owing to the years they would be working together. There were three finalists who traveled to California to give presentations.

"We wanted to sit and chat with them," said Theirgartner. "We needed to decide if we liked them." He added that all three candidates were perfectly qualified. The committee had an overriding question in its collective mind for the presentation each candidate gave. As he explained, the committee was made up of people who know what they are doing in their individual areas of expertise but had never done anything like creating a cathedral. "So, the question was, help us understand what we need to know as we embark on this."

It was Brother William Woeger who stood out as the right personality mixed with the right knowledge.

"It just struck me that the way Brother William dealt with us, described it to us, came to us with that information, was a far better thing," said Theirgartner.

Woeger would influence every aspect of the transformation of the Crystal Cathedral, its art, and its Catholic Christian meaning. It was a selection that met with the approval of Kevin Vann, the bishop designate of the Diocese of Orange, who was just a few weeks from his installation. He wrote in a letter to Rob Neal that he had heard good things about Brother Woeger. He had also met him once.

"Rob, as the Bishop designate of Orange, I thank you and the committee for your hours and hours of work and dedication. This is not only work of Faith, but also a historical and most significant exercise in what can be called 'ecclesial communion.' How we work and pray together in these most significant and providential times is an essential 'foundation stone' for the House of God that will be a witness to Christ the Lord, and thus to the unity of Faith for our Diocese and beyond. One Bishop recently told me that 'Kevin, the whole world is watching'! That is indeed the case, and therefore is a great responsibility before the Lord for all of us. Thank you and the committee for being such an essential part of this journey of Faith."[11]

The Wall Tumbles Down

For nine months, since the close of escrow, much of the restoration planning for the arboretum had been in the early stages. Most of the work to that point was administrative and organizational rather than physical. It was not a matter of misplaced priorities, but it was based on factors including time and the condition of the infrastructure. As it turned out, it was an education in property acquisition where existing buildings were concerned and more so for historic renovation. It was about to become painfully clear that there was not going to be as much time to complete the project and there would be multitudes more work required.

At first, it was all coming together as planned and there was plenty of time to make it all work out perfectly, God willing. On campus, most of the physical activities on the part of the diocese were small. The first person to occupy an office was episcopal vicar and rector Father Christopher Smith, who took over a space on the fourth floor of the Tower of Hope. It was a space he shared with Crystal Cathedral Ministries' cemetery operations. It could have been an uncomfortable situation, but Smith recalled being welcomed right away and made to feel at home. It was the beginning of a long relationship where Smith felt a bond develop between Crystal Cathedral Ministries and the diocese.

"I got to know some of the pastors who were still there working and a lot of the people," recalled Father Smith.[1] "I started getting invited to talks at some of their gatherings," some very special invitations from the young minister Reverend Bobby V. Schuller, the grandson of Dr. Schuller. He had been hosting the *Hour of Power* and would invite Father Smith to join him for interviews. Smith would also preach in the Crystal Cathedral for the TV program and have the honor of pushing the red button that opened its great glass wall out to the parking lot.

Crystal Cathedral Ministries still occupied most of the offices, and the committees and teams from the diocese, when they assembled for meetings, had to make arrangements for conference rooms through the ministry or use empty windowless office space beneath the cathedral, literally sitting on the floor. It was not a cruel burden. It was a necessity, and the teams made it work.

A couple of events challenged just how well the campus could handle two ministries at once. Crystal Cathedral Ministries' services, the *Hour of Power*, staff, and tourism continued as usual on the campus. They intermingled with mini-tours, surveys, and various managers with or representing the diocese. It was a pair of larger Catholic events that served to help inform diocese planners as to how well the campus in its current state was prepared to handle large events.

The Orange County Catholic prayer breakfast was the first test and saw a large influx of visitors for a single morning event that took place primarily in the arboretum. The next was a greater challenge because it lasted all day and took place in the arboretum, cathedral, and a large portion of the outdoor area of the campus.

The Magnificat was a worldwide organization, so its Day of Faith was an international event and at least three thousand attended. A year earlier, where the event would be held was a perplexing question: Somewhere in California?

At the time, late 2011, Berni Neal was the California point person for Magnificat, and she had been desperately trying to organize the Magnificat Day of Faith in Southern California. She preferred Orange County and encouraged the organizers to look there first. It offered many benefits, including being a central location between San Diego and LA. It was well known that important bankruptcy hearings regarding the Crystal Cathedral were happening the day Berni Neal and others, some of whom had traveled from France, went out in search of a location for the conference. On that trip, around-the-county talk of the Crystal Cathedral came up, so Neal circled the group through the parking lot. The visitors from France were very curious. Like so many others around the world they had heard of Schuller and the Crystal Cathedral. It was a drive-by tour, and Neal explained that plans to buy the cathedral had begun to raise hopes, but on that particular day many were resigned to accepting the court's decision, which seemed destined to favor Chapman University.

"Oh well," she told the visitors.[2]

Later that day, after she had dropped off the visitors, she was driving alone. They had been looking for a place that would work as a religious retreat and could be converted into appropriate liturgical space. It was not easy. The phone rang. It was Tim Busch.

"We got it!" Busch shouted.

"What?" she said, confused. "Uh, you probably want to call Rob."

"Yes, but we got it! The judge said that it's coming to the diocese."

"Oh my gosh. You gotta call Rob!"

When the call ended, Neal contacted the Magnificat team and told them, "We now have a location for Magnificat Day; we have a location that can seat three thousand. Everything we need."

The *Magnificat Magazine* was a pocket-sized magazine, printed and shipped monthly to Catholic bookstores and other distributors and platforms around the world and intended for daily use, "to encourage liturgical and personal prayer," according to the organization's website. It was often used to celebrate Mass more fully and to enhance the spiritual experience both before and after Mass.

During his talk to attendees who had packed the glass cathedral, the *Magnificat Magazine*'s editor-in-chief said that it was a wonder to see thousands of people gathered there.

"It's just an awesome testimony to faith," said Father Peter John Cameron.[3] "And one that would make the Holy Father very happy." Cameron was referring to Benedict XVI, who was pope at the time, and his call for "a year of faith."

"We will have opportunities to profess our faith," Cameron said, quoting Pope Benedict XVI, "in our cathedrals and in the churches of the whole world, so that everyone will feel a strong need to know better and to transmit to future generations the faith of all times."

The event was inspiring, and there was a general sense of spiritual optimism, not just in the general Christian faith, but in the way the faith would be practiced at the diocese's new cathedral in the future. The infrastructure handled it, at least on the surface, despite the strain on campus systems and resources. There did not seem to be anything it could not handle, according to Rob Neal, whose wife, Berni, organized the event.

"I was walking around seeing how the campus handled the load," said Neal.[4] "They had set up all of these tables inside the arboretum, and just handled it effortlessly. We hadn't done anything to the arboretum yet." As the chief organizer and restoration lay leader for the diocese, for Neal it was helpful to see the campus tested.

"It started to give me an appreciation that this is a campus unlike anything I'd ever seen, a facility, a project, a place I'd ever been associated with before. And all I've ever done for forty years is real estate."

For good reason, Rob Neal had high hopes that there would be plenty of time for the restoration of the arboretum so that St. Callistus and Crystal Cathedral Ministries would both have a home to worship in when the time came. Sure, the campus had seen better days maintenance-wise, and the arboretum required a little more work, but the Magnificat Day of Faith showed him that the campus was well designed. He had also received word that Tim Busch had secured a $1 million commitment for the restoration fund from the John L. Curci Foundation. It was to be paid over three years. Fundraising had been going well with donations large and small from across the diocese. The donation was great news for the renovation budget, but the timing of the project changed when Crystal Cathedral Ministries abruptly announced a change of plans.

The phone rang at Jim Wirick's desk at LPA, a prestigious architectural design firm in Irvine, just a few miles from the Crystal Cathedral. It was Rob Neal. Joe Novoa at the Diocese of Orange had recommended Wirick and knew he was likely available. Novoa had noted the extreme wear and tear on the arboretum and pushed Neal to get a dedicated architect for the job.

"Rob, we really need an architect. We really need to get an engineer involved with this thing. It's got all kinds of issues here," said Novoa.[5]

"Who would you recommend?" asked Neal.

"The only one I know of that has the horsepower to handle something like this right now, LPA." Novoa and Wirick had worked on several projects together for the diocese, mostly dealing with building or improving parishes and schools going back to the year 2000. This project was different. It would put Wirick in the middle of two of the most significant challenges facing the restoration of the newly acquired Crystal Cathedral campus under a tight timeline, limited funding, and daunting scrutiny. Already difficult, it was a task easier said than done, as they soon found out.

Jim Wirick had about three decades of experience in architecture and design. It was a passion he had been called to early on. He recalled how, as a boy growing up in Pasadena, California, he had turned on the TV one Sunday morning and caught the glimpse of something spectacular.

"Saw this parade of glass next to these fountains," said Wirick, "jets shooting up to the sky and the camera pulling away from the building. So, I kind of met the building before I knew of Reverend Schuller."[6]

He was just nine years old at the time, and not quite sure what he was seeing, but his appreciation for the structure and the scene of the spouting water was an early indication of his interest in building design. The house he was sitting in was also part of that inspiration. It was a midcentury, post-and-beam structure designed by renowned architect Cal Straub. Wirick said it became an architectural case-study house and "was very cool." He knew he wanted to be an architect in fourth grade. His mother and grandmother saw that interest and did not discourage him.

Wirick stayed on that path and earned his bachelor's and master's degrees in architecture at Cal Poly, or formally, California Polytechnic University, in San Luis Obispo, 190 miles north of Los Angeles. As he grew in his education and career, Wirick followed famed architect Richard Neutra's work with Robert Schuller. He'd gone to the campus to see all of the buildings just after the Crystal Cathedral was built and later, as a member of the American Institute of Architects (AIA), listened to a rousing speech Schuller gave to its members that ended in a standing ovation.

"Anyone who knows architects, knows that's not an easy thing to accomplish," said Wirick.

The call from Rob Neal was thrilling for several reasons, and his early interest in Neutra and connection to Schuller was not lost on him. Wirick and Novoa had spoken about the Crystal Cathedral once before. But that was when the prospect of the diocese buying the property was just a "pipe dream" that would take a "miracle." Wirick expressed interest in that unlikely event.

"I just mentioned as a sidecar to Novoa," explained Wirick, "if you're ever interested in doing anything interesting with that Neutra building, give me a shout. We'd love to be involved."

He was serious, but like most people figured it wouldn't happen, so he was half-serious when he suggested that the diocese should just build a cathedral in one of the old historic blimp hangars in Tustin, just up the road. It so happened that the option of considering a hangar was something Joe Novoa had suggested to Bishop Brown, to no avail.

The *shout* to Wirick came in the invitation from Rob Neal.

"Hey, get to the arboretum, next Tuesday at ten," Wirick recalled the instructions. There was no question about it, Wirick was going. It was December 2012, and although it had been ten months since the close of escrow, there was a tone of urgency in the call tantamount to if escrow had closed last week.

Tuesday morning, Wirick drove to the campus and met with Rob Neal and Joe Novoa. Together they ventured into the Neutra Sanctuary, the original indoor/outdoor church, that had become known as the arboretum. There were several other people inside the building. While Wirick was the architect, there were some contractors, subcontractors, and consultants.

"Everybody was just walking around," said Wirick. "It was like some sort of info fair." But he hardly had a chance to think about it when he stepped into the cavernous hall where the *Hour of Power* had been launched.

"The arboretum is just in shambles," he said. Many of the tables that had been set up for the Magnificat Day of Faith were still in place, and the full cleanup had been delayed, so it also appeared to be cluttered as well. "It was sort of deflating," he said.

Everyone from the diocese who had ventured into the building after access was granted had the same sinking feeling. What they saw was known as deferred maintenance—not an entirely unexpected reality considering the Crystal Cathedral Ministries' financial problems for so many years. Due diligence in the bidding process for the sale put Joe Novoa inside the buildings with inspectors, but there was only so much that could be learned without digging into walls and the kinds of under-the-skin evaluations that tell the whole story. There was a cost analysis done; there had been no professional inspection that went beneath the surface, because that kind of work causes damage in the process.

"The carpet looked like it hadn't been cared for since the Reagan Administration," said Wirick. He was not being facetious or critical.

The building had not been used in any meaningful way for an awfully long time, and the age showed as well as the wear and tear.

After spending the summer and fall putting together a team and a plan for the arboretum, there were two major projects that Rob Neal had decided were a given. He was resigned to the fact that it was a little more than just a "paint and carpet job." Joe Novoa was right. There were "issues." It would require air-conditioning and a seismic retrofit. "No problem," he said. But then the deadline for the work shrunk significantly.

"Jim, this needs to be finished by July," Rob Neal told Wirick. "We don't have a lot of time, and we don't have a lot of money, and it needs to be air-conditioned." Neal had a similar awakening to the realities presented by the arboretum as Wirick. He had hoped for an easy renovation. But there were more challenges in-store. But how much more was the big unknown.

Starting the restoration in the arboretum was a decision that had been made for them. Crystal Cathedral Ministries had a three-year option to remain in the Crystal Cathedral or move to St. Callistus in June 2012 rent-free for the first year. It was a time frame for the ministry to swap with St. Callistus that might have worked if it was just a carpet and paint job. But the ministry opted to stay in the cathedral. By November of that year, something had changed. The ministry decided to take the early move-out and informed the diocese it intended to occupy St. Callistus beginning in June 2013, which afforded it a rent-free period of six months.

Two obvious requirements immediately came into play. One was they were moving out in seven months, and then there was the parish at St. Callistus: it would have to be cleared out and its congregation moved also in seven months. The arboretum was to be St. Callistus's new worship space, and the church, school, and offices at St. Callistus would be turned over to Crystal Cathedral Ministries. The call to Jim Wirick was the first step in meeting that tight new timeline. It would be less than six months by the time the first physical work on the arboretum could begin. Again, the sudden rush was not in itself an emergency. The only complicated parts of the renovation, air-conditioning and seismic retrofit, seemed doable. Of the two, air-conditioning was the most complicated. If Wirick and LPA had the horsepower Joe Novoa was talking about, Rob Neal was going to need it.

Rob Neal had said there was not much time and not a lot of money. Wirick could work with that, but air-conditioning would require some design work. Wirick looked around at the infrastructure, thinking about that requirement, and nodded. "If you don't have a lot of money, would you consider ventilating it?"

In response, Neal just restated the situation about time, money, and the air-conditioning.

"Okay," said Wirick, who was up to the challenge.

A time was set for them to reconvene in a week at Rob Neal's office so that Wirick could present some design options for air-conditioning. They met the following week as planned, and it very nearly ended Wirick's involvement in any part of the restoration plan.

As promised, Wirick presented Rob Neal and Joe Novoa with two options for air-conditioning the arboretum. The first involved the installation of two massive air-conditioning units on the top of the Neutra-designed building and blowing the cooled air downward. This was typical for how modern construction dealt with air-conditioning. The other plan was more costly: to demolish the existing concrete floor and replace it with a concrete tub that would blow cold air through a perforated floor upward. Not too surprisingly, the first option seemed to make more sense, and Rob Neal nodded.

"We'll take option number one," said Neal. "We'll just squirt the air in from the top like a conventional system."

"I completely understand," Wirick replied. "But ..." It was the moment he knew the air was going to get sucked out of the room like one of these air-conditioning plans in reverse. "I can't be involved in that," Wirick said apologetically.

He knew what the architectural community in Orange County and beyond would do to him if he were to go through with a plan that fundamentally altered the entire look of the building. As expected, the declaration did not go over well with Rob Neal.

"He said, 'Rob if you put this on the top,'" Neal recalled, "'you will destroy the envelope of this building and LPA will not have its name attached to it.' I was thinking, *Who the hell is this guy to tell me what to do about this building?*" Neal continued. "He literally got up in my conference room like he was gonna leave."

But Neal convinced him to sit and talk. It was not a long conversation, and when Wirick left he assumed LPA had been dropped from the restoration commission. Neal was genuinely upset, and that was the end of the conversation—for the moment. Neal went home; he was frustrated and pressed for time. To Neal, these decisions happened all the time in restoration work, and what professionals did was deal with the circumstances and move on, particularly architects.

"Architects are not well compensated," Neal said. "They don't have the luxury of turning down jobs. Even the successful firms like LPA." That was the situation, however. Then something inexplicable happened. Neal was a Catholic and attended church regularly, but there was no reason to expect a moment of conversion in this atypical crisis. It was not unlike many restoration projects he had dealt with in the past besides a significantly tighter time crunch and less money than it required. Other than that, and the fact that it was a Catholic diocese and a cathedral campus, it was just another day to Rob Neal. So why was he so self-absorbed and indignant over a little matter of business and what felt like a snub from an architect firm?

"There haven't been many times in my life when something went into my mind so clearly that it changed everything about what I was doing," said Neal. "But I swear it was just that intense."

Rob Neal went from frustrated, a little angry, and stymied in this important project to a realization that the cathedral campus was not just some other project. It was intended to last for centuries. Neal bore the responsibility, and the time had come.

"I realized this building is a treasure," Neal said of the arboretum. "This was built by one of the greatest American architects that's ever lived, Richard Neutra, and it's ours. We can't screw this thing up."

To Neal, making a mistake here was more than just a crime against architecture. It was a defining moment that would send a "signal to the community about the kind of stewards that the Catholic Church was. I'm convinced that was the Holy Spirit. That's really what created in my mind this guiding principle that whatever we do, it must be best in class, so as to demonstrate that the Catholic Church was reassuming its mantle of leadership in art and architecture." This would be not just a statement to the local community, but to the world.

Neal called Wirick and said the second option, demolishing the original concrete floor and installing the tub, would work. So, LPA was back on the job. Wirick said that was when everyone jumped in with "both feet."

"Let's bore into this project," Wirick remembered thinking. "And we went after it."

It was a good attitude to have, but the real surprises and costly challenges presented by the arboretum had yet to be discovered.

Meanwhile, Rob Neal and his wife, Berni, went to visit Robert Schuller in his office on the twelfth floor of the Tower of Hope, the same room where Schuller met with the team from the diocese during the bankruptcy proceedings. Arvella Schuller and the couple's daughter Carole Milner joined them. Rob Neal felt a sense of duty to assure the Schullers, in what he called his "own imperfect way," that he understood art and architecture.

"I told him that my own particular vision," Neal recalled, "that I think had been shared with me through the Holy Spirit, was that the Catholic Church had been a leader in art and architecture for two millennia and it had only been in the last hundred-fifty years that it had surrendered that leadership. It was my intent with this particular project to reassert that leadership. To do it in a way that was completely compatible with the vision that originally guided the development of the [Crystal Cathedral campus] project. To do the highest standards of preservation and restoration. To bring these great buildings back to their majesty."

Neal sought to explain that it was not about just restoration, but about the future and what would happen on the campus. It was an area his wife, Berni Neal, would play a significant role in, and Rob Neal told Schuller that his legacy would continue in ongoing missionary work at the campus and be preserved in its architecture.

"We saw [this vision] as a continuation of the promise that he had ignited for that campus."

"The phrase was, 'We will be Vatican West,'" said Berni Neal. "We offended a lot of Catholics with that," she said with a chuckle.

Berni and Rob Neal recalled Schuller's response. "You're not thinking big enough!"

The task was complex, and there were unknowns and surprises ahead that no one could have predicted. But Neal's sincere effort to communicate this noble purpose to Schuller set a tone that influenced the restoration teams going forward. From unavoidable significant changes, to restoration with an eye toward preservation, this attitude and intention was up front.

With Crystal Cathedral Ministries eyeing a move-out date in little more than five months, the arboretum was about to be swarming with crews. On that first day there was a small crew gathered at the arboretum for a blessing led by vicar and rector Father Christopher Smith for a safe and speedy restoration project.

"Rob and his team had to really get on the ball fast," Smith said in a later interview. He laughed at the understatement. "The whole project of Christ Cathedral became very real for me that day."

Real as in *reality*.

The first of the major projects was the removal of the building's concrete floor. The foundation was to remain intact, but the floor had to go so that the air-conditioning tub could be inserted. There was a very tight deadline that was about to become even more difficult.

"And the guys started tearing into the building," said Rob Neal. "I saw there was an area of the glass that sort of reflected and sagged." So, Neal pointed it out and asked the crew "to check it out and fix it up." He thought it was a minor thing.

LPA design project lead Jim Wirick was watching as the glass contractor started to work on the giant sheets of glass to repair the connections. "And the curtain wall started to heave out. That's when the caution tape went up and the contractor said, 'I'm not repairing this.'"

"They got into it and they found that the entire interior of all the walls was rotted," said Rob Neal. "Water had been seeping in over years because the building hadn't drained properly. It was all shot. And all that glass was just hanging by a thread." Neal was shocked. He said the glass was not safety glass, just single paned, so if it had collapsed, it could have killed someone.

Neal and construction managers had a decision to make. So, they committed to a demolition project to take the building down to a shell. They needed to have a true picture of the situation. That picture surprised everyone.

"It changed everything," Neal recalled. "There's nothing but dirt and steel. The roof was intact; the walls were completely open other than the steel columns." Even with Neal's traditional contingency in mind, this level of demolition was extreme. "We had never anticipated anything remotely like that," he said. And he added, "It was the single wildest, most amazing six months of my life."

Bishop Vann

Seven months after the sale of the Crystal Cathedral to the Diocese of Orange was finalized, bishops and cardinals from around the country were participating in the Knights of Columbus National Convention in nearby Anaheim. A group of them stopped by the campus for a tour to learn a little for themselves about the ten-thousand-glass-pane church and the famous campus they had heard so much about and only seen on TV. Escorted by Rob Neal, the interim COO of the Christ Cathedral Corporation, they toured several buildings and listened to the harmonic sounds of the famous Hazel Wright Organ in the sanctuary. Reporters interviewed the bishops, curious about what they thought of the shimmering megachurch built for television and its future. Could it ever equal the traditional church appreciation the Catholics were known for? What about the production studio? Would it be used?

The response was overwhelmingly positive, at least publicly. There had to be at least some realization that as fine as the campus was, it was in disrepair and the church needed substantial work to be transformed into a Catholic cathedral. Among those clergymen who put on a good face and spoke positively about what he saw was Kevin Vann, the bishop of the Diocese of Fort Worth, Texas. He wore a white Stetson, as was the custom for such social and informal events in his diocese back home.

"The campus was extraordinary," Vann later recalled; "it was beautiful." It was huge and in need of work. "It's going to be a lot of work for whoever gets it." A similar quote appeared in the major local paper in a story about the tour.[1]

Vann was aware that Bishop Brown was set to retire. It never occurred to him while surveying the campus that he would preside over the dedication of Christ Cathedral.

Kevin William Vann was raised in Springfield, Illinois, as part of a large middle-class Catholic family. He was the oldest of the six children, spanning twenty years, blessed to William Vann Jr. and Theresa Vann. William was a World War II veteran and a postal worker with two additional jobs on the side. Theresa was an obstetrics nurse. For Vann, being the big brother forced him to play leader early in life, but also to develop a heart for helping and nurturing. The kids were raised to care for others.

"My father always taught us to do the right thing," said Vann.

But it was his mother's influence that persuaded him to pursue a career in the medical field. Vann recalled his parents' attitude of selfless service. His father was known to brave the terrible Illinois December weather to make special trips to pick up and deliver Christmas packages by request. His mother made nursing house calls whenever she got the call.

"I'd say I'm a combination of both of them."

Vann earned a degree in medical technology from Millikin University in Decatur, Illinois. But he had longed for something else—something deeper that called him to the Church even before he went to high school.

"It evolved over time," he said.

There were strong ties to the Church within the family, and religious vocations were common among the people he knew growing up. His aunt was a Dominican sister, and the family had a good relationship with the local parish priest. It was common for some of the priests from the parish to have dinner at their home.

"They inspired me," said Vann. "They inspired all of us."

While working as a medical technologist at night, he studied at the Immaculate Conception Diocesan Seminary. Then he left his job to complete a four-year course of study in theology at Kenrick Seminary in Missouri.

Vann was ordained in 1981 and was immediately called to Rome for canon law studies. He called it an incredible time in his life, as he was there when Saint Pope John Paul II was still active. They were his formative years, and he found he had a knack for speaking Italian. While there, as what amounted to be a rookie priest, he met another American priest who was quite a bit older. Tod Brown was there on a sabbatical program. They were housed in the same residence at the Casa Santa Maria of the North American College, where they studied together. Vann returned to the United States and took several assignments, including as pastor of small and large congregations. While on one of those assignments in Decatur, Illinois, he studied the text for the Spanish Mass, and the language came easy to him. He established a Spanish Mass before leaving. Eventually, Vann headed back to Missouri to teach canon law at his alma mater, Kenrick.

By 2005, he was on his way to Texas to take over as the bishop of the Catholic Diocese of Fort Worth. It was there he turned Texan and became known for his stylish cowboy boots adorned with an embroidered image of Our Lady of Guadalupe, along with his initials. The special boots were made in the stockyards on the north side of Fort Worth and were a gift from some close friends. Vann had a well-established devotion to Our Lady of Guadalupe. A pair of matching cufflinks later followed. In sheer size, Fort Worth was a massive diocese with twenty-five thousand square miles, but it had relatively few Catholics for its size at just seven hundred thousand.

Seven years later, just three weeks after Vann's photograph adorned the cover of the local newspaper in Orange County marking his visit to the Crystal Cathedral, he got the surprise call from the papal nuncio to the United States. The nuncio revealed Pope Benedict XVI had chosen Vann to replace the retiring bishop of Orange, his old friend from Rome, Tod Brown. It was Brown who first entered Vann's mind at that instant.

"Oh, I know Bishop Brown!" he recalled his first words after the news.

It was hard to imagine that so much could change over a matter of weeks, but Vann obediently packed his boots and headed west to the Golden State to its most Orange of counties with its glistening church of glass. It was a challenge to be sure, but he called it another step in his journey as a priest. Despite appointment as bishop, he had always considered himself a priest first.

"You have to take life in stride," said Vann. "My mom and dad did, and God has his surprises. I'd already had the earlier surprise bringing me from Springfield, Illinois, to Fort Worth. I love Fort Worth. I love Texas. I love the people. But when you're a priest you move. You're asked to move, you go."

Compared to Fort Worth in size, Orange was ridiculously small, but it had far more Catholics at 1.3 million, estimated by the diocese to be 40 percent of the county population. But that did not mean it would be a fish-out-of-water situation for Vann. Vann had already mastered Spanish by the time he had arrived in Fort Worth, which had a sizable Spanish-speaking population, but Vann's parish also had an Asian immigrant population from Vietnam and Korea. The experience in culture and language set him up as an appropriate choice for the job in Orange County. He did not see the population as all that much different, just a lot larger.

Vann traveled to Orange County to make his statement to the media about his appointment. Sporting his cowboy boots honoring Our Lady of Guadalupe, he recalled his friendship of thirty-one years with Bishop Brown and how they met so long ago. He also talked about family. The Family of God.

"When bishop or a priest is transferred," Vann said, "from one parish to another or one diocese to another, they leave one family behind and gain another." He would miss the Fort Worth family, and in a deeper meaning for Vann, his mother had died only months earlier.

He promised, "As we grow together in this exciting and dynamic time of the Diocese of Orange, I will love you and do my best to serve you, with the Lord's help."[2]

There was excitement with his arrival, because of what was ahead with the Crystal Cathedral. "We are at an exciting time here in Orange. With the acquiring of what will be Christ Cathedral, we have the opportunity, with the gift of God that this is, as Bishop Brown has said, to continue to preach the Word of God here."[3]

He did not offer any plan for what he would do next. He said he did not have one, but he was sure "God's purpose and plan will be shown to us each day."

In Pope Benedict XVI's appointment decree naming Kevin Vann bishop of the Diocese of Orange, the pontiff was clearly mindful of the challenges Vann faced as he was to shepherd the diocese through renovation and transformation of the newly acquired Crystal Cathedral, so that it would become the center of Catholic life for 1.2 million Catholics.

"We know for sure, that the most Blessed Virgin Mary of Guadalupe to whom the spiritual welfare of the church in Orange, California, has been entrusted, and whose virtues like crystals, reflect the divine light, will with her loving glance watch over you, as you come to meet the flock entrusted to your pastoral care," Pope Benedict said in the official apostolic mandate and decree.[4]

Bishop Vann flew from Texas to Orange County to prepare for installation and settle in, but he was so curious about what was going on when he heard about the campus design charrette under-way that he joined in and spent part of the day with the team orga-nized by Randy Jackson.

Landscape and design architect Randy Jackson was president of PlaceWorks in Santa Ana, California. He was one of the first to join Rob Neal in the planning stage. Jackson was one of many people involved in the project who had some past connection to Schuller and his ministry. As a boy, he went with his father and brothers to the drive-in to hear a sermon. It was in the early days of the ministry in the mid-1950s. They were a Catholic family and enjoyed the novelty and the sermon, but they never went back. Jackson's relationship with the cathedral campus project began as an invitation to sit in on the architectural design committee. He called it an honor to be involved.

Bishop Vann went to Jackson's office and found the charrette was well underway. A charrette has its origins in a sixteenth-century French art and architecture school. There were a series of rooms in a long hallway. Inside each one was a designer architect. The profes-sor would submit weeklong assignments and at the end of the week would send a cart up the hallway ringing a bell. The architects put their drawings in the cart; some sat on the cart and rode it back down the hallway. Jackson organized the charrette for the Christ Cathe-dral campus with about twenty team members. Each worked in his own space, or in small groups.

The charrette Bishop Vann witnessed, and participated in, was an effort to pull together the major elements of the campus design. They were trying to answer basic questions, such as how to keep it Christian, how to address the architecture, plazas, and outdoor spaces, and finally, access. That latter part dealt with signage. There were no signs to direct visitors around—an apparently intentional omission by Schuller. There were a lot of ideas going into the cart, and Bishop Vann stayed there for four hours.

"With all the ten thousand things he had to do in his three-hour flight from [Fort Worth]," said Jackson, "to come and think about the cathedral and its organization and function, I think was a major statement about his commitment and the church's commitment to do something special."[5]

Bishop Vann did have a lot to do. He was formally installed as the fourth bishop of Orange shortly thereafter. The ceremony required a much larger space than what was available at the eight-hundred-seat Holy Family Cathedral. Instead, it was held at the Bren Center at the University of California Irvine. It was a dilemma the diocese would not have to contend with in the future due to the purchase of the Crystal Cathedral. The sports-venue basketball court, with its close-in arena seating, was transformed into a temporary cathedral sanctuary with the altar at its center. That put the dais and bishop's chair at one end some distance away. The rest of the seating was in artfully arranged folding chairs to mimic traditional church design. The focus was on the center of the makeshift cathedral for the Eucharistic celebration. Fittingly, suspended over the altar was a large crucifix known as the Christ the High Priest cross. It depicted the resurrected Christ with his head tilted down, dressed in priestly vestments, and his unpierced palms outstretched as if in blessing. Detail such as this to turn a gymnasium into a place for Eucharistic celebration was easy compared to the restoration of the Christ Cathedral campus.

The day after the installation ceremony, Vann sat down for his first full meeting about the cathedral and the status of the campus. He had had little time to figure out a plan. It was merely a matter of months between his campus visit, where he gathered initial impressions, without foresight of his future responsibilities, and his assumption of duties. True to his earlier commitment, he let circumstances dictate, as he had said, according to "God's purpose and plan … each day." He was fortunate to have already met many of the people at the diocese, and he was well acquainted with some of the priests with whom he had attended graduate school. For the first few weeks he was happy to get to know a lot of new people and get involved as soon as he could. There was no doubt the diocese and laypeople had done extraordinary work; but the centerpiece of the campus and the heart of the diocese, Christ Cathedral, had years of work ahead.

"My objective was to be the pastor the Lord wanted me to be," he said. "And to grow in love and to know the people that were all here together. That was my first objective. You can't do any construction unless you, kind of, all go together to be the people the Lord wants you to be."

Chief among Vann's immediate senior managers was Father Christopher Smith. He was the reliable episcopal vicar and rector of Christ Cathedral who had been appointed by Vann's predecessor in March. Smith had a depth of knowledge and experience Vann could rely on, but there was also an easy trust and comfort that developed between the two clergymen. Smith was also from a large family, strongly influenced by his parents, and had a skill and love for playing the piano.

For most of that year, Smith had been working with Bishop Brown and diocese laypeople and experts to pull together the restoration plan and management of resources going forward. The St. Callistus Parish and school were well into planning the eventual move to the diocese. The diocese appeared to have everything under control. Money had been raised to get started, between $20 million and $30 million of Brown's $100 million capital campaign for renovations and diocese parish improvements. Key people were working on delicate design and construction plans and actively engaged. Among them was Rob Neal, who was involved in both renovation management and fundraising. Estimates were that the capital campaign would take a year and a half while the renovation would extend to twice that or longer.

There was not much for Bishop Vann to do with regard to what was already underway and the many parts that were in motion. Even if he wanted to, traditionally, the incoming bishop was not eager to make major alterations to what the retiring bishop had planned. As such, Bishop Vann let the plan play out while staying informed.

The restoration of the Crystal Cathedral campus, the arboretum, the Tower of Hope, and the Christ Cathedral was about to begin with a head-spinning six-month odyssey focused on one building. What many had prayed would be according to God's plan was set to move forward, and it did with all the requisite surprises and challenges one would expect and a lot more no one saw coming.

The Neutra Arboretum

Renovation fundraising by Cindy Bobruk of the Orange Catholic Foundation and Tim Busch had gone well and accelerated to meet the new time demands for getting started on the arboretum. But while there was money for the work, there were three buildings, including the cathedral, that required renovation. So, by December 2012, there was careful watch on the budget for the first major renovation. The revelations that were yielded by getting into the walls of the building found that all of the glass and sagging wall had to be replaced, which meant the ticking seconds of a clock loomed louder and larger than the bells of Schuller's carillon. The pressure was intense, and some in the diocese still wondered if the arboretum was going to be done by the July 4 deadline. After he saw the growing list of what would be required to get the arboretum done, Rob Neal was momentarily frozen by the gravity of the situation.

"Within a week," said Neal, "I almost fell into a depression. I thought, what are we going to do? What *are* we going to do? And then I thought, there's nothing we can do but do it. We'll just simply have to do it."[1] Neal said the restoration of the arboretum, on a difficulty scale from 1 to 10, went from a 1 to a 10. "In terms of complexity, involvement, and of course the budget was blown to pieces."

And it happened overnight.

"Everything had to change," said Neal.

Neal had assembled an architect and planning committee. Among its responsibilities was to select an architectural design contractor to do the work. Mary Kay Westbrook joined the board. She was an attorney with many years' experience working for developers and master planners.

"The call from Rob Neal was out of the blue," she said.[2] "I did not know him. I don't know why he called." She suspected there may have been an effort to add women to the team for diversity. Even if true, there was no questioning her qualifications when it comes to development. She had also served on a diocese board many years ago at the invitation of Bishop Brown.

"Let me think about it," she told Neal. "I'm very, very interested. Let me think about it."

"Okay," said Neal. "I'll call you tomorrow."

It had not occurred to her at that moment, but by the next day, she had decided it was an opportunity of a lifetime.

After the selection of the architectural firm LPA, Westbrook was invited to co-chair the Master Planning Subcommittee with Randy Jackson, a master planner and architect.

The brutally short deadline for completion of the arboretum really put the onus on Neal to recognize needs versus wants, requirements versus quality, and to put in countless little prayers in between. Quality revealed itself as a strong partner to the goal of historical preservation married with modern technology. Neal was well suited to bear the responsibility. He had already discovered the hidden deferred maintenance problems at the arboretum and begun to absorb the new jobs he had encountered. These were, after all, hiccups in renovations he had seen before. The difference was the solutions and design work had to be not just done but done second to none and in less than six months.

"We do a lot of heavy renovations," said Neal. "I have a very large contingency on our renovations." That can be 10 to 15 percent or higher for Neal's firm, and that has drawn criticism from outsiders who have accused him of not knowing what he was doing. "I say, 'No, I'm a developer, I know exactly what I'm doing.' Because when you're renovating existing buildings there's almost always a situation where you find something in the field that was not anticipated. And in [the arboretum], we ran into it in spades over and over."

The solutions to these situations were sometimes costly, and often innovative. The air-conditioning and glass walls were both.

The contractor, Canon Building, stripped away the layers of what design firm LPA had determined were unsuccessful modifications that had been made during the life of the building. LPA relied on historical data and photos to find Neutra's original design he created in 1961. There was talk of bringing in a historian, and there was a local Neutra scholar by the name of Barbara Lamprecht nearby. The debate centered on the wildcard nature of that decision. A historian could slow down progress, and they did not have time to waste. There was already too much to do and no time to do it. LPA's Jim Wirick suggested it would help and won Rob Neal over, so calls were made to recruit Lamprecht.

At the same time, the glass panes were ready to fall out, and there was the catastrophic failure of the walls' support structure that required disassembling. The capital campaign raised money as the work continued, and time was not a friendly companion. The metaphorical ticking of the clock manifested itself in every setback. But there was an energy and optimism that ran through everyone involved. The removal of the cement floor for the purposes of installing the tub for air-conditioning and the demolition of the walls and glass took the building down to the bones. When Bishop Tod Brown saw the extreme demolition, he called Rob Neal in a panic.

"Why are you tearing down the building?" asked Brown.

"I'm not, I swear I'm going to build it," replied Neal.

The arboretum had two major walls made up of glass panes, so the greenhouse effect made for some ridiculously hot days. It was a departure from architectural norms to design a building with east- and west-facing glass walls. There was no air-conditioning at all for the arboretum. During a Schuller indoor/outdoor service, there could be six hundred cars in the parking lot for rolling worshippers to listen and watch and more people on folding chairs beneath Schuller's elevated platform. Inside, more than a thousand people in theater seating would be sweating, many of whom wore sunglasses. The best that could be hoped for was a breeze fueled by the massive opened panel that allowed Schuller to be inside and outside at once. There was a vent or louver-type window later installed in hopes of creating a draft, but it was largely unsuccessful. For worshippers of the diocese celebrating Mass, air-conditioning was a must.

As the building was reduced to its bare steel bones, the job of rectifying the problem got underway. The installation of the tub was for what was known as an underfloor air-distribution system or displacement ventilation. It was the first innovation that showed the restoration was a commitment to restoring the arboretum to its former glory but also bringing it into the twenty-first century technologically. This system required a lower velocity of air distributed through vents in the floor. With the cool air rising naturally with lower fan pressure, it was highly energy efficient. The installation of the newly designed glass walls would further illustrate the point and enhance the climate-control system.

Each quarter-inch-thick sheet of glass was two feet by five feet stacked and offset, one on top of the other. They were "resting on top of each other, going down, and the moldings were held in place by screws up in the top of the wood," said Jim Wirick. "How it stayed together for fifty years, nobody knows."[3]

To improve safety and durability crews installed dual-pane glass in prefabbed curtain installations, which provided increased protection from the penetrating heat of the sun. Great care was taken to replicate the look of the floor-to-ceiling glass walls. The glass was one-inch-thick insulated, glazed units, installed "in a way that looked like they looked originally. And that was a chore," said Wirick.

But there was another structural surprise.

While looking at the drawings, it was noticed that there was a large X brace behind the wall at the head of the room—the end of the building where the organ pipes were located and the altar would be installed.

"Steel rods that are keeping the building from racking in the east and west direction," noted Wirick.

This was part of the original design, and in the original drawings. But for the architecture and design team looking for the brace in the structure, it was not there. The structural engineer was so surprised, he quipped he did not know how the building was standing.

"So, again, in real time," Wirick said, "we had to design a moment frame to be attached to that all behind the organs, to be slipped down on the north side of the building in between the new HVAC unit, and all the ducts coming in underneath this floor. Then that's put on micropyles to keep it from racking. All this was a surprise.

In spades ...

Beyond the building there were other repairs that needed to be done, including the Fountains of the 12 Apostles—the array of fountains that run the length of the arboretum glass wall between the parking lot and the building. They were not operating when the diocese took possession of the building. And that raised a larger exterior question of what the campus would look like. The arboretum phase included figuring out signage and the lettering that should be used to identify buildings. It was not hard to imagine that signs were important, but it was work that proved the value of the ethics and attitude that breathed unique life into every task.

Mary Kay Westbrook, Randy Jackson, and the Master Planning Subcommittee had been tasked, as one of its major responsibilities, with planning the flow and signage for campus navigation. Schuller seemed to have an aversion to signs, and while the Neutra buildings had names on them, the rest of the campus lacked signs. This was known in the planning vernacular as "way finding" and would be essential to the general operational needs of the campus.

"You would arrive on campus here," Westbrook explained, "and there was no sign if you were looking for the office or arboretum. That's the way it was inside the buildings as well. No signs."

The process of master planning and the intricacies of not just placing signs but deciding what they would look like was Westbrook's major takeaway from that hard work. But there was more.

"There's no question what it brought to me," she said. "I was not alone in this, the uniqueness of these people working together, the committees, of both laypeople and [clergy] that, to a person, were attempting in life to mirror what God wants us to do. Compassion and love and forgiveness. I had never worked ever in that kind of environment. You wanted to bring you're A-game."

And not just with the signs, but with everything they did together. It was infectious and intoxicating, which spread to everything in Westbrook's life.

"Your A-game as a human being. Not just there, everywhere. It was like, wow; this is an experience." It was spiritual growth so profound that she wondered why she had to have this experience to recognize the "A-game of life." For that she credited the many mentors she worked with on the project.

It was with that spirit that she tackled way finding with signs. Her co-chair Randy Jackson said it might seem strange to fuss over signs, but it was important work.

"You can go get signs knocked out downstairs at one of the printing shops," said Jackson. "But here, to be able to go back and inventory the signs, understand why and the placement of them, work through the way finding as well as the story telling of the sign, was a commitment to respecting the building and the architect."

There was an early movement to put the way-finding signs in but remove the names on the buildings. That idea did not reach any level of consensus over objections that to do so would violate the historic restoration. So, what they did was identify the font for the Neutra-designed letter on the building and re-create the original look.

"It's actually his letter style that he created," said Jackson.

Meanwhile, the dedicated crew working on the arboretum eventually resembled an ant hill. During a gathering of workers, Rob Neal talked to them about the importance of their work. Always stay on schedule if the work can be done safely. Then, he told them something that seemed to emerge from within his heart. Something he had not planned on saying.

"I think, guys," said Neal, "you're gonna look back, fellas, and you're gonna say this was the finest work of your life." He later recalled, "How many times do you have an opportunity to know that in advance? That wasn't me. That thought just boom, popped in my head. And I felt that. It was the finest work of my life. Not just me, but hundreds of others."

History as a Guide

Rob Neal had a uniquely personal involvement with this already inimitable project. It was a campus unmatched in its collection of architectural examples from legendary architects, and it had a larger-than-life identity across the globe. Neal came to an appreciation for that and was convinced it was God's intent, an endorsement through the Holy Spirit, that whatever the project required would be provided. Planning and design architect Randy Jackson, who set up the architectural and renovation subcommittee, recognized right away that the culture Neal fostered for the fast-moving campaign of restoration was dedicated to preservation.

"They actually bought an architecturally historic place," said Jackson.[1] "It has three major buildings by three different architects that are world class. They are all within one hundred yards of each other, and there's no other place in the world with that much quality of architecture in one place."

The architecture and historic value were just two dimensions of the obligation Rob Neal's team and the diocese had grown to understand. The cathedral would be the center of the campus, and the other buildings preserved. There was a history of life and Gospel preaching on the campus embodied in the founder of the campus, Robert H. Schuller. The reverend's appearances on campus tapered to almost nothing, but he occasionally showed up and could be seen walking around greeting people. One day, Rob Neal and Schuller were walking across campus when a group of Korean tourists spotted the old pastor, now in his mid-eighties, and they swarmed him.

"There must have been thirty or forty of them," said Neal.[2] "He was very gracious with them all."

Neal was surprised and recalled talking to Schuller about the excited crowd.

"Reverend, those were all Koreans."

"Yes, yes," said Schuller, "we had a special audience in Korea. We had a special affection for our Korean friends."

That was when it occurred to Neal that Schuller had a special relationship like that with people around the world. And he thought, *We better get this right. We better really get this right.* What Rob Neal needed was to keep it moving forward, passionately committed to the standards that had been set for restoration and preservation. To achieve the goal, design architect Jim Wirick suggested a historian, a move most architects dread because historians tend to slow projects down to a crawl. Rob Neal could not afford to slow down, but he could not afford to not hire a historian—not when the perfect person was readily available and lived locally. True to the needs of the campus restoration from the start, when project managers sought expert help, the perfect person for the job was available and eager to assist.

Barbara Lamprecht was a distinguished Neutra scholar and architectural historian who had published several books on Richard Neutra's body of work. After receiving a master's in architecture at Cal-Poly Pomona, she went on to complete her PhD at the University of Liverpool. Her contributions to the restoration of the cathedral campus were to be many, but the most visible was the discovery and reimagining of Richard Neutra's most stunning and rare design elements: color, something that had mysteriously vanished from the exterior of the arboretum some years before.

By late spring, about halfway through the arboretum restoration, the focus had begun to shift to interior and exterior design aesthetics such as paint, artwork, and drapery. There was still major work being done, and meeting the deadline was not assured. Crystal Cathedral Ministries was set to trade campuses with the parish at St. Callistus by the end of June, which seemed like just weeks away. A lot of moving had already happened. Students at Crystal Cathedral Academy and St. Callistus had traded spaces a few months earlier. There were already discussions about what to do if the arboretum/sanctuary was not quite ready. One solution was to hold Mass outside. It was a feasible solution, and there was some certainty that the outdoor Mass would be a onetime event. Holding Mass outside became a certainty when it was estimated some three thousand worshippers would attend. The arboretum could only hold a crowd a third of that size.

Jim Wirick and Rob Neal reached out to Barbara Lamprecht to invite her to join the restoration team. Lamprecht was familiar with the Neutra-designed buildings on campus and had once enjoyed lunch with Robert H. Schuller and Richard Neutra's son Raymond Neutra. The lunch took place in Schuller's Tower of Hope office before Crystal Cathedral Ministries publicly unraveled. It was an affirming meeting for Lamprecht, because Schuller already knew about her from her book *The Complete Works of Richard Neutra*, published in 2010. In the two years that followed, Lamprecht noted the occasional news story that chronicled the financial decline of the ministry.

"It was a very difficult thing to hear about," said Lamprecht, "given *Hour of Power* and Schuller's monumental impact on American culture."[3]

Lamprecht was excited to join the restoration team and was tasked in two ways. One way was as problem solver. When a committee or group identified a visual or architectural problem that impacted the historical restoration, they turned to her for advice and suggestions. And for the second way, she was tasked with providing more free form as it related to observations and research.

The addition of a historian commonly followed a firm commitment to restore a classic structure and earn historic designation. That was not the case for the Neutra buildings. Rob Neal, nevertheless, wanted to follow the same federal standards for historic rehabilitation. There was a consensus that it made sense to be that meticulous.

"And that's very unusual for a client," said Lamprecht. "This was exemplary on the part of Rob Neal, Jim Wirick, and the diocese."

Lamprecht saw herself using her depth of knowledge to channel Richard Neutra inasmuch as that was humanly possible.

"Nobody can channel a great architect, but we can determine what would be appropriate, what would be compatible."

What Lamprecht accomplished in the discovery of color was a combination of channeling Neutra and the freedom of observation and research in which she excelled. Part architect, part archaeologist.

The adventure in color began with an old blurry and cloudy photo of the arboretum's east-facing exterior façade where the glass wall terminated on the north end. This was the side facing the parking lot that was in the style of a drive-in. More specifically, it drew attention to the part of the interior/exterior pulpit that jutted out like a balcony where Schuller preached. The source of the photo was lost to time. Lamprecht explained that she may have found the picture herself, but it might also have been given to her. Regardless, it was a fascinating image that offered a glimpse of an original Neutra-design element that had been erased. It was a bright orange panel. In the terrible photograph, it appeared to Lamprecht to be something not particularly appealing.

But what was it doing there? Why had it been removed? At the time of renovation, crews demolished the walls. It had to be done. That section of wall was a large rectangle of reflective glass. It was not orange. In her research, Lamprecht failed to find any information about when that swath of orange was covered up by the mirrored glass. No one seemed to know anything about it. But there it was. Not a great photo, but proof that the orange wall was there, and Lamprecht knew instinctively it was what Neutra intended.

Richard Neutra was famously a midcentury modernist and utilized his own inspiration for design of "biorealism," which meant that many experts did not connect Neutra to bright colors. Instead, what was expected in a Neutra design was more subdued like the tones and hues used everywhere else in the arboretum.

"Browns and whites, and silvers and creams," said Lamprecht. "In other words, a repertoire of a spectrum of neutral colors." But Neutra used to dramatic effect orange, persimmon, and teal.

In Lamprecht's view, to dismiss the use of a bright-color panel in that very intentional location would be to dismiss the original intention of a master architect at work. She asked restoration designers and planners to imagine Dr. Schuller in his robe moving deftly back and forth between the congregants inside and the congregants outside in their cars. All the while, that bright orange panel, visible from the parking lot, silhouetted Schuller's sturdy figure.

Lamprecht's essay on the subject, published online later that year, described how Neutra employed color to make the silhouette pop.

"To this most theatrical event," wrote Lamprecht, "the robed pastor addressing a sea of cars, the architect's goal was to attract one's eye immediately to Schuller. How to do it? Neutra employed Gestalt aesthetics, especially 'figure vs. ground,' a form against a backdrop.

This was a technique he had learned decades earlier and refined at the Bauhaus in 1930, when Neutra taught there in 1930."[4]

There was no doubt, the orange panel had purpose. "An instant visual magnet," said Lamprecht.

There was also little doubt that the original color was undesirable at the very least, and incompatible with Catholic aesthetics and symbolism at worst. Once Lamprecht and the restoration team concluded that the color panel should be restored, the real work began. The strict historical restoration guidelines they had been following required that the color be in the spirit of the original, but it did not require an exact match. The mantra was "compatible but differentiated." To find that color, Lamprecht had to further channel Neutra, but also leaned on something that transcended the cognitive and tapped into the spiritual. When the restoration team tasked Lamprecht with finding the right shade of orange, it required "a trust as bold as the color itself."

"Compatible, both with history," she said, and with "the type of dynamic spirit that the diocese was promoting."

The mandate was logical, intentional, and complex. The color must meet the Secretary of the Interior's Standards for Rehabilitation, capture and express Neutra's "convictions about the role of vision and cognition, emotion and the senses," and finally, be "an orange that could meet the liturgical needs, rituals, vestments, and ornaments of the Catholic Church."[5]

Lamprecht dove into Richard Nuetra's archives, but there was not even a hint about the original color specifications. There were additional photographs that captured the colored section of wall, but few revealed helpful detail. One picture, however, provided enough of a sample, in the proper light, to help an expert paint analyst find a sample swatch that closely matched. From there, the search for a new color was another painstaking process, researching and looking at colors by different manufacturers. Lamprecht had to discern nearly imperceptible subtle differences over many hours of research. The first alternative orange lacked energy, a muted orange that reminded Lamprecht of highway safety vests.

"It had little to say about the radical offer of redemption, which was, after all, the point of all this effort," wrote Lamprecht in the 2013 essay. So, she kept on looking.

"What orange could be a welcome participant throughout the liturgical calendar, which relies on colors to notate significant events, holy days, or periods for the Church: white, purity; red, blood; black, mourning; violet, penance; and the warm green of 'Ordinary Time'— that is, most of the Church year?"

What she found was "a wonderful color for processionals with those crimson details and robes that Catholic clergy can use sometimes."

It was called "untamed orange," a color created by Dunn Edwards. Lamprecht described it as a fiery orange, a color that can "lift the spirits on a gray and rainy Sunday morning in February or match the color of a rising or setting sun."

When painted, the orange stood out and was worth the many hours of work. For Lamprecht it was the result of a job well done, but her labor of love in campus restoration was the placement of boulders around the arboretum and campus. Some of them were incredibly important, having been shipped from the Holy Land by Reverend Schuller. The large stones were relocated to a storage area to make room for construction equipment. Lamprecht used historical data, pictures, and finesse to identify the rocks and place them in close approximation to their original locations, while considering the changed landscape designed by Rios Clemente. Research included a handful of images taken by legendary architectural photographer Julius Shulman. But even those focused on structures and unsurprisingly overlooked the boulders. Locating boulders was one of the most unusual requests she had received in her career.

"I was quite intimidated," she said. "So, I had to kind of wing it."

The process took heavy equipment and hours of labor for the workers. One day, when there were many more boulders to place than she would imagine, Lamprecht wore work clothes, not her usual business attire. She knew she would get dirty. She also brought with her several books on Richard Neutra containing pictures of what Neutra did with boulders in landscapes.

It was not just helpful for Lamprecht's eyes and understanding; she used the photos to help the laborers understand what she was looking for in the stones and where they might go. It created a team approach to the task that helped her avoid coming across as a bossy interloper on the construction site. Lamprecht said it embodied the best of historic preservation that was the creation of a collaborative team.

"That felt more Christian to me," she said, "than that dictatorial attitude." And they had fun in the process.

One of the boulders caught the eye of a team crew member. Something in it inspired a reminder of the Virgin Mary. Lamprecht said she agreed to let him do what he was inspired to do. The stone was placed prominently near the arboretum balcony and the "untamed orange" panel.

The interior of the arboretum was fully restored, with only a few minor exceptions. A horizontal rod piece that was there in the drawings perplexed Jim Wirick. The bar that ran the length of one of the walls was part of the original design.

"Jim was pulling his hair out," said Joe Novoa, "trying to come up with a solution to get that back in. Then Rob said, 'No, we can't do it. We've got to get going on this thing.'"[6]

What it was, how it should be replaced, and what exactly should be done were all perplexing questions; finally it was decided it would just be left out. Additionally a row of large chandeliers ran the center of the ceiling in the early pictures, but unlike painting the one wall section, chandeliers seemed extravagant.

"Everybody was budget conscious, because we did have a budget," said Joe Novoa. "Changing the color doesn't impact dollars. But trying to find chandeliers, putting in chandeliers, getting them custom made was a big deal. Big money."

Otherwise, it was transformed into a renewed version of the original. But it also became a Catholic worship space. That would be the final touch, and it would feed the work of Christ Cathedral designers as they worked to redesign the Crystal Cathedral and make it a Catholic worship space.

Close the Path Behind

For months, the sprawling twenty-acre campus at St. Callistus had been in transition. A team from the Diocese of Orange, headed up by Susan Stoneburner, had arrived to help coordinate, arrange space, schedule dates for major moves, and overall make it easier for the parish and school. It was a two-way street, so coordination was closely tied to work being done in concert with Crystal Cathedral Ministries. Both teams described it as seamless. The first and biggest change was the move of the students of St. Callistus School and Crystal Cathedral Academy as they swapped campuses. The Family Life Center, which housed Crystal Cathedral students, was the four-story, 132,000-square-foot building built in 1990. It was move-in-ready, as was the school at St. Callistus, so the quick exchange of space made sense. Change, transition, adjustment—some of it methodical, some of it beholden to the calendar, but all of it infused with mixed emotions as two families shed the past to embrace the future.

"It was months of preparation," said Christ Cathedral vicar and rector Father Christopher Smith.[1] "Not just the physical renovation of buildings, but all of the spiritual preparation and psychological preparation for making this move."

Before anyone moved from St. Callistus, the diocese team held retreats and evenings of prayer and reflection. Parishioners were given many opportunities to join in question-and-answer sessions, all to help provide and smooth transition.

There were many changes for which to be prepared. St. Callistus Parish staff moved out and into temporary space beneath the Crystal Cathedral, the only open space that would accommodate them. St. Callistus priests who had lived at the home at the fifty-two-year-old parish moved to another house, about five minutes away, that was purchased for the purpose. So, when Father Tuyen Van Nguyen, pastor of St. Callistus, woke up that summer morning, it was not in

181

his old familiar surroundings. The home he shared with the other priests was fine, but he had not yet gotten used to the change. He had lived at the other house for ten years, and it still felt like he was away from home. It was Saturday, and the sun was shining. The forecast predicted a hot day, which was typical for Orange County in late June. It was the day for which they had prepared for the better part of a year, the biggest day for St. Callistus since it was founded in 1961. Father Tuyen Van Nguyen had mixed emotions, but he was far too involved in preparing for the closing ceremony at St. Callistus to dwell on his feelings. It was going to be a busy, emotional day—a day to remember, to say goodbye, and to rejoice in fellowship that today is "the day which the Lord has made" (Psalm 118:24).

Song lyrics from the American pop-rock band Semisonic assert, "Every new beginning comes from some other beginning's end."[2] The beginnings that ended for many Christians in Orange County in late spring and early summer that year went back decades. Each ending had its own bud-to-blossom story that yielded a bounty before the fall came and the season had passed. The moments of transition as one beginning's end became the commencement of something new for these Christian families moving in different directions were both sad and inspiring. After all, to leave the comfort and security of a childhood home, with all the memories, hopes, and dreams of the past, inevitably resulted in an emptiness, not easily filled. But filled it was as new hopes and dreams began to bud beneath the Orange County sun.

The cascade of endings started with Sheila Schuller Coleman as she moved the Hope Center of Christ ministry, established a year earlier in a rented movie theater, to a new site. She reportedly took with her about a hundred Crystal Cathedral Ministries' congregants. As the eldest Schuller daughter, she was with Robert and Arvella Schuller in that highway roadside diner where her father began drafting a list of possible places to hold services—the list that led him to the drive-in. Schuller Coleman's life growing up was spent participating in the family business, which was the preaching and ministering to the unchurched of Orange County and eventually the world. While the young ministry hosted by the preacher on top of a drive-in snack bar grew, Schuller Coleman grew up in a humble house that acted as church offices, a place for Bible studies, and choir practice—just to name a few of the activities that were part of her daily reality. Eventually, that humble beginning became a privileged, secure life with a ready-made career. Not only was she cutting ties with the cathedral campus that she saw built by her father from the ground up, but she was also permanently leaving the ministry she had temporarily led. Her husband, Jim Coleman, also worked for Crystal Cathedral Ministries as director of creative services. That had also ended a year earlier. Still, as "hope" in the new ministry's name suggested, there was reason to be optimistic.

"All the lessons that my dad taught me have been worth their weight in gold," Schuller Coleman told the *Orange County Register*. "Dad said: 'When things are tough, go out and help other people.' We are blessed. We have our faith. We have our health. We have our family."[3]

The new ministry reportedly planned to take over a kitchen ministry that provided groceries for forty families weekly.

Around the same time, Schuller Coleman's nephew Robert V. "Bobby" Schuller, son of Robert A. Schuller, and grandson of the founder, had his own ministry called Tree of Life Community Church in Garden Grove, born just after the Crystal Cathedral opened its doors; Bobby Schuller was raised around the ministry and was a youth pastor to bring younger congregants. That was over the few years his father was pastor. He became the accidental heir apparent when his cathedral sermons and appearances on the *Hour of Power* began to gain interest. Crystal Cathedral Ministries changed the name to Shepherd's Grove in preparation for the congregation's move at the end of June. While he would eventually take over as senior pastor and merge Tree of Life with Shepherd's Grove, he was strictly a volunteer called to lead the final sermon at the Crystal Cathedral.

Bobby Schuller had proven himself a capable leader and an inspiring minister for the program and the ministry. That did not mean vacating the campus and the glass cathedral was easy and without its costs, financially and emotionally. For Bobby, the memories ran deep and included growing up around the campus and getting married in the Crystal Cathedral in 2003.

Crystal Cathedral Ministries had worked for much of the past year to prepare for the move, and on June 29 final preparations were underway for the last *Hour of Power* and last Sunday service at the Crystal Cathedral. Pastor Bobby Schuller found himself torn between the dread of closing what his grandfather built and the desire to be certain his final sermon at the Crystal Cathedral would buoy the spirits of the congregants whose lives and fortunes had supported the ministry. In many cases, over several decades. But it was also about the *Hour of Power*'s worldwide audience. They were the financial divers behind what became the Crystal Cathedral campus. He faced a difficult challenge to lift them up on a trying and sad day.

"I had people constantly telling me that if we moved out of the Crystal Cathedral, we wouldn't have a shot," Bobby Schuller said in a later interview. "So, I had that weighing on me as well."[4]

Just up the street, at St. Callistus, the congregation had gathered to say farewell to their home.

Anyone passing the St. Callistus campus that afternoon would have noticed the crowds, parking lot full of cars, and buses, correctly assuming something big was happening. There were easily six to seven hundred people in attendance, but some estimates put it at around a thousand. Anyone wondering about the diversity of the ten-thousand-strong parish did not have to walk around and listen for accents or languages spoken. Diversity exploded in colors and international festive attire. Mixed among those with traditional, conservative, and mostly California casual church attire was clothing from around the world.

Children in bright yellow Vietnamese ethnic clothing and hats carried long red ribbons in preparation of ceremonial dance performances. Women with shared origins or ancestry wore equally colorful *ao dai* (pronounced "ow-zye"), sometimes adorned with elaborate embroidery. In contrast to the slender styles of Vietnam were the traditional Mexican dresses with flourishes of embroidered flowers and wide abundant full skirts that went all the way to the ground. Some men wore traditional Mexican white clothing and wide-brimmed hats. Spanish influence and North American Native cultures infused.

Father Nguyen, a Vietnamese-refugee-turned-American priest, embraced the multicultural parish in what he called his rookie assignment. He said he entered the job just wanting it to go well as most new priests do. He did not know he would one day be closing its doors. The pastor of St. Callistus for the past ten years was also closing the doors on that "rookie assignment."[5] It was his last day as pastor, and by the end of the day the pastor of the transplanted parish would be Bishop Kevin Vann. The parish priest of the cathedral of a diocese was the bishop. So, the event of the day was also a passing of the baton. It was Bishop Vann who would lead the congregation down the street and perform Mass.

They gathered to pray and say farewell to St. Callistus. Bishop Vann, Father Christopher Smith from the diocese, and St. Callistus priests Father Joseph Thuong Tran and Juan Navarro joined Father Nguyen as they led attendees around the campus for the ceremonial closing. They were dressed in full Sunday Mass vestments. Bishop Vann wore the tall miter (hat) of the bishop of Orange and carried the crosier, which is the traditional shepherd's staff for the bishop.

Father Smith had a long-standing personal relationship with the parish at St. Callistus. He had for years been a supply priest who helped with Spanish and English Masses. He expected it to be an emotional day but was still surprised at just how emotional it was for so many in attendance.

"People were weeping," said Smith. "Of course, looking back, of course it was, because that community was just asked to move. The church they had been worshipping in had only been built twelve years before, so there were a lot of fresh memories of building that church. We're all tied to our homes that we love." Bishop Tod Brown had presided over the dedication of that new church in 2000.

The clergy, accompanied by nuns from Lovers of the Holy Cross, led attendees around the campus in a carefully choreographed route to stop and pause at each door. In English, Spanish, and Vietnamese there were blessings, along with puffs of incense and anointings with chrism. Bishop Vann closed each door on the way to the church sanctuary and eventually to the gate of the St. Callistus property. It would be the final closure.

"To close the path behind," said Father Nguyen, in a later interview. "To move forward to across the bridge."

The crossing was symbolic of God's chosen people going to the Promised Land. It was a theme that would continue throughout the day.

"To assure the people that the future would be better and bigger and there will be ample opportunity," he said. "There's the past and there's the future. There's the present and the future and where's the Church? Where the people are, we are the Church." He said he told attendees, "We have to take pride in who we are and who we've become under the leadership of the bishop."

They processed from the chapel, to the parish office, each school classroom, and the rectory. Emotions accompanied the solemn affair and there were tears. Father Tuyen Nguyen had only been at St. Callistus for a decade, while some in attendance were there for decades and longer or represented generations that knew no other parish home. It was understandable to see many tears, and there were many.

The longest single stop was in the shining church sanctuary with its white-tiled walls and angular vaulted ceiling. The solemn silence and the smell from the wood of the purple-cushioned pews remained familiar. It could have been any Sunday. The multicolored light refracted from the long stained glass window that ran down the center overhead and filled the room with light. The crucifix faced the congregation as they filed in to sit in the sanctuary. The bishop and priests took seats next to the familiar altar and candles. As always, the altar was draped with a white cloth and the candles flickered brightly. But there was the feel of a house, once a childhood home, moments before the moving trucks arrived.

Father Nguyen could feel the rise and ease of emotion, ebbing and flowing, throughout the closing ceremony. But he was also participating in and orchestrating a planned event. Staying on time, and on plan, meant he did not dwell for much time on any certain emotional response—that is, until he stood for what he knew was the last time at the place of the altar.

"I could not, oh, I almost cried," said Father Nguyen. "We like that church very much."

It was a sanctuary built by parishioners and dedicated in the year 2000, just three years before Father Nguyen arrived. The story of St. Callistus was of humble beginnings, from starting out celebrating Mass in a former bowling alley, to a six-hundred-seat church, to a modern sanctuary with twelve hundred seats. It was a home they had built together over many decades. There was a kinship, no doubt, on an emotional and spiritual level, between St. Callistus parishioners and Crystal Cathedral congregants that weekend that had to be felt to be fully understood.

Father Nguyen circled the altar. As he did, he swung a thurible that extended from a chain. Its contents, burning incense, distributed a cloud of smoke that wafted up toward the ceiling, reminiscent of the day the altar was dedicated. Like the altar, other important sites received special attention. The confessionals had been the site of countless reconciliations. The baptismal had seen the christening of babies nearly weekly since the church opened. Some of those babies, now adults, had their own kids there to say goodbye. Each held special meaning for the priests and the laity alike and were blessed. When the church cleared, there were roses left on the altar as farewells and humble offerings.

Still holding the thurible, dangling from its chain, Father Nguyen faced the altar with the crucified Christ in front, above him on the wall. He leaned forward and kissed the altar where he had performed Mass on thirty-six hundred Sundays, and countless weekdays.

Every new beginning comes from some other beginning's end.

They filed outside and began the procession to their new home across the freeway. Only a handful actually walked. Logistically, a parade-sized crowd walking the entire distance was not practical. Lewis Street was on the border of two cities, and it would have required permits and police coordination that would have been difficult at best. Most climbed into cars and buses. Parishioners with classic cars lead the rolling procession carrying Bishop Vann, Father Christopher Smith, and Father Nguyen. Yellow ribbons streamed from the motor vehicles, a signal they were part of the St. Callistus procession. As they drove past, they saw the two columns that processed on foot as one colorful flock along the sidewalk on Lewis Street.

About a mile, at an average pace, it was a twenty-minute walk in the now-blazing afternoon sun. It was not a straight road either and went through a mix of residential housing on the left and a large outlet mall on the right. The first Catholic Mass to be held on the former Crystal Cathedral campus was set for 4 p.m. and was anticipated to be standing-room only with at least three thousand people. Row after row of white folding chairs faced the temporary outdoor altar. Even if the arboretum had been ready, it lacked the capacity for such a crowd. The slow procession and getting everyone parked and moved to their seats gave diocese staff time to make final arrangements for Mass. There were important last additions.

As throngs of worshippers arrived, they were welcomed by mariachi music and the sight of men transporting and placing the wood altar from St. Callistus, the one Father Nguyen had kissed not long before, at the front. It would be the altar for the Mass and eventually moved into the arboretum to be its permanent altar. Next, the candles from St. Callistus were placed on the right and left of the altar just as they had been earlier that day. Likewise, those candles would become permanent fixtures next to the altar inside the arboretum. It was part of Bishop Vann's promise to the parishioners, that while St. Callistus was gone it was not going to be forgotten.

There were other promises. The dedication plaque for the new church at St. Callistus, just thirteen years old, was to be preserved for later display. Vann promised a new chapel on the campus to be named St. Callistus Chapel and that the plaque would be preserved there to remember the old parish. St. Callistus School would be renamed Christ Cathedral Academy, and Pastor Father Nguyen would take the job as vice rector of Christ Cathedral. He would work with rector Christopher Smith.

The Mass was standing-room only, but a few seats toward the front were left empty, the occupants driven out by the direct sunlight. Thoughtfully, and a show of intense planning, the outdoor altar was placed under the awning of the circular Welcoming Center building so that the shadows of the arboretum and the Tower of Hope mercifully protected many worshippers from the relentless sun to the west. Some of those still unprotected used umbrellas or large brimmed hats to ease the heat. The choir sang "The Ode to Joy."

The Gospel was Luke 9:51–62, about the Samaritan village that refused to receive Jesus and the eager followers of Christ who put conditions on that commitment. In a surprise for Father Christopher Smith, Bishop Vann asked him to preach the homily with him in tandem, trading off as it progressed. While Vietnamese was spoken off and on during Mass, the homily was in English and Spanish. The collaboration between the two clergymen would develop as an occurrence for special events.

"Many of the parishioners of Saint Callistus," said Father Smith, "know that, for these past several months, we've been talking about our pathway to transformation. And today we've literally taken huge steps on that pathway to transformation of Saint Callistus

Parish eventually becoming Christ Cathedral Parish.... Today, as we remembered, as we gave thanks and as we prayed in the buildings and on the grounds of Saint Callistus parish, we knew that something new was about to happen."[6]

"As disciples of Jesus," continued Father Smith, "in one way or another we are always on the road, we are always on the way, by the Lord's grace, to becoming new and better people. To building a new and better Church, to becoming a new and better world."

Bishop Vann called to mind some of the great "journeys that have been made throughout the history of salvation so that something new could happen."[7] Some of the examples he gave were Abraham and his family traveling to their new home, Moses and his people moving from slavery to the Promised Land, and Joseph and Mary traveling to where Jesus was born. "In today's Gospel," said Bishop Vann, "we are told of the journey of James and John on their way with Jesus to Jerusalem. They along with others were tempted to turn back, but were told by Jesus in clear terms that it is precisely in staying on the journey and not looking back that the kingdom of God will be found."[8]

"The journey down Lewis Street," said Father Smith, "proclaims that we as a community—that was as a Church—are being called to do something new and great and to be something new and great in the name of Jesus Christ."[9]

"You didn't ask for this," said Father Smith. "You didn't ask for this, and some didn't even want it. In fact, what we are doing here today, no matter where we have been in our emotions and in our thoughts, we know in fact that God is calling us to do something wonderful with our community."[10]

Bishop Vann pointed out that on one recent evening he was traveling to St. Callistus and saw two illuminated crosses. One was atop the Tower of Hope and the other atop St. Callistus, as if one becoming the other. "Just like the lit cross of St. Callistus," he said, "and just like the cross here, you will be an example to the world, what it means to always grow new. What it means to always show the light of Christ."[11] For Vann and Father Smith it was a day of solemnity and sadness; however, they also remember that after the procession from St. Callistus, over the highway, "the mariachis who were present at the first Mass on campus were greeting everyone with joy and welcome, as only the music of mariachis can! Another sign of God's providence!" Vann later wrote.

During the afternoon and Mass, the Crystal Cathedral doors remained open. For some it was to escape the sun; for others it was an irresistible curiosity. Like tourists, visitors snapped pictures, pointed, and marveled at the immense space and the 190-foot ceiling at its peak. Its stunning transparency, and the Hazel Wright Organ that was typically awe-inspiring, did not disappoint. Sitting nearby was Tom Leonard, the Crystal Cathedral organist, who had been planning his role in what was coming in less than twenty-four hours. Sunday, the organ would sing out one final time for the *Hour of Power* when the grandson of the founder led the final service in the Crystal Cathedral.

The next morning, the final service was taped for the *Hour of Power* TV program but would not air for months.

"I would say it was a very special experience, but it was just incredibly sad," said Pastor Bobby Schuller in a later interview.

The event drew about two thousand to the glass cathedral, easily making it the most attended service in recent memory. Although, since taking the job as full-time pastor and *Hour of Power* host, Schuller reported a rise in attendance and donations. It was a positive sign for the future, but too late to change anything. Schuller later disclosed that at the end there was no escaping the reality that more than $50 million was overwhelming and a lot of debt.

"It was a heavy day," said Schuller. "I spent that day with my wife and my dad. It was sad to me that my grandpa couldn't be there." The elder Schuller had been suffering the effects of dementia. "I just feel like symbolically it would have been so great to have him there. I know he would have loved to have been there."

"This is the day the Lord had made," Bobby Schuller said in his sermon, "let us rejoice and be glad in it!"[12] Schuller likened the last service in the Crystal Cathedral to a commencement: the end of one thing and the beginning of another. There was no shortage of special guests, including the oldest living charter member of the ministry who had begun attending services in the drive-in in the 1950s.

Robert A. Schuller, onetime pastor, son of the founder, and Bobby's father, spoke to the congregation. He chose to read from Joshua about the death of Moses and the encouraging words from God that He will be with his people wherever they go.

Bobby Schuller's message was titled "Moving Together with Joy."[13]

"God has new memories for us," he told the assembled congregation. "God has a future for us, and those memories are not going to be here! There are new, wonderful, exciting memories to be had for this ministry but they're not going to be here anymore. And that's painful, in a way, but I hope that's encouraging to you. Because now we're not a church that has it all anymore and that's just a good thing."[14]

He told them to smile and be glad because they were a church that was on the move and headed to a better place, as the flock following the shepherd.

"I really trusted and believed," he said in a later interview, "that God was trying to teach our congregation what it meant to be a church that's not so associative with a building but more a church with a mission."

When the emotional final *Hour of Power* and service at the Crystal Cathedral ended and the crowd was headed for the exits, a couple of priests could be seen headed up the steps toward the stage. At the top, Pastor Bobby Schuller greeted them in what was a planned moment, off mic and camera. Christ Cathedral rector Father Christopher Smith and Pastor Schuller had invited clergy of both churches to gather. There were the other Crystal Cathedral pastors, joined by Father Smith, who brought with him Father Nguyen of the now former St. Callistus for mutual prayers and quiet personal blessings.

"Me for Bobby, in their new home down the street," said Smith, "and him for us in our new home here. We gave a blessing to everybody that was gathered there. It was just really, really beautiful."

A Mass of congregants and Crystal Cathedral staff hung around to ask Bobby Schuller for an autograph on the fiftieth-anniversary commemorative coffee-table book that celebrated the founding of the ministry in 1955. *A Place of Beauty, a Joy Forever* was written by Dr. Robert H. Schuller with pictures of the campus and glass cathedral by James Coleman, published in 2005. The ministry had been handing out free copies for congregants to take home. Many wanted more, a personal touch to remember the important occasion. Bobby Schuller was the face of the ministry, and they were excited to get his signature. And while they were at it, why not complete the night's

Christian unity with a signature from Father Smith? It was like they had co-written the book and it was their book signing.

"It was the first time I ever did that!" said Smith with a laugh.

Bobby Schuller and Father Smith may not have written a single word of the elder Schuller's book, but they were authors of a powerful message to Orange County Christians that weekend. Two families bid goodbye to the homes they had known for five decades, crossing paths to begin new stories and weave new tapestries.

Restoring Hope

The intense time constraints for the arboretum's restoration required rapid decision making, sometimes overnight. The circumstances were less than ideal for the diocese leadership because major decisions were usually not made rapidly in any Catholic Church bureaucracy. The miracle here was that a special kind of teamwork permeated the effort, and it was palpable. Church leadership was part of this unusual partnership and process.

"There was a period of about twenty-four months," said Rob Neal, "where the Diocese of Orange was operating at light speed, and I mean *light speed.*"[1]

Renovations were also moving fast and sometimes outpaced collection.

"Money was being spent almost as fast as it was coming in," said Randy Redwitz, who managed accountability of the pledges.[2] "So, we were actually using construction lines of credit to gap that difference over time." Redwitz said U.S. Bank, which supplied the diocese with the original $50 million purchase loan, and Farmers and Merchants Bank made it possible through very favorable interest rates.

St. Callistus, no more. The parishioners who moved to the Christ Cathedral now had a new place to worship. One week after grieving the closure of their old home and celebrating rebirth in a new place, parishioners in the renovated arboretum sanctuary held their first Sunday Masses. Father Christopher Smith and the other priests held services in English, Spanish, and Vietnamese. They were well attended, and there was a sense of enthusiasm and optimism across the campus. Rob Neal could not have been more pleased as attention turned toward completing a complex seismic retrofit of the Tower of Hope while simultaneously finding the right architecture firm for the cathedral.

The Tower of Hope got its name from Schuller's twenty-four-hour suicide prevention call center. It was a first of its kind as a dedicated crisis help line. When the Crystal Cathedral Ministries moved out, it left the operation of the fourth-floor call center to Catholic Charities of Orange County. The tower, topped with a ninety-foot cross, was once the tallest building in the county. While it had thirteen floors, it was fourteen stories tall. The Chapel in the Sky on the top floor was two stories high. Some buildings had been known to skip the thirteenth floor, but to get to the chapel, Schuller embraced thirteen as if thumbing his nose at superstition. The tower was built in 1968 as a design collaboration between Richard Neutra and his son Dion. It was a slender, concrete reinforced building. Tall for a building with a small footprint—meaning fourteen stories was high sitting on a two-thousand-square-foot foundation—made for a complicated restoration and seismic retrofit. It also meant that at thirty-two feet wide by fifty-eight feet long, the usable floor space on each level was unbelievably valuable.

"There were serious suggestions that it was too costly, and it would be better to just demolish the building. While the Diocese recognized the Tower's architectural and cultural significance, it decided that the safety of its large parish population must ultimately take precedence. It was at that time that contingency plans were made to demolish the Tower of Hope and replace it with a modern office building in case a viable seismic retrofit solution could not be devised."[3]

There was logic in that idea. It was a building that, for all intents and purposes, could have collapsed in a major seismic event. Neal convinced the diocese it was worth it to complete the retrofit, to maintain the integrity of the campus and preserve what it had been entrusted.

As they had for the arboretum, Design Architectural firm LPA, headed up by project lead Jim Wirick, had to be both innovative and meticulous about preservation. He supported Neal in the argument that keeping the building was the right thing to do. It would also preserve what Wirick believed was the most moving feature on the whole campus: the Chapel in the Sky.

"Come through those elevator doors," said Wirick, "look through the veil of the 2×4 Douglas fir. You just see light beyond. An intimate space. Those simple pews."[4] With its sky-high ceiling and glass walls with 360-degree views, it did give one the feeling of being in the sky.

The dedicated construction team was led by Kevin Pitzer of MATT Construction. MATT was the builder for Schuller's final campus project, the visitors' center designed by Richard Meier next door, completed in 2003.

Unlike the arboretum, the Tower of Hope's major problems were well established, and the seismic retrofit was necessary to prevent a collapse in an earthquake. There were multiple serious deficiencies identified in the screening phase. While the building had a seismic-force resisting system that was considered abundant for a structure of its size, serious risk existed because of the concrete system that was used.

In a published case study from architecture firm LPA, Bryan Seamer, S.E., and Daniel Wang, S.E., said LPA worked closely with the diocese on the following priorities, beyond the highest priority, which was the safety of the congregation and staff:

- Respect the period of architectural significance and historical context of the tower by not adding structural elements to the first floor, twelfth-floor offices of Reverend Schuller, or the thirteenth-floor Chapel in the Sky.
- Limit new seismic-force resisting elements to the perimeter column lines to maximize usable interior space and allow for future flexibility.
- Avoid the need for adding new foundation elements in order to minimize construction costs.[5]

Neutra historian Barbara Lamprecht continued to assist and advise the various boards and committees and worked directly with LPA to meet those goals. She recalled the retrofit and one of the early discoveries about the movement of the neighboring bell tower as it manifested itself in the six-inch gap between the bell tower and the Tower of Hope.

"The staircase, because of earth tremor, it and the bell tower were knocking together," said Lamprecht.[6] Continued unabated, the knocking together may have caused a catastrophic failure. There were a couple of solutions, both of which required some level of demolition. The Neutra Bell Tower was strictly for aesthetics and had no actual function. It consisted of a five plaster-column and steel-beam structure with fifteen gold plastic bells. The wind also contributed to the contact between the structures. One solution they considered was removing the column, next to the Tower of Hope. Lamprecht said there were hours spent agonizing over this aspect of the project.

"We decided, after much discussion," Lamprecht recalled, "to take a notch out of the bell tower, so it's acknowledging the reality of what's going on, but nobody notices that a little piece is gone."

The notches saved the five elements of the bell tower campanile. Preserving the original look was a major part of the restoration, and the notches were a necessary compromise. The seismic retrofit of the tower, if done the way most buildings were reinforced, would be far more noticeable.

Diagonal or cross bracing at the ground floor, for example, would be too noticeable. The huge steel braces would be easily seen from the outside and the inside of the tower lobby. "That would compromise what we in historic restoration call a character-defining feature," said Lamprecht. "And a character-defining feature, in Neutra's work, is an uninterrupted view out to the savanna, if you will, the grassy features, the reflecting pools." In essence, the building was designed to embrace the ancestral relationship of primitive man and the natural surroundings of the African savanna. "So, visually for Neutra, it was an imperative to maintain the relationship between nature and the human being in the building."

Where Lamprecht's expertise and depth of knowledge proved most valuable was in divining what Neutra was thinking, what his ideals were, and how they were manifest in the building. As a result of this and other factors that were considered, LPA's innovative solution preserved the building's character.

"This lobby was awesome," said project lead Jim Wirick of LPA. "We brought in our guy Bryon Seamer, who said, 'This building doesn't have everything we need but it has something. Let's use what it is giving us.'"

Saving a defining feature and supporting the building ended up saving $2 million. It was the kind of value that engineering renovation head Rob Neal cherished. It was not an easy task to convince some critics that renovation of the tower was worth the expense. But he was persuasive, and when he could point to a savings of a couple million dollars it certainly helped.

LPA's design engineer Bryan Seamer had come across some seismic building solutions that had recently been used in Asia. They adapted the technology to the requirements of the Tower of Hope. The engineering team used a performance-based strategy with the help of Saunders Commercial Seismic. By placing custom-designed shock absorbers, fluid viscous dampers, on floors four through thirteen, the views from the lobby were preserved, as were the panoramic views from the Chapel in the Sky on the thirteenth floor.

"They were magicians," said Jim Wirick. "This was really hard work."

The viscous dampers had to be anchored to plates that were two inches by twelve inches by sixteen feet. The plates had to be anchored to the concrete floor, which required precision drilling using x-ray equipment to avoid the rebar in the concrete. Then the plates had to be bolted together.

"And you're inches away from glass," said Wirick, "and they never broke any glass."

Once installed, the only way to see the dampers, or shock absorbers, was to take a ride up one of the glass-backed elevators and watch them pass by. The retrofit included what Wirick described as a kind of rebar wallpaper. One of Wirick's tasks that was not structural was the installation of the television studio on the fourth floor, and thanks to the rebar and the dampers, usable floor space was maximized. The only floor that remained untouched and off limits was the twelfth floor, Schuller's office and study.

Rob Neal surveyed progress on the Tower of Hope while communicating with Bob Theirgarten about progress on finding an architect for the cathedral. There was a major decision to be made.

Brother Woeger, the liturgical design consultant, was not an architect, and the future Christ Cathedral needed one who could work with the design committee. So, a new committee had been formed almost immediately after the search for a liturgical consultant had ended. It was many of the same people who chose Woeger, and it was going to be yet another difficult search for the right people. Bob Theirgartner used the same liturgical consultant RFP format to send the same requests out to about twenty architects. Immediately a few declined, turned off by a church with modern architecture.

"One guy said we should make the Crystal Cathedral a performing-arts venue and build a gothic church in the parking lot next door," said Theirgartner. "Ridiculous."[7]

The Request for Proposals asked for electronic submissions to start. The majority responded with enthusiasm. Through a process of review and discussion, the field was reduced to about five, then three. Over a day or two the three candidates made their final presentations, not just in front of the architectural selection committee, but in front of a much larger group of various committees and managers overseeing the design and restoration of the cathedral. It was the first chance to see what these candidates might do with the design, including some 3-D modeling.

"At that point in time, they had spoken to us," said Bob Theirgartner. "They had toured the property. They toured the property and talked to Brother [Woeger]."

After the presentations it had come down to just two: Johnson Fain and Rios Clementi Hale Studios. But which one became an agonizing decision as difficult as all the other steps rolled into one.

Founder and managing partner at Johnson Fain, Scott Johnson, spent a couple of weeks in the late 1970s doing some glass wall drawings for famed architect Philip Johnson in his New York office. They were not related in anyway. Scott Johnson's task was to come up with some concepts with which Philip Johnson could work. The project was the Crystal Cathedral in California.

"I probably have insights to the building that others wouldn't necessarily have because I worked in the office when it was being designed and I knew what the elements were," said Scott Johnson.[8] "I was very close to Philip. We talked a lot about it. I knew what the projects in the office were at that point. I knew what ideas mattered to Philip." But the selection committee saw that as an interesting coincidence rather than a tie breaker.

Mark Rios of Rios Clementi had a stellar reputation with a master's of architecture and master's in landscape architecture from the Harvard University Graduate School of Design, the same school attended by Scott Johnson. Rios Clementi had also worked on cathedral landscaping. It had completed work at Our Lady of the Angels in Los Angeles and Christ the Light in Oakland, California.

"Johnson Fain's presentation was best," in Theirgartner's opinion, "and Rios Clementi's spirit was best."

"They were both great," said Rob Neal, who chaired the selection committee. "We just didn't know what to do. One was stronger on the outside, and one was stronger on the inside."

This is where the collective group, the committee, did some sleuthing of their own to do fact finding and see samples of work around the Southern California region. Theirgartner rented a large SUV. The committee had six or so members, which included Theirgartner, Father Christopher Smith, Rob Neal, Kory Kramer, Brother William Woeger, and Monsignor Art Holquin. Theirgartner had already visited some of the candidates' properties. But this trip allowed them to make the visits together and talk along the way—a rolling meeting, to solve a perplexing question: Johnson Fain or Rios Clementi Hale Studios?

In the morning, the group met with Johnson Fain at two of its projects, an apartment complex near Staples Center and an office building. Then they went to the offices of Johnson Fain for a meeting. In the afternoon it was the same thing for two projects with Rios Clementi, the renovation of the Mark Taper Forum and LA's Grand Park, which it had designed, followed by another meeting.

The preference between the two came down to fractions in a variety of categories, and in each one a different firm was slightly ahead. They were more informed than ever about the two finalists and more certain of their qualifications, but somehow, no closer to deciding which one should design Christ Cathedral. After hours of contemplation, phone calls, and talks there was a decision. The diocese would hire both firms: Johnson Fain for the cathedral and Rios Clemente for landscape design.

The architect announcement from Bishop Kevin Vann, who had been at the helm of the whole process since taking over ten months earlier, came at the Eighth Annual Orange County Catholic Prayer Breakfast. The event included a blessing of Scott Johnson and Mark Rios by Bishop Vann inside the famous glass sanctuary. The breakfast was both outside in the plaza and inside the Meier visitors' center.

"These two firms," said Vann in his formal comments, "see this important work as more than a renovation project, but as a reflection of God and his people on earth."[9]

At the same event, the update on the Christ Forever Capital Campaign was positive. A year after launch, Cindy Bobruk, executive director of the Orange Catholic Foundation, told attendees at the breakfast that the campaign had raised $60 million of its $100 million goal. The campaign was successful, in large part, because it was an opportunity for members of the diocese "to be part of the living history of our diocese—to be able to watch this transformation take place, and actually invest in the transformation," as Bobruk told Catholic News Agency at the time.[10]

What appealed to the design architect selection committee was the professional and intricate concepts and modeling Johnson Fain brought to its presentation and the exemplary exterior design record of Rios Clementi and his vision for Christ Cathedral. The firms had collaborated before and they agreed to the challenge. Prayer breakfast attendees were able to visit the completed arboretum and see progress on the Tower of Hope.

The exterior around the tower was already getting a facelift. LPA restored the water feature, just outside the lobby. The pool was designed to reflect the building in the afternoon and the lights at night. It was a shallow and wide pool with fountains and a statue of Jesus walking on the water. LPA's integrated architecture and interior design team was led by Jim Wirick and Maria Louie. The interior, now fixed with seismic retrofitting that preserved the exterior look of the building, and interior floorspace, became a complex matter of a stacking plan—something Father Christopher Smith had never heard of before the restoration of the Tower of Hope.

"That's the architectural term for it," said Smith.[11] "We had to come up with the stacking plan when we were redesigning the spaces in the Tower of Hope. I learned a lot of new terms from Rob Neal in this process. The first floor remained the lobby. The second floor had a couple of small conference rooms but was mostly home to Schuller's New Hope Crisis line. When Crystal Cathedral Ministries asked us to take it over because they couldn't finance it, we did. It's a program of Catholic Charities." There were conference rooms on the third and fourth floors. The fifth, sixth, and seventh floors were the parish offices, which became available in 2014. When St. Callistus closed, the parish moved to the less-than-ideal space in the undercroft of the cathedral. So, the move to the Tower of Hope represented a second big move.

The eighth floor was more work completed by Jim Wirick, and LPA as the architect designed a television studio and radio station. The diocese would use the radio station, and the TV studio became home to EWTN's West Coast Studio. EWTN coming to the Tower of Hope was largely the work of diocese legal advisor and prolific fundraiser Tim Busch and the host of *Father Robert Spitzer's Universe*, Father Spitzer. It was an advantageous relationship that gave the building a tenant and further raised the profile of the cathedral campus.

The ninth floor became Dynamic Catholic and the Magis Institute, where Father Spitzer had an office. Some of the space had become available for temporary rental use of various organizations. The team office for the diocese's facilities and events were placed on the tenth floor. The eleventh floor became the parish vicar's office for Father Smith and other staff, including Sister Katherine "Kit" Gray, who was in charge of Mission Integration and Ongoing Formation at Christ Cathedral.

The twelfth floor, long home to the office, study, and conference room of Dr. Robert H. Schuller, would remain as it was, until his passing. The stacking plan had it one day converted to the music ministry. And finally, the thirteenth floor, at two stories high, was the slightly reconfigured and fully renovated Chapel in the Sky.

Phase One

The Tower of Hope, as an office building, did not occupy much of liturgical design consultant Brother Woeger's time, although he discussed various aspects of both the tower and the arboretum with Rob Neal and with the various groups or subcommittees if a question came up. While cement poured, welders bonded supports, and crews labored on the arboretum and the tower, Woeger worked diligently laying the foundations of what would become Christ Cathedral, although he was doing much of it alone, or with Monsignor Art Holquin. Woeger would become central to the Sacred Art and Design Committee with a focus on the cathedral's transformation from a Protestant house of worship to a Catholic Cathedral. When the first design teams assembled, they already knew what Woeger was thinking because they had the information from Woeger's briefing with the selection committee.

Back in late 2012, before Rob Neal found himself in a sudden rush to complete the arboretum, the liturgical design consultant selection committee he chaired held in-person interviews and presentations of the three finalists. The eventual selection, Brother Woeger, gave a professionally researched and detailed presentation and impressed with his personality and understanding of the project. It all had to be there. It was liturgically focused and would become the building blocks of the design phase of the Crystal Cathedral. Woeger defined a list of principals important to achieving that goal as it related to a cathedral, in part, that "our participation in the sacred liturgy is a participation in what God is doing, namely that our worship has as it source, the Blessed Trinity, not simply human initiative and creativity. Our Eucharistic remembrance is most fruitful when experienced as a participation in the work of Father, Son and Spirit, and understood as a past act made present which affects the future. Our worship, by its very nature, has a sacrificial aspect, and so we the Church is what is offered joined with the once for all offering of

Christ for the sake of the world. Our worship is efficacious to the extent that it empowers."[1] In that spirit, Woeger asked a series of questions aimed at establishing the fundamental liturgical considerations of the existing Crystal Cathedral compared to its potential as a Catholic worship space. Among those questions were the following:

- Does this structure inspire Catholic imagination?
- Does this structure gather the worshipping community as a Body rather than as individuals?
- Does this structure create an environment of awe and wonder—a sense of holy ground?
- Does this structure support the various liturgical functions (ministries)?
- Does the structure support the sung Mass?
- Does the structure support the spoken Word?
- Does the structure provide a sense of place for the various actions: initiating, reconciling, waking the dead, confirming in the Spirit, ordaining for diaconal and priestly ministry, witnessing of vows in religion and in marriage, and most importantly, doing what Christ said we can and should do, take, bless, break, eat, and remember?
- Does the structure tell of those who have gone before upon whose shoulders we stand and with whom we are in communion? In short, will it tell the Story and support the devotional life of the people?

Woeger explained that there were merits to the Crystal Cathedral, including the price for what was a thirty-four-acre campus of five buildings. It was a sizeable space, so it offered appropriate seating capacity. He recognized the building's design with a "20th–21st century vocabulary and material," and called it "bold." But there were challenges. Woeger pointed out that the lighting and speakers with the jumbotron created an intrusion of technology. The massive organ dominating a focal point was a further intrusion. The building shaped like a four-point star was a "symmetrical plan on an asymmetric footprint," and there was no control of the natural light. One of the complaints among Catholics was that the cathedral's glass structure was not at all Catholic. But Woeger dispelled that idea by providing examples such as St. Patrick's Church in Oklahoma City, which was a five-hundred-seat, glass-enclosed sanctuary built in the 1960s.

These were difficult hurdles but not insurmountable, even if each affected in some way something else. The seating arrangement, which was theater seating at present, would have to change because of the placement of the altar, which was another question to be answered: then what does that mean for the placement of the ambo? And so on.

One approach to seating was a circle with aisleways forming a cross with the altar in the middle. Woeger gave examples of how that design had been used before for Catholic churches. There were merits to that design, and he gave two examples that placed the altar in the middle. Additional options moved the altar to the area near the rise beneath the pipe organ. For each, Woeger offered a slide showing what that seating might look like and the sight lines for worshippers in the pews.

Woeger finished his presentation by asking some questions of his own, about what ideas others had to tackle, about various concerns, including the important Bishop's Doors, which would require a clever and innovative solution. It would be one of many. Woeger titled the presentation *A New Vision for the Crystal Cathedral.* Since then that "New Vision" had been percolating in the minds of many. The addition of the design architects Scott Johnson of Johnson Fain and Mark Rios of Clementi Hale Studios put the designers in full motion. The goal was to get the design done and reveal it publicly by September 2014 and complete renovation within a year.

"We learned a lot by redoing the arboretum," said Monsignor Michael Heher. "We learned a lot about different elements that need to be there, just to be able to have Mass there. I think it seasoned us to make better decisions when we went for the cathedral."[2]

"The conditions that made it successful to Reverend Schuller's ministry were entirely different than what one would think of if you imagined a Catholic cathedral," said Scott Johnson.[3] "As an architect, as a young man, you go to Europe and you see all these magnificent cathedrals which are carved out of stone. Maybe they have a rose window. Maybe they have tales of the Scriptures. But they're solids and they are dark and they are musty. Then you walk into a building and it's all glass, and the sun is beaming through."

"There's a job to do," he said, "to reconnect it with kind of the Catholic mentality and the lineage of great cathedrals."

But it would not be dark and musty, and it would not have stained glass. What then might it look like, and how to get to the design that says to the diocese and Bishop Vann, this is it? It came to weaving a new tapestry, beginning work with a goal in mind but no idea what it would look like when it was done.

The Richard Meier Building, also known as the visitors' center or cultural center, was where these questions got answered. The third floor of the campus's white five-story oval building had the space to handle the expansive design team. When finally assembled, the design architects Johnson Fain and Rios Clemente, with the diocese architecture committee, and all the other related groups from the diocese, numbered about forty. Depending on the day or the gathering, it could be more or fewer. But when they gathered it was a unique, dynamic, creative experience even for the most seasoned professional on hand.

They would gather for the day's work, and if the agenda began with lighting, they would talk about lighting and look at a dozen or more lighting schemes pinned to the walls. Lighting vendors, who were experts, would answer a slew of questions and offer advice. They worked directly with the architects. Depending on how long that lasted, there might be a lunch break. When they returned there was another subject to cover, another set of sketches, models, or presentations. It might be for the overall site, which was the responsibility of Mark Rios of Rios Clementi Hale Studios. Unlike lighting, which was narrow in focus, when the team from Rios Clementi had a turn it could last for hours because there were so many issues to cover. There were the Memorial Gardens, statuary in the Legacy Gardens, signage, parking, flow, and where the stones go, just to name a few. There was no question about the importance of the site work. It impacted every other design aspect.

It was Rios Clementi's design work that fed the early revelation that the altar inside the cathedral was the most sacred area of the entire campus. This may seem obvious, but it was a matter of looking at the entire site as one in relationship to this sacred spot. As the designers moved out from the altar, areas became less and less sacred. The church remains intensely sacred, and just outside the doors as an extension, because of the church's long history of beginning worship outside and processing in—but then beyond the doors to a lesser degree and so forth to the plaza and too the rest of the campus, which becomes mostly ordinary and not sacred at all. A colorized visualization of these areas was called a heatmap, which created a fundamental understanding that helped design the whole layout.

One of the early questions was, how do the designers tie all of these different structures together? But Rios Clementi's heatmap challenged the question.

"Don't try to tie the buildings in," recalled Father Christopher Smith, but "make the cathedral the center of the campus by building a plaza around the cathedral. Nobody had thought of that before and it was like 'oh wow, now that's an idea.'"[4]

As their day continued, and they had moved on to something else, there could be a presentation from Scott Johnson of Johnson Fain on the cathedral design. The Johnson Fain team could easily number as many as seven all by itself. There could be small models carved of wood, more sketches pinned to walls, concept renderings, and color or material swatches. Often it was a well-curated presentation, by Scott Johnson himself, or another key designer, incorporating all of the examples.

"They would move from one to one," said Rob Neal. "We'd sometimes be seated and want to leap up and run over and touch and feel. We'd all have to sit down and try to compose ourselves again. It was very didactic. It was very interactive."[5]

Neal described it as electric with the design architects feeding off the architecture committee and the architecture committee feeding off the design architects. But as anyone would tell you, the excitement was about the creative process and the passion for building a cathedral. Because designs were never on target at the beginning.

"I would sometimes take Scott Johnson aside and say, 'This isn't it,'" said Neal. "I'll know it when I see it." Neal was not the final authority—none of them were—so input was the name of the game. Scott Johnson said he felt like he had all the support he needed to make bold choices.

"You have two approaches in life," said Johnson. "You can either take a building like that, or some building, and make it look like the thing people expect. Or you can make it so different that they have to redefine what it means to be a Catholic building. And that's a very risky thing to do. That's a risky thing to do, but they were willing to do that. I obviously admire them and thank them for that."

And there were no tasks to be taken lightly. Parking for example had depth. There were questions like, how will this relate to transportation ten, twenty, one hundred years from now? But then there were, as mentioned, more sacred aspects to a cathedral than a parking lot.

As design work went on the third floor, the second floor of the Meier Building became a museum of sorts. The place for models that had been created in the process. To view them was to view the progress over time for everything from the interior layout, to the Hazel Wright Organ, and the most sacred altar. There were a series of carvings on ideas for the altar. The only early altar features that generated interest right away were its size and material. When finished, it would be eight feet by eight feet and be made of marble.

A baldachin was proposed. In Catholic cathedrals, a baldachin is a kind of canopy over the altar. But that was problematic because of the high ceilings. Columns were common for baldachins, so that was a possibility. But Scott Johnson explained that "we" do not obstruct views. So, he suggested floating the baldachin instead. Johnson had a plethora of liturgical advice to lean on, starting with Brother Woeger and Monsignor Art Holquin. They were indispensable resources. But there were great minds among the clergy from the bishop on down, who informed the process.

"We had a lot of conversations with the priests, the bishop, and the building committee," said Scott Johnson, whose firm had done some religious buildings but never a cathedral. "They were very generous with their knowledge. They are truly people of great faith, because they had great faith to figure that we would somehow make something they'd be happy to be in. And that takes great faith."

All of the creative energy and excitement surrounding progress, setbacks, and more progress easily made the team forget about everything else. But, once in a while, there came a moment to stop what they were doing and reflect.

On a late Tuesday afternoon in February 2014, there was a small crowd gathering at the arboretum. They were there to pay last respects to Arvella Schuller, who had died on the eleventh at eighty-four years old. She was often called the brains behind the church that became an international television ministry. She was, after all, the one who suggested her husband choose the drive-in. She was the producer of *Hour of Power* for most of its run and programmed much of the music for the church. She was laid to rest in a prepared plot in the Memorial Gardens in the shadow of the glass church she had helped build. It remained much as it had when she last saw it, but it was destined to change.

Addressing some of the major priorities environmentally inside the cathedral was difficult. Like the arboretum, it had to be air-conditioned. Fortunately, because of the design work and learning experiences the diocese had with the arboretum, air-conditioning was not a problem. It was also true they were dealing with a better infrastructure for getting it done. But it was not without its technical challenges. The ceiling was nearly one hundred feet high.

"We introduced both heat and air at the pew level, where the people are," said Scott Johnson. "You know, the top 94 percent of the building, nobody's there. We're on the bottom 6 percent of the building. That's where we stand and sit, so that's where the comfort has to be."

There were hours agonizing about the interior color, but the design architect's instinct on the color white for much of the interior was proven correct. Sometimes, for inspiration, they would leave the confines of the fourth floor to venture over to the cathedral en masse. They would go inside and just stand there and look around. There were wall mock-ups to look at different design examples to get a feel for the floor level tranquility. The sun shined through the ten thousand panes of glass onto the open floor—a surreal experience. It had become a blank canvas. But when it was hot outside, it was noticeably hot inside with the greenhouse effect. If there was a loud clank or shout, it echoed dramatically. If they went in at night, the light was dull because it escaped out the windows and was not reflected down. Lighting, temperature control, and acoustics were known issues and handled, on the design front, separately—that is, until there was a breakthrough that solved several dilemmas at once.

"The quatrefoils," said Rob Neal. "When I saw that, I knew it was right."

"I wanted to pick an idea that was both related to Philip Johnson's original idea and solved all these problems," said design architect Scott Johnson. He figured it was not very aspirational to have people show up to a building and see all the problems that were solved. "We wanted to solve all those problems and have someone walk in and just go, 'Oh, wow,' and they wouldn't think about the light and they wouldn't think about the heat and they wouldn't think about the acoustics. They would think that it was heaven inside the building." They wanted to solve the problems in such a way that says more about the ethos of the building than the problems the quatrefoils solved.

Johnson developed this concept of a series of triangles that would be white, slightly opaque, and perforated. They would need to cover the entire inside ceiling at alternating angles. The gaps would allow sunlight and shadow to coexist in scattered patterns across the interior. They would reflect sunlight out to further enhance climate control and reflect interior lighting downward to the floor to light the space.

"Now that we had the quatrefoils, we could not only throw light down, but throw light up into the vault and it would reflect back down, so we could get a glow in the evening and have [the cathedral] illuminated by night," said Scott Johnson.

Liturgically, the quatrefoils would create a more intimate space so that the focus, instead of on outside distractions through glass, would be on the altar.

There were a dozen models of floor plans, pew arrangements, and mock-ups of every type. Every feature was visualized. Over the course of more than a year, the collaboration went on, until a final model had been built, a computer simulation created, and a new vision was ready to be revealed.

In September, Bishop Kevin Vann revealed the design plans that had been, in some form, taking shape in the minds of the design team since 2013. The results of exhaustive work by the Architectural and Renovations Committee with Scott Johnson's interior design work, collaboration with Brother William Woeger, and Mark Rios's work on an expansive plaza were all part of the unveiling.

The altar had been set in the center of the cathedral on a three-step predella. Across from it on the same platform was the cathedra, or bishop's chair, against the rise housing the pipe organ. The ambo was on the opposite wall, partitioned off from the main doors. The pews were set in straight lines on each side of the altar platform facing inward in what is called an antiphonal layout with each side facing the altar. The alternative was radial, which is a kind of half circle with isles like spokes. The setting was like one of the layouts presented by Brother Woeger to the selection committee. The design also showed the proposed size and square shape of the altar. The images previewed the crucifix to be suspended from the Johnson-designed hanging baldachin above the altar, with a reliquary underneath. Both the cross and reliquary were designed by Brother Woeger.

The virtual reality video showed a room shimmering with the kinds of angular shadows predicted by Scott Johnson from the white quatrefoil ceiling at play with the sun. Johnson said the interior design was like building a ship inside a ship.

"The exterior of the building is widely acknowledged as a landmark architectural specimen as are other buildings on the site. So, I didn't want to alter that," said Johnson. "But once you enter on any side of the building, we did a white frame, so we delineate very carefully between the whole exterior, which is virtually the same restored and conserved. Once you walk through a white frame it all changes, everything changes. The quatrefoils are the ship inside the ship. The ground plan, which is no longer a diamond, is actually a huge rectangle. The sides are in gray limestone. Everything's on the floor."

Within the building, the transformation was complete with the old Crystal Cathedral only recognizable on the outside.

Mark Rios designed an expansive tree-lined plaza with Christ Cathedral at its center to create a cohesion between the sanctuary indoors and the experience outdoors. Brother Woeger had asked questions about the sanctuary in his application presentation. He asked, "Does this structure gather the worshipping community as a Body rather than as individuals?" The design committee actively pursued a sense of unity and oneness as people of Christ.

"Through this innovative design process an insightful plan has emerged that will establish Christ Cathedral as a place for involvement in the sacraments, a place to hear the Word of God proclaimed and a place for personal prayer and devotion," said Bishop Vann.[6]

The design was well received and, if it remained as scheduled, dedication would be set for sometime in 2017. Generous donations had supported the effort since the beginning, but none like what was coming. A surprise donor came forward with a sizable gift, which many considered a "game changer."[7]

Tim Busch, who chaired the development committee of the Cathedral Board, had spent much of his time seeking out the large donors. There was a separate part of the capital campaign that sought smaller donations across the parishes of the diocese, but Busch was responsible for attracting donations for the Bishop's Circle. Eventually, it totaled about $20 million. Fundraising pledges from both the parishes and the larger benefactors did not automatically reflect in the fundraising bank account. With money going out as fast as it was coming in, there was always a danger of needing loans to keep up. A loan equaled debt, and it was a noble effort for the diocese to avoid increasing long-term credit obligations that drained capital needed for renovation.

In December, Richard "Dick" Pickup and his wife, Donna, decided to contribute $20 million from the family trust, a gift to the diocese. A very modest man by nature, he would typically keep his donation secret, but for this publication he agreed to allow his name to be released. It was a multiyear pledge to the Orange Catholic Foundation, which was the chief fundraising apparatus for renovation. It was the single largest pledge gift ever given to the Diocese of Orange and was said to be earmarked for completion of the new Christ Cathedral. In a 2017 interview with the *LA Times*, Pickup made his motivations clear.

"Most of my life, I've been trying to build an estate," said Richard "Dick" Pickup, "but when you reach your 80s, you realize that material things pale in comparison to what mankind can do with these monies."[8]

Testimony to just how important the renovation was to the larger Christian community: Pickup was not Catholic. He was a Protestant. He had been a business partner with Tim Busch for twenty-five years, so they knew each other well, and the donation, in part, reflected how the Pickups felt about Busch's commitment to the cathedral project and their long friendship. Pickup was a man of faith who frequently used his means to support his own church. But after the diocese purchased the Crystal Cathedral, which he called a brilliant move, he wanted to support the restoration of the cathedral and promote Christian dialogue. He had hoped to see the diocese set aside the cultural center for that purpose. His donation came just when it was needed the most, and when the project was saying good-bye to one of the project's leaders.

Not long after the remarkable donation was announced, Rob Neal, the lay leader of the effort, and interim COO of Christ Catholic Cathedral Corporation, had decided to leave. It really was not his decision. His body and his mind were spent. He was simultaneously running the restoration and his own company. By late 2014, it had been a four-year stretch for his significant involvement in the Crystal Cathedral becoming Christ Cathedral, in one way or another. Those who knew him said he had clearly reached a physical and mental end and had no choice.

"It almost killed me," said Rob Neal. But, like he had told the crew working on the arboretum, it was the best work of his life. "It really was the greatest thing I've ever done in my life."

The work of Christ Cathedral was never about one person any more than the Crystal Cathedral was about one person. But, while Christ was at the center of both, there was no escaping that the name Robert H. Schuller was synonymous with the cathedral and the campus.

On May 2, 2015, the diocese prepared to celebrate Holy Thursday Mass. Then came word that Dr. Robert H. Schuller died. The Thursday before Easter, also known as Maundy Thursday, marked the night of the Last Supper, but it was also the anniversary of John Crean's $1 million gift to Schuller's ministry, which launched construction of the Crystal Cathedral. It also happened to be the tenth anniversary of the death of Pope Saint John Paul II, who had blessed the cathedral drawings at the Vatican. It had been a little over a year since Schuller's wife, Arvella, died. Schuller was eighty-eight, but had also suffered from esophageal cancer since the fall of 2013. He had most recently been in the care of a facility in Artesia, California.

The following day it was news across the nation. Locally, the *Orange County Register* headline read, "'It Was a Life Well-Lived': Rev. Robert Schuller, Leader of Crystal Cathedral and 'Hour of Power,' Dies at 88"; *LA Times*, "Rev. Robert H. Schuller, Who Built Crystal Cathedral, Dies at 88"; *New York Times*, "Rev. Robert Schuller, 88, Dies; Built an Empire Preaching Self-Belief."

A week and a half later, the plaza at the gutted Christ Cathedral was jammed with more than two thousand people, there to pay respects to the one-of-a-kind pastor, preacher, builder, husband, and father of five. The memorial service and funeral included the casket with Schuller's famous preaching robe outstretched, laid flat on top. All the local media was there to record the event. The parking lots and surrounding streets were jammed. A cruel group of protestors, a group known for grandstanding, attention-starved criticism, carried signs and made disruptive noises. For what? Nobody really knows. A requisite group of counterprotestors made disruptive noises back. In the plaza, the service was somewhat isolated from the circus outside.

The family insisted that the elder Schullers lived on Social Security income alone and relied on volunteers to care for their home. Funeral expenses in part were covered by a GoFundMe campaign that had raised nearly $6,000.

Bishop Vann and other members of the Diocese of Orange were there to pay their respects.

"He has built bridges between people, faiths and between the rich and poor," Vann said.[9]

Vann had visited Schuller once in the hospital.

"I was a pastor and he was a pastor," said Vann, "and I went to make a sick call, which is part of my life. So, I wanted to go and be with him and pray with him as I would with anybody. But I knew this was important that I went because there was that connection between them and us."[10]

The Schuller family played a major role at the service, but it was officiated by Honolulu reverend Dan Chun, Schuller's friend.

The Memorial Gardens, now operated by the Catholic Diocese of Orange, had been declared interfaith as a promise to Schuller. They sit in a large area that drops fifteen feet down from street level, surrounded by walls that block noise from the clogged roadways for the solace and reflection of visitors; stairs lead down into the first tier of the cemetery; walkways split left and right along memorial walls. Straight ahead are a set of large burial plots—each with manicured green grass and their own low stucco walls owing to their prominence and importance to the history of the Christian campus built by Schuller's life's work. Notably, on the right, are John and Donna Crean, longtime Christian supporters and donors to causes large and small, including Schuller's ministry. The couple donated the first $1 million to guarantee the successful fundraising campaign that paid for construction of the Crystal Cathedral. On the left, Arvella DeHann's marker where she had been laid to rest described her as wife, mother, pastor. Added to the marker next to hers was the name Robert Harold, husband, father, pastor. Beneath the marker, a long rectangular hole had been prepared. Robert H. Schuller's casket was lowered into place in the peace with which he had intended the cemetery.

In Schuller's final sermon in the glass church that he had built in 2012, and the final sermon for the international ministry known as the *Hour of Power*, Schuller spoke of God as one's personal self-esteem booster.

"I had the idea years later to come here and begin a church," he said. "Talent? I don't know. Money? No. Members? None to begin with. But dream the dream that God has put within you!"[11]

The broad marble wall fixture facing visitors was engraved with a soaring eagle beneath the name SCHULLER and the quote, "This is the day the Lord has made. We will be glad and rejoice in it" (Psalm 188:24).

His final resting place was in the cemetery that his church built and that was now operated by the Diocese of Orange. It gave visitors a chance to visit and pay their respects—as much an attraction for the visitors seeking to connect with the late pastor as anyplace else on campus. It was a changing environment, outside but more so inside the cathedral. With the design announced publicly, it was time to think about starting the work and selecting the sacred art and liturgical necessities that would have to be ready when the time came.

The sacred artwork did not require an architect, and that was an ongoing project. Since joining the effort, Brother William Woeger had been part of the Sacred Art Commission, made up of himself, Bishop Vann, Monsignor Art Holquin, Father Christopher Smith, Lesa Truxaw, Monsignor Michael Heher, and Tony Jennison.

In May 2015, following the funeral for Dr. Schuller, the diocese had secured the tabernacle designed by Egino Weinert. Monsignor Arthur Holquin, S.T.L., Diocese of Orange episcopal vicar for divine worship, had traveled to the German studio of the artist Egino Weinert, who had died in 2012. Weinert was renowned for his work with gold and bronze, focusing on religious subject matter. But he was also a master painter and sculptor. Holquin took a particular liking to Weinert's bronze and enamel pieces.

"Egino Weinert was very much committed to art integrated to the service of worship," said Holquin.[12]

In search of a tabernacle for the cathedral, the most sacred vessel in any Catholic church, Holquin and Brother Woeger, his regular collaborator, reached out to Weinert studio representatives in the United States. They contacted Weinert's wife, who had a tabernacle in the Weinert museum. But it had a deep sentimental value, and she did not want to part with it. But over time and after a few conversations about its intended prominence in the new cathedral in California, she agreed to sell the tabernacle, its bronze pillar, and two bronze candelabras to the diocese. On its pedestal it stood nine feet tall. The painted images on each side depicted moments in Christ's life. It was placed in a glass case and put on temporary display on the second floor of the Meier Building with the other design displays until the adoration chapel in the cathedral could be completed. As it turned out, that was more years away than anyone had predicted.

Phase Two

In a small, mid-nineteenth-century Pennsylvania town, just north of Pittsburgh, there was a bustling German Catholic community. There was a sizable monastery founded by the Capuchins and a nice church with a cemetery. St. Mary's of the Assumption Parish was dedicated on July 6, 1845, on donated land. Although the original chapel was erected in 1841, construction on the monastery and church improvements were nearly nonstop for the next decade. The goal was to complete the buildings needed to establish St. Fidelis College sometime in the 1870s. There had developed a Capuchin pipeline of sorts that led religious and laypeople alike to immigrate to the township. Among those settling in what is now called Herman, Pennsylvania, was a young German named John Heim. He was born about 1810 in Baden-Baden, Germany, and eventually made his way to the New World, attracted to Herman by common cultural comforts and an established Catholic community. The names of parish members read like a German phone book, had there been phones at the time: Schmidt, Eichenlaub, Koebel, just to name a few. It was easy to understand why John Heim, a ship's carpenter by trade, chose Herman to raise his family. He often took jobs plying his skills on projects at St. Mary's. One of those projects was for the cathedral at the monastery. One day, while working on the steeple, precariously high above the ground, he slipped and fell. He was in his mid-fifties and was buried in the St. Mary's cemetery. He had a son, Martin Heim, who grew to be a highly skilled carpenter and made his living building some of the finest homes and schoolhouses in nearby Butler Township. He was a member of St. Peter's Catholic Church. Martin Heim's son William became an architect, having migrated to Highlands County, Florida. It was a bit of a culture shock. He left his home in a largely Catholic community and settled in a place where there were so few Catholics in the primarily Protestant South, Mass was held in the Heim household. A priest had a scheduled route he traveled to provide services. William Heim designed and supervised the construction of the first Catholic church in Highlands County, where he remained a parishioner for the rest of his life. William's son Ralph Heim continued the family tradition and became an engineer who was involved in church construction as a volunteer for Christ the King and Resurrection parishes, and Holy Spirit Catholic Church. It was this history and lifelong Christian faith that enchanted Ralph's son Richard when the bishop of the Diocese of Orange called with a request: "Would he be willing to become a direct advisor to the bishop and see the renovation of Christ Cathedral completed?" Of course, he would.

Richard Mark Heim was division president and CEO of the Western Region office of Clark Construction Group in Irvine, California. He was a busy man, with projects up and down the state. He had most recently been involved with projects that were historical renovations, including LA City Hall, LA County Hall of Justice, and the Supreme Court Building in San Francisco. Heim had a bachelor of science degree from the University of Florida and an MBA from Auburn University. Bishop Vann liked Heim's resume and his history of supporting the Catholic Church. Bishop Kevin Vann awarded Heim the Bishop's Award for Exemplary Business Ethics.

Bishop Vann called Heim in late June 2015. He wanted someone who understood complicated renovation and construction projects and could look closely at what the renovation of Christ Cathedral was going to cost. Vann, a typically frugal child of the Depression, had been growing uneasy about being too lavish with the renovation to the point of diminishing returns and at the expense of the rest of the parishes in the diocese.

"Everything comes across my desk," said Bishop Vann. "I was very much conscious of what's important and what has to be the priority and what do you need versus what you want. Mom and Dad lived that. My grandparents and I did. I do know all the priests were very supportive and the cathedral is very significant. But it's only one part of the whole mission of the diocese."[1]

Vann's goal was to find a balance. He wanted the cathedral to become the center of Catholic life in the diocese, but also to keep up the mission of all the sixty-eight parishes and four ethnic centers.

"My dad always taught me to do the right thing" he said. "My mother did too."

Vann extended the invitation to Heim, who accepted the post as a volunteer. He was nearing retirement from Clark Construction.

A month later, Heim received a letter from Bishop Vann, outlining his responsibilities as special advisor to the bishop. Heim called them mandates: get the cathedral renovation completed; do it within the limitations of the budget; maintain the architecture; and finally, bring people together. Chief among his duties was a review of the Phase One design and the need for an accurate assessment of the finite costs when the cathedral was complete. For this, Heim worked with the contractor McCarthy Construction to establish the Guaranteed Maximum Price (GMP), based on the current design. That included wood specifications, where marble was sourced, air-conditioning, and every expense associated with the renovation. Heim would take that number and factor in soft costs—that is, anything not directly connected to construction. For example, that could be expenses for inspections, accounting, fees for permits, and legal fees and taxes. These were already considered by the Phase One committees and teams along with diocese construction manager Joe Novoa. But Heim's mandate from the bishop was simple: the budget for the renovation of Christ Cathedral would be capped at what was already in the bank and or pledged. That number was just over $72 million. When the contractor, McCarthy, returned a GMP of $67 million, it might have seemed like a good number, considering the budget. But Heim found that when adding in the "soft costs" the total budget was more like $108 million.

"I told the bishop we had basically two options," said Heim.[2] "One option would be to delay the construction, hold on to the Phase One design, until we had raised enough money; we had raised the available funds." That was unlikely, considering Vann's growing impatience with the costs so far. So, Heim proposed option two: a redesign, a Phase Two design, to reduce costs and bring the design within the budgetary limitations. "He selected the second option," said Heim, "and it was my recommendation."

The enlistment of Richard Heim also had the added effect of filling a void that was left after the departure of Rob Neal. After years of managing the restoration of the arboretum and Tower of Hope, as well as launching the cathedral design, the intensity, workload, and pressure of managing a major business and a complicated project like the cathedral campus proved physically and emotionally draining. Rob Neal had been the face of the project and the lay leader. The committees that remained were not rudderless or incapable, but Neal's influence was missed. Heim took some of the team members left over from Neal's tenure and added them to his own design oversight committee. The core of the team was Randy Redwitz, Tim Psomas, Kent Peterson, and Rand Sperry.

Bishop Vann hosted what Heim described as a critical meeting with the architectural firm Johnson Fain. Heim explained what they had planned, and Johnson Fain's Scott Johnson enthusiastically accepted the redesign challenge. Brother William Woeger remained as the liturgical design consultant, and Joe Novoa continued in his role as construction manager for the diocese.

At this point, nothing had been done in the cathedral other than the removal of the Hazel Wright Organ and the theater seats. Otherwise, remained as it was during the final *Hour of Power* taping in June of 2013 and would for a while longer. Phase Two, the value engineering of the Christ Cathedral design, was underway. The plan was to take the design, which was universally popular, and preserve its essence while saving money.

"The goal was to preserve the original design to the point that a Phase One committee member could walk into the finished cathedral and say, 'Yes, that was our vision,'" said Heim. Bishop Vann recalled a meeting he had with Heim and Scott Johnson about the architectural concerns. To Bishop Vann, Scott Johnson did not seem concerned and, in front of BishopVann and Richard Heim, took a page from that day's *Orange County Register* and personally drew a proposed layout, which eventually became the new plan.

The hard part was figuring out how to do that and still slash about $26 million from the projected construction and soft costs. Over a nine-month period, Richard Heim and his team looked at every design detail in search of every nickel-of-cost savings.

Heim said there was an old saying: "If you want some good ideas, you're going to need a lot of ideas."

So, they went in search of creative, quality ideas that would make a difference and still be true to the inspiration that was the Crystal

Cathedral and the Phase One Christ Cathedral design. One design feature caught Heim's eye right away. The quatrefoils were an innovation by the architect firm Johnson Fain, but to Heim they left a lot to be desired.

"When I first saw it," said Heim, "I thought, boy, we gotta get rid of these things." But he admitted he had a lot to learn about quatrefoils.

Heim's team found ways to trim the budget. Ten million dollars in savings came from an early critical decision to use the existing structure. Forego major concrete work and adapt the needs of the cathedral design to what was already in place. That meant reconfiguring the air-conditioning plan so the air would come from the walls and not underneath as it had been with the arboretum. Air-conditioning was a must. It was incumbent upon the diocese to ensure that it had mitigated one of the major complaints of Crystal Cathedral Ministries' congregants that it was too hot and dreadfully uncomfortable. Electrical infrastructure was to be moved off-site because of noise, but that also changed. The expense of moving electrical infrastructure to an area some distance away, then running it underground, was more costly than focusing on noise mitigation. Then there were the concrete columns that supported the main sacristy floor. Most people never saw and did not think about the space under the cathedral, but there was equal space underneath the church as existed inside the sanctuary. Every column that was removed had to be supported by a beam to support the load to the adjacent columns. Each one had a price tag of about $80,000. So, the architect worked out a design of the undercroft that mitigated the situation and reduced the number of columns, requiring removal from fifteen to just one.

The original contractor, McCarthy, had declined to continue the work in Phase Two. Through a selection process, the general contractor Snyder Langston was hired. This was not as easy as it might sound. The construction marketplace was tight. Construction projects kept everyone busier than they had been in a decade, and finding organizations that had the time to take on smaller projects was next to impossible. Snyder Langston had a history with the Diocese of Orange and was a welcomed addition. Richard Heim was more worried about subcontractors who, in the extremely competitive marketplace, could ask astronomical budget-busting sums. Because of the likelihood that the marketplace was going to work against the budget, Heim could not help but see the power of the project move subcontractors to act contrary to financial concerns. In the subcontractor-selection process, Heim appealed to the desire by these firms to be involved in something important. It was a cathedral, he would tell them; how often can you say you were involved in something like that? The Christ Cathedral was a once-in-a-lifetime project, and the subcontractors accepted the responsibility of controlling estimates.

By mid-2016, still, the only major work that had been done was in gutting the cathedral, including the removal of pews. The restoration work that had been completed on the cathedral was all on the exterior. This included the rehab and sealing of the eleven thousand panes of glass. The Hazel Wright Organ, which was removed in January 2014, had completed its eighteen-month restoration in Italy and was sitting in storage in Orange County. From disassembly to installation, the whole process to restore the rare and colossal instrument to all new glory was itself an odyssey. With the indispensable help of Gabriel Ferrucci, the Ruffattis of Padua, Italy, who built the organ in 1980, were back for another chapter in the legend. The delayed cathedral renovation meant that the organ had to sit in storage for an unplanned and extended time. The pipes had to be regularly rotated by hand to prevent strain and avoid damage. It was the same kind of care the craftsmen took at every step along the way, even as the Ruffattis installed the sixteen thousand pipes. More on that later.

In early 2017, five years after acquisition of the Crystal Cathedral, the ambitious restoration of the now Christ Cathedral was formally launched. It began with Bishop Vann's blessing of the sanctuary and construction crews. Vann had added Eric Flynn as construction-phase emissary of the bishop. The kickoff celebration saw attendees from around the diocese invited to use large permanent markers to sign names and messages to the walls and cement floor. The messages would eventually be covered by carpet and wall coverings, but they would always be there hidden away. Weeks later, Bishop Vann was back in the sanctuary for a signing ceremony with John Rochford of Snyder Langston, the general contractor. The budget for the contractor, the hard costs starting point, was \$44,795,539—more than \$22 million lower than the guaranteed maximum price quoted by McCarthy for the original Phase One design.

By June, the scaffolding was in place and Christ Cathedral was a formidable construction zone with a target completion date of early 2019. Already in use was one of the redesign team's innovative workarounds. Because there were lightbulbs and sprinklers scattered all over the interior ceiling of the cathedral, those areas needed to be accessed for ongoing maintenance. The 50,000-hour LED bulbs, which the team also found, would not be enough. The original plan called for a network of catwalks and bosun's chairs to meet that need. (A bonsun's chair is a harnessed web that hangs from pullies and suspends a person from a rope.) But the cost assessment was such that the team found a better way. What they did was buy a specialized lift from Germany that could telescope a cherry-picker basket up to the ceiling and reach 90 percent of the area. The move saved \$3 million, and it stood to reason that it would also come in handy during construction and ongoing maintenance. But the equipment required easy access to the cathedral floor, which called for rethinking the pew arrangement.

The pew arrangement had been a matter of long discussions. Some of the pews would have to be removable so the German lift equipment could roll in and roll out. But there was something not quite right and it came down to the placement of the altar. The original design called for the altar to be in the middle of the cathedral. The placement was liturgical and had precedent in other major churches. The Vatican had its altar not quite in the middle, because its space is so large, but worshippers were on all sides. The idea was that with the altar in the middle, Christ was at the center. But some of the diocesan priests had concerns that it was not practical to conduct services with their backs to half the congregation. It was a matter of pragmatism and preference and, unlike most concerns for Richard Heim's team, was not about cost savings. But the decision to place the altar at the wall in front of the bishop's chair, next to the ambo, raised new questions about pew configuration. The change raised new questions about how to design a pew pattern that would maximize the ceremonial, processional tradition of large church events. Auxiliary Bishop Timothy Freyer said when the request went out to the design committee to take some time to rethink the pew pattern, the reaction was not positive.

"They said, 'That train has left the station,'" he said. "I was like, 'Give us a week.' I remember saying this is going to affect us for generations. A week to ten days won't be the end of the world."[3]

The most expedient way to visualize the different options was to lay blue painter's tape on a floor. A gathering of priests laid out several patterns.

"It was a week of trying to get as many people in there with the bishop just to say 'What do you think, will this work, will that work, will this work?'" said Freyer.

The consensus on a final pattern harkened back to another option presented by Brother Woeger during the selection process. It was a radiated pattern that gives multiple processional options.

"So, you can proceed through the Bishop's Door north [entrance], or you can proceed through the radial spokes of the aisles," said design architect Scott Johnson.[4]

The layout did not impact the budget, but the construction of the pews, the type of wood, was a significant cost savings. The design called for English Black Walnut, a hard, durable wood with a deep dark color. With seating for twenty-two hundred, it was a considerable amount of wood. But Heim's committee determined that another hard, resilient wood was less expensive, and the millwork company developed a dark stain that matched the look of the English Black Walnut. The contract for construction of the pews with the stained oak went to a company based in Idaho. Pews were ordered and scheduled to be among the last projects for installation.

Another area that had frustrated the priests and that they had to petition to change was the placement of the Our Lady of Guadalupe mosaic in the chapel in the undercroft.

"So again, the priests were really upset," said Auxiliary Bishop Timothy Freyer. "They said we had to have an image of Mary in the church. That's what makes it more Catholic. So, it was moved to the Blessed Sacrament Chapel." But that would not work either; it was moved to the place where it is now. "I think it's at the best place," said Freyer, "where she's right there looking at the altar. And as Father Christopher says, it's a sign of her as the first of the disciples as she's with us adoring Jesus."

Marble featured prominently throughout the cathedral, but the most prominent marble designs were the bishop's chair, the ambo, and the altar. The redesign committee worked with the architect to source less expensive marble.

"For example," said Heim, "in lieu of travertine floor from Italy, we could get travertine from Turkey at a third of the cost."

The original source was a single quarry in Italy, but by sourcing the same-quality marble from five countries including Turkey, there was a positive impact on the budget. The savings was between two and three million dollars. But the stonework and polishing were still done in Italy. Bishop Vann had traveled to Italy while the Hazel Wright Organ was under restoration to get to know the Ruffatti family and the people doing the work. When the marble was ready, he went to Italy to approve the stone and returned to check on progress and meet the artisans.

"The veins in the stone, the grays and the whites and the black, just struck me as being very beautiful," said Vann of his purpose. "To see the stone cut, but then as well to see the people who were doing the work, because it was their life cutting the stone. So, when you see the stonework you see the folks who did it for us." Vann said the experience helped forge friendships that continued years later.

In late spring 2018, Cardinal Timothy Dolan, archbishop of New York, visited the cathedral campus, and Bishop Vann gave him a personal tour and updated him about progress. Two months later, he would have seen the cathedral's most dramatic feature installed: 10,400 quatrefoils designed by Johnson Fain.

"This was a rigid piece that was developed by us," said Scott Johnson, "and manufactured in Germany. We did mock-ups, we checked the mock-ups, and then they made them all. They came out, they installed them. We watched the installation."

Richard Heim was skeptical about the quatrefoils. The white triangles seemed to be too modern and potentially controversial aesthetically. But there was no arguing the need to further reduce echo in the church and, if successful, the innovative design was supposed to help with climate control. The quatrefoils worked better than anyone thought. Under the blazing early summer sun of 2018, the glass building was like a greenhouse inside. But in the first few hours of quatrefoil installation, the temperature dipped noticeably and continued to cool. They put scaffolding throughout the whole building. It took months to install. The heat mitigation worked exactly as it had been designed. The sunlight and shadow cast alternating slivers across every surface in the sanctuary; previously only imagined in design concept, they dazzled. Incorporated with and enhanced by the ceiling lights, the quatrefoils illuminated magically inside and out.

In the fall, Bishop Vann held a blessing of the quatrefoils, which was the first public unveiling of the results of the installation. Donors and many who had worked on the campus restoration were invited to view the sanctuary lighting. This was a moment that gave Richard Heim butterflies. He had been won over by the designers and engineers, and with the effectiveness of the quatrefoils proven, he was also pleased he trusted their work. But he was never enamored with the appearance and worried the reception would be a negative one. He did not have to worry long. The feedback he received was universally positive; he felt it was a blessing that it had worked out so well. That early evening it had rained. As the rain stopped, the sun came out and a rainbow appeared. Bishop Vann later recalled that he thought of the rainbows in sacred Scripture, which are a sign of God's blessing.

Among those at the lighting were Tim and Susan Strader. The husband-and-wife team had been named co-chairs of Christ Cathedral Task Force a couple of years earlier to raise the final dollars needed to complete Bishop Vann's campaign goals. They wasted little time and approached the effort with enthusiasm. Because it was a fundraising campaign aimed at individual donors, and not parishioners in more than sixty parishes across the diocese, the Straders' were tasked with making individual appeals. By the night of the gathering for the lighting and blessing, the Straders had been doing well, but to their work was not done. They took the opportunity to reach out to potential donors to close the final $4 million gap. Tim Strader told a video-journalist with the diocese why the cathedral attracts such generous donors. "This particular cathedral on the West Coast will be as important to the Catholic Church as St. Patrick's Cathedral is on the East Coast."[5]

It would also be musically important, a House of God that was designed to sing praises like trumpets from heaven. Come January

2019, the floor of the cathedral was filled with sixteen thousand organ pipes for installation and it left no room for much else. Liturgically, the art, ambience, and construction worked together to make the church a Catholic place of worship. But with all of the other considerations, the interior design had a hidden and complex cohesion created to perfect the sound of the Hazel Wright Organ. There to supervise the complex installation, as he had in 1980, was Piero Ruffatti. It was a bit of a surprise to get the call about the restoration in 2013, three decades after the original installation. The invitation came at the behest of Bishop Vann with the help of an old countryman of Ruffatti's, Gabriel Ferrucci. Farrucci fled Fascist Italy, to start over in America, so the two grew up in different worlds along different paths. They did not know each other, but were contemporaries in many ways, and Ferrucci spoke fluent Italian. Bishop Vann did not need a translator, owing to his own skill in the language and Ruffatti's proficiency with English. What he needed was a man who could help coordinate a project working directly with the Italian craftsman over a long period of time. As it happened, it was more than six years and started out with a few surprises.

"Harsh conditions in the building," Francesco Ruffatti, a tonal designer for the firm Ruffatti Brothers, wrote in an essay for *American Organist*, "including rainwater leaking from the ceiling's glass panels, as well as the severely reduced maintenance in recent years, caused the whole instrument to fall into severe disrepair."[6]

The Diocese of Orange gained from the partnership with the Ruffatti Brothers, the coordination work from Gabriel Ferrucci, the design work of cathedral architect Scott Johnson, and the work of the sound consultant. There was a great deal of excitement around the undertaking as the renovation's first major project and the cathedral's final major installation. The organ was the original Ruffatti from the arboretum. It still had five manuals or keyboards, and there were still sixteen thousand pipes in 270 ranks, but the total renovation resulted in a complete transformation. The original organ was copper tones and brown, with silver pipes. The only color that remained unchanged, because of the sensitivity of the instruments, was the silver pipes. Otherwise, like the interior of the cathedral itself, it was nearly unrecognizable. The pipes blended in with the opaques and white tones that made up the quatrefoil ceiling. Everything from the quatrefoils to the sanctuary walls was designed in close consultation with a sound designer and done to make the organ sound better.

"The different stone that you see on the walls. It's all different size and beveled at different angles. That's also to help with the sound of the organ," Greg McClure, superintendent of Snyder Langston, told OC Catholic TV at the time.[7]

Those who worked closely on the project were taken aback, not just because of the results, but because of what it meant to rebuild a great instrument designed to sing the praises of God.

"It was a great honor," said Gabriel Ferrucci.[8]

Ferrucci noted modestly that many people made it financially possible for the restoration to happen. It was true that, like the other projects, every donation mattered. But Ferrucci gave more than his volunteer time, and there was a lot of gratitude from the diocese.

"I think Gabriel's dedication, love for organ music, knowledge of the Italian language and culture, and his business acumen contributed enormously to the Hazel Wright Organ restoration project," said Bishop Tod Brown. Ferrucci served on Brown's Board of Directors for the earlier Christ Our Savior cathedral project.[9]

As the final months of restoration approached, the endless string of deadlines that never seemed to ease up continued the high pace of work. Richard Heim noted the safety record of the work crews. Identifying a long string of consecutive days without a time-loss accident, he hosted a family barbecue. The purpose was twofold: one, to thank the crews and their families for their hard work and dedication. The other purpose was more personal: like his predecessor Rob Neal, who encouraged construction crews with the message that this will be the best work of their lives, Heim wanted to underscore that their work was a once-in-a-lifetime kind of job.

"We had a little contest to see who could come up with a slogan for the safety signs, the message to the workmen," said Heim, "that, not only was it asking them to be safe for themselves, for their families and for God, but also, to understand that they were building the House of God and that they were part of it."

The Sacred Art Committee had its own deadlines and a task to seek budget relief if possible. Many of the central pieces, like the stone altar and bishop's chair, were ordered and being made by craftsmen known for staying on schedule. But there was a hiccup, to say the least, with the image of Mary that Brother Woeger had worked so hard to obtain.

"It was a devotional object that countless people had prayed in front of for centuries," said Woeger. "So, it was a venerable object."[10]

Brother Woeger found the painting in Sante Fe, New Mexico, and conducted appropriate due diligence. The painting came with the correct paperwork. But once the painting was secure back in Orange County, further investigation revealed additional clues as to the painting's history. At one time, in its distant past, the painting had been "misappropriated," a nice way of saying it had been stolen. That was enough for the diocese to return the painting and search for a suitable replacement for an image of our Lady appropriate for permanent display inside the sanctuary. It was decided that a large mosaic would take the place of the painting.

Bill and Helen Close funded the work as a gift to the diocese. Bill Close was well known for financing mosaic pieces depicting Our Lady of Guadalupe in other churches, including in the Archdiocese of Los Angeles. He sponsored nearly three dozen such works. He had a well-established relationship with mosaic artisan Atelier Lenarduzzi Mosaici, in Pordenone, Italy. The image of Our Lady of Guadalupe was to be ten feet by seven feet and require fifty-five thousand tiles. To meet the dedication deadline, multiple artists were assigned to just the one project.

The diocese benefited from long hours from volunteers over the years of work, but the mosaic was made possible by the significant generosity of Catholic families like the Closes and the Jilots. Dennis Jilot was a longtime Catholic and a man of faith. He and his wife, Lynne, were parishioners at a church within the diocese, and when Bishop Vann called and asked if he would join the board of Christ Catholic Cathedral Corporation, he said it would be an honor. It was a short tenure during a time of a lot of changes in the process, but he said some of the meetings were fun. For the Jilots, who had supported the diocese and Catholic Charities over the years, the opportunity to sponsor the primary crucifix above the altar was one they could not pass up. It was a sizable commitment, but paid over five years, so it was financially workable. It was a chance to contribute to the long-term beauty of the church sanctuary and its art collection. "It was one of many contributions, large and small, that made the renovation and transformation of the cathedral possible."[11]

"I think it was one of the largest contributions we'd ever made to anything," said Dennis Jilot.

Brother Woeger's knack for sourcing Omaha craftsmen to save money, but still get the desired quality, paid off in several liturgical features—including the altar candles and the crucifix sponsored by the Jilots. Woeger chuckled about the candles, saying, "I'd bring them the prices and they would ask me if 'that was just for one?'"

Woeger and the art committee set out from the beginning to ensure that the pieces placed in the sanctuary, as unique as they were individually, felt like a family of objects. So, each one related in some way to the others. And the inspiration began with the acquisition of the midcentury bronze—like the candlesticks and the crucifix. The candlesticks were tall and bronze to make a statement in the large sanctuary, and each, about halfway up, was adorned with large cabochon gemstones. The crucifix, in the shape of a Greek cross, called a *Crux Gemmata*, gets its name for being jewel-encrusted. It had emeralds and crystals, which seemed to fit its new home. It was more than a nod to the history of the building.

"There's a huge fifteen-pound chunk of quartz in the back of the crucifix," said Brother Woeger. "It's a historic precedent of a jeweled cross, that the instrument of death is the glorified cross—that is, means of our salvation. In other words, it's a double idea. That something as horrible as crucifixion is glorified because it resulted in the salvation of all the world."

The bleached-white carved cedar image of Christ on the crucifix called the corpus was done by the Ferdinand Stuflesser Studio in Ortisei, Italy. But the brass and stonework were done in Omaha.

"It's three different shades of bronze," said Brother Woeger. "Some of it's high polish and some of it's low polish." It weighed a thousand pounds and had to be assembled in the sanctuary the day it was installed. The builder of the cross, Dave Fitzpatrick, traveled from Omaha and glued the gems in place himself.

Brother Woeger also designed the reliquary to hold the sacred relics of the saints that had been donated. Small, shaped like a house, it had as its future home the space the designer provided for it under the altar, but visible between its large marble legs.

The walls were adorned with the traditional fourteen Stations of the Cross, which were in bronze relief. And there were twelve dedication lights, representing the twelve apostles, around the perimeter walls of the sanctuary.

For the final artistic touch, Brother Woeger turned to Brother Martin Erspamer, a monk at the Saint Meinrad Archabbey in Indiana, to craft an image of Christ that could be woven into a tapestry. He designed and painted the original image that was then sent to Belgium to be woven. The colorful Christ, Lord of Creation tapestry was thirty-two feet long when completed and, when placed high above the sanctuary floor, was the cathedral's only flash of color against the monochromatic quatrefoil ceiling.

Like the long history of the Crystal Cathedral that became Christ Cathedral, Erspamer's work was a tapestry woven from the back. But it was also so large that it illustrated how, even from the front, things are not always what they seem.

"If you look at it from the front," explained Brother Woeger, "you just see the warp and the woof, you know." The threads that run lengthwise were the warp and the threads that run crosswise were the woof. "It doesn't look like anything. You have to keep backing away and backing away to get the long view. Then you realize that it's actually a picture. And certainly, that's the way a lot of life is; you don't see how it all fits."

Dedication of Christ Cathedral

The grand glass structure was no more than colorful renderings on paper, signed by one of America's preeminent architects, when Reverend Schuller inquired about seeing Pope John Paul II at the Vatican in Rome. The renderings were tucked up under his arm as he marveled at the world's great examples of art and architecture. There was the Sistine Chapel, the Gardens of Vatican City, and St. Peter's Basilica. As he went along, he used his astute instincts to find people who looked like they knew what they were doing. Then he asked if he could see the pope, a task harder than it might seem.

The visit was without announcement or appointment, and, as most people who had ever been to the Vatican knew, the best anyone could usually hope for was to see the daily papal blessing from St. Peter's Square as the pontiff stood on the balcony. While it was difficult, nearly impossible, to get such an opportunity, unbeknownst to Schuller word had gotten around that the reverend from *Hour of Power* was at the Vatican and asking to see the pope. In most situations, this would open doors for Dr. Schuller, but not at the Vatican—not when a key press office bishop was working behind the scenes to thwart a face-to-face meeting.

Bishop John Patrick Foley took it upon himself to make sure that meeting never took place. His reasonings were not recorded. Foley was working in the press office and aided with papal visits, particularly abroad. According to the Vatican Press Office, "He served as news secretary for the meetings of the National Conference of Catholic Bishops in the United States and as English-language press liaison for the visit of Pope John Paul II to Ireland and the United States in 1979 and for the Synod of Bishops in Rome in 1980."[1] This was the time when Schuller visited the Vatican. Foley represented the kind of opposition that virtually guaranteed there would be no meeting.

231

For most people that is. On the day Schuller was there, the pope was not in his balcony, but rather on the street level of St. Peter's Square. Exactly how Schuller managed it was not entirely clear. Yes, he was an international figure. So, perhaps he was recognized by someone unaware of Foley's efforts. Schuller ended up beyond the barriers and face-to-face with Pope John Paul II.

A photograph shows Schuller with the image of the Crystal Cathedral under his arm as the two shook hands. He asked for and received the pope's personal blessing of the Crystal Cathedral architectural work. The picture of them together was one of Schuller's most prized mementos. The pope's blessing was priceless beyond that of a keepsake. The story of Foley's intervention was only known because, just weeks after the purchase of the Crystal Cathedral, the then Cardinal Foley called Bishop Brown and left a voicemail. He conveyed the story of how he tried to stop the blessing of the cathedral drawings. He also said he came to understand why the Holy Spirt prevailed. Cardinal Foley died an hour after making the phone call.

Schuller set out to build a cathedral but knew formally that designation was reserved for a house of worship with a cathedra, or bishop's chair. The Reformed Church of America in which he belonged was not structured for bishops or cathedrals. He called it the Crystal Cathedral. It was a cathedral to many around the world. Then it became Christ Cathedral, a real cathedral and "a place for Christ forever."

Dedication Week, as it was called, was a series of events large and small that bookended the Dedication Mass. There were moments with great meaning, like the vigil with the relics, prayers, and blessings, and an evening gala. Youth gathered for their own events to share in the week's festivities. High school students gathered for one such event, with tours, speakers, and pronunciation discussions among young guides for such terms as *Crux Gematta*. It all represented a multifaceted transformation beyond the obvious aesthetics.

"You know high school kids are reading the script off their phone now rather than paper," said Auxiliary Bishop Timothy Freyer, vicar of priests since 2012.[2] There was also instruction about the meaning and importance of the historic moment. "I remember telling them that for decades Jesus Christ had been proclaimed in this building.

Very well by Dr. Schuller and others. But for the first time, Jesus Christ will actually be adored in this building. We'll have the adoration of the Blessed Sacrament."

The night before the Dedication Mass, outside Christ Cathedral's festal doors, sat a well-guarded box containing the relics of ten martyrs and saints. They had been placed there the night before by procession after a vigil in the arboretum. Among them was a relic of Saint Pope John Paul II. The placing of the relics was to mark a major moment in the dedication of the cathedral and blessing of the altar.

Vann spoke in his white, priestly vestments, trimmed in gold, under his amaranth red cap. He was to the right of Christ Cathedral's splendid marble altar at a portable podium. Typically, the homily would be delivered from the raised marble ambo, further right at the top of a short stairway. But this was hardly a typical Mass or homily. It was a joint homily with Reverend Christopher Smith, the rector for Christ Cathedral, and the Mass celebration was historic.

Vann's quote from Benedict was not his first reference to the Virgin of Guadalupe, nor was it the last. While Vann read from his prepared words, he stood opposite the tall mosaic bearing our Lady's image that faced him. He and the mosaic, and the thousands gathered at the Dedication Mass, bathed in a mix of crisscrossing light and shadow produced by the cathedral's remarkable renovation design. The light entered eleven thousand glass panes, dispersed by the white quatrefoils.

"That quote of the crystals reflecting the divine light," continued Vann, "certainly can lead us to the light that is being reflected today through these quatrefoils onto the floor, here in the House of God. You can see that clearly. This light of Christ symbolized by this light spilling onto the floor today ... helps us see the path that God marks out for all of us. To see clearly, where we are going and where we are being led."[3]

The light of Christ provided a well-illuminated path to arrive at this point in history under the bright summer sun of Orange County, but who could have imagined Christ Cathedral as it came alive that day?

It was impossible to imagine that anyone, but God, knew where it had all started or what each one of His divinely inspired workers would accomplish. Robert Schuller knew only that he was headed to Orange, California, to preach to the unchurched, or next that he could do it from the rooftop of a drive-in theater, or next that he'd build a worldwide ministry with a glass church as its picturesque backdrop. But even he did not start down a path that had not been set in motion two thousand years before with the Resurrection of Christ and the gift of the Holy Spirit on the day of Pentecost.

Schuller built the campus and the Crystal Cathedral to be a place of worship, and his last official act as founder of the ministry was to make sure it stayed that way. There were many critics, worriers, and naysayers to say that the transformation of a worn-out glass church could never result in a true cathedral sanctuary worthy of the Catholic Church's celebration of the Eucharist—almost as many who said the diocese could never buy the campus in the first place.

Too often, the path was illuminated only by divine light that is well known to present a clear path without revealing the intended destination—just like Bishop Fulton Sheen's tapestry analogy. The labor of the faithful relied on a clear path and the acceptance that where it led was up to God. Bathed in sunlight, on that July afternoon, the cathedral reveled in the presence of Christ and in the fellowship of the Holy Spirit, to see forward, not back, in the hope that this day too was only a beginning to a million newly inspired paths.

The dedication ceremony began with an invocation by Bishop Vann and the reading of a message from the Vatican Secretary of State, Cardinal Pietro Parolin. In the message, Cardinal Parolin wrote greetings from Pope Francis in Rome.

"The Holy Father prays that the cathedral may serve as a tangible sign of our Lord Jesus Christ's presence in your midst, and help deepen your missionary witness to the broader community, and lead souls to an experience of his abiding mercy and divine light."[4]

The procession into the Christ Cathedral was led by the Knights of Columbus, who entered from all three major entrances and processed to the main altar. Deacons in red followed among lay oil lamp bearers who were dressed in traditional clothing representing the diverse cultures who call the diocese home. The choir sang the entrance songs backed by a full orchestra. Also carried in were the relics of the martyrs and saints.

Saints Charles Garnier, Jean de Brébeuf, and Gabriel Lalemant are among a group called the North American Martyrs. The three

Jesuits lived during the sevententh century among the indigenous people of North America in the area that is now upstate New York. They were killed during the war of the Iroquois Confederacy.

There were three Mexican saints: Justino Orono Madrigal, Atilano Cruz Alvarado, and Rafael Guízar y Valencia. Madrigal and Valencia were murdered by Mexican government soldiers in separate crackdowns on religious freedom. Alvarado was wounded while caring for the sick during the Mexican Revolution.

Saint Andrew Kim Taegon was a priest and the patron saint of Korea who was among thousands of Catholics in Korea who were killed for their faith in the mid-1800s. Saint Andrew Dũng-Lạc was among more than one hundred Catholics in Vietnam who were persecuted and killed during the same era.

Also included was Saint Junípero Serra, known as the Apostle of California. The Franciscan friar established nine missions in the state.

The relic of Saint Pope John Paul II was a droplet of his blood.

Despite skeptics and worries over beloved cathedral processions, seating the large number of clergy and Church leadership from the three main aisles at Christ Cathedral worked as hoped. Bishop Vann took his place in his chair and from there it was like a traditional Mass, ahead of the long-anticipated blessing of the altar. Bishop Vann took his seat without kissing the unblessed altar. The first-ever celebration of the Eucharist would also wait until after the blessing.

Readings included Ephesians 2:21–22, which carried a special meaning about the united Church. "In whom the whole structure is joined together and grows into a holy temple in the Lord; in whom you also are built into it for a dwelling place of God in the Spirit."

The Gospel reading was from the Book of Luke, about God's divine mercy. Zacchaeus, the wealthy tax collector, was so desperate to see Jesus, he scaled a tree. Jesus insisted that he stay at Zacchaeus's house. This drew immediate and severe criticism.

"'He has gone to be the guest of a man who is a sinner.'" And Zacchaeus stood and said to the Lord, 'Behold, Lord, the half of my goods I give to the poor; and if I have defrauded any one of anything I restore it fourfold. And Jesus said to him, 'Today salvation has come to this house, since he also is a son of Abraham. For the Son of Man came to seek and to save the lost'" (Luke 19:7–10).

In the homily, Bishop Vann said, "Our presence here today is not by our choice or actions, but I believe what I would call the providence of God, who has brought us here today … as the Family of God."[5]

Because it was such a unique situation and Reverend Christopher Smith, the rector for Christ Cathedral, had such a large involvement in the transformation of Christ Cathedral and the campus since 2012, Bishop Vann took the unusual step of having a joint homily. It was unusual but not unique, because Bishop Vann and Fr. Smith previously had preached together on a few special occasions.

"The joy of today," said Smith, "is that with the generosity, efforts, the talents, and love of God's people, you, we, have built a house for Jesus and His Church."

In preparation for the celebration of the Eucharist, first the relics were placed in the reliquary beneath the altar. The relics were not a requirement, but a blessing for many who have loved and admired the sacrifices and example of the Christians they represent. In the box they had been transported in, they were placed in the reliquary tent by deacons who knelt and moved their upper bodies into the space between the legs of the large marble structure. Then the bishop was called to prepare as the pitcher of oil called chrism, which contained balsam, was brought to the altar. It was a combination reserved for blessing the altar and the walls of a new church. Of the three holy oils, it was known as the premier oil.

One of the intricate features of the altar top was the five cruciform engravings representing the five wounds of Christ. The oil would be poured out over those locations, but intended to cover the entire eight-foot-square surface. Assistants helped Bishop Vann remove his outer vestment and replace it with a white apron, then they flanked him while he prepared to distribute the oil. Vann hoisted the pitcher.

"May the Lord," said Vann, "by His power, sanctify this altar in this house, which by our ministry we anoint, that as visible signs they may express the mystery of Christ and the Church."

The assistants held the bishop's sleeves, as he began to pour the oil on the altar, to prevent inadvertent soaking and spreading the oil onto the floor. As a very large surface, it took a foot stool for Bishop Vann to reach the middle. He circled the altar clockwise once again, using his bare right hand to smear and distribute the oil evenly over the whole surface.

Spread out across the altar in this manner, the chrism acted as a symbol of Christ as the Anointed One. "For the Father anointed him with the Holy Spirit and constituted him as High Priest, who on the altar of his Body would offer his life for the salvation of all."[6]

Chrism from the pitcher that had been reserved and separated into smaller portions was passed out to several members of the clergy who dispersed around the cathedral. Most notably, first, Bishop Vann himself, carried chrism to the only other person in the sanctuary wearing the tall bishop's cap. Bishop Emeritus of Orange Tod Brown had been seated in the pew near the wall to the left of the altar since before the procession. At eighty-two years old he was struggling with mobility and still showing signs of recovery from a life-threatening illness.

Vann handed his predecessor a vessel of chrism. They exchanged a few words.

"I really wanted to acknowledge him in some personal way," said Bishop Vann in a later interview. "I mean in the days leading up to it we all did that, but I wanted to acknowledge in some personal way, to accompany him as he anointed the walls."[7]

Then Brown, the man who had believed deeply that God had called him to build a cathedral, stood and made his way over to a point on the wall. To Brown, the dedication was a culmination of all that had happened. His place in the moment was emotional. He resisted the temptation to reveal too much about how he felt as he walked in short, halting steps.

It was no more than twenty feet when Lesa Truxaw, who had been instrumental in the cathedral's restoration, directed Brown to the designated location on the wall and pointed. It was high up the wall, above Brown's chin. Using two shaking hands, unable to raise his arms up enough, Brown boosted himself on his toes. He dipped his thumb into the chrism and made the Sign of the Cross on the wall. When he was done, Vann welcomed him back to his seat.

The anointing of the walls was the second part of the blessing for the preparation of Christ Cathedral as a worthy place for the celebration of the Eucharist. It was followed by the incensation of the altar, which had Bishop Vann burning incense, which was then distributed to deacons who made the rounds of the pews. It symbolized the Sacrifice of Christ and the prayers of the faithful rising to heaven as the bells from the carillon bells outside chimed.

The oil was cleaned from the altar and the altar dressed in white cloth. Then the candles were lit, symbolizing the lighting of the cathedral. The sanctuary was ready for the first celebration of Communion in Christ Cathedral.

It was a week of events, looking forward, rejoicing, and worship in preparation for the dedication. But it was also a time of reflection and sometimes understated or overstated claims of influence and participation in seeing it all come together. Bishop Vann's homily at the Dedication Mass was unambiguous and inclusive.

"Then to experience, with the eyes of faith, the gift of gratitude to the Lord of the work of so many hands," said Vann.[8] As is often the case in blessing a new church, because of its profound meaning, Vann quoted from a sermon by Saint Augustine of Hippo. Saint Augustine's full text is included in italics for further context. "The work we see complete in this building is physical; it should find its spiritual counterpart in your hearts. We see here the finished product of stone and wood; so too your lives should reveal the handiwork of God's grace.

> *Let us then offer our thanksgiving above all to the Lord our God, from whom every best and perfect gift comes. Let us praise His goodness with our whole hearts. He it was who inspired in his faithful people the will to build this house of prayer; he stirred up their desire and gave them his help. He awakened enthusiasm among those who were at first unconvinced, and guided to a successful conclusion the efforts of men of good will.* So God, who gives to those of good will both the desire and the accomplishment of the things that belong to him, is the one who began this work, the one who has brought it to completion.[9]

"We have all been instruments of that," Vann pointed out. "This work of God is our place for Christ forever."

CONCLUSION

Neither Crystal nor Gold

Bishop Tod Brown was convinced that the cathedral was providential and a gift from God for the diocese and its 1.3 million Catholics. As Dr. Robert H. Schuller noted, it was anything but free, of course. There may be more than a few congregants of Crystal Cathedral Ministries that might wonder why. How could it be a blessing, part of God's plan, when another group of God's people had to lose? In an interview for this book in 2020, Bishop Brown said the question was a difficult one. But the story, taken in its entirety, allows one to see how it all turned out. To understand the benefit to what became Shepherd's Grove and what the diocese did with Schuller's legacy, with the Christ Cathedral and the campus with its carefully preserved midcentury architecture by Richard Neutra—isn't this the tapestry?

Oranges were abundant across Orange County in January. The major orchards were long gone, but citrus trees were everywhere in the yards of homes new and old. To drive down almost any residential street was to see orange bulbs dangling among the dark green leaves, as a sweet temptation to just go up and pick one. It was also a sign that spring was just around the corner when the very same trees blossomed.

On the campus of Christ Cathedral, Sunday mornings smelled of pancakes and syrup. Hot and cold breakfast food and snacks awaited Mass attendees on tables placed under awnings. They were under canopies like a small farmers' market. They were in the plaza, noted by rector of Christ Cathedral Christopher Smith to be one of the campus's most stunning transformations. As Mass ended, those who so desired walked to the tables and snacked, with the proceeds going to support the Christ Cathedral parish formerly known as St.

Callistus. They spoke in English, but also Spanish, Vietnamese, and Mandarin depending on which Mass had just ended. Sundays were that busy. Smaller services in other languages were also held. Ten thousand worshippers came every Sunday.

There were three Vietnamese Masses starting as early as 6:15 in the morning. Three Spanish Masses and two English Masses filled out the Sunday schedule. But do not look for a missalette. Those slots on the back of the pews are empty. Instead, note the large screen that allows everyone, whether on the floor level or up in the raised sections, to see everything from the songs to the Gospel. On one January morning, the screens lit up and it was live video of the main entrance and Bishop Kevin Vann. He was standing with a group of catechumens and their sponsors. Brown welcomed them to the church and invited them in. They processed together into the cathedral singing the entrance hymn with a massive choir. The pipe organ, excluded, was still in the middle of a yearlong process of voicing.

It was not like any other Catholic cathedral, but as a house fitting the glory of God, it was completely unique with beauty and attention to detail in every respect. It had become a "place for Christ forever."

The title of this book, *Neither Crystal nor Gold*, was drawn from references in the Book of Job to answer the question, *where can wisdom be found?* "Wisdom," as it was revealed, was the Holy Spirit of God that cannot be found by dredging through mines for precious stones and cannot be purchased with gold. It cannot be seen by man. In spring 2020, as these pages were being composed, Pope Francis spoke about the true guide of a "good Christian." According to the *National Catholic Register*, "Pope Francis explained that the early Christians were guided by the Holy Spirit, who provided them strength to pray with courage and boldness."[1]

"Being a Christian is not just fulfilling the Commandments. They must be done, this is true, but if you stop there, you are not a good Christian. To be a good Christian is to let the Holy Spirit enter into you and take you, take you where he wants," Pope Francis said.[2]

Like the tapestry, woven from the back, Dr. Robert H. Schuller never saw his path from Christian preacher in a drive-in to pastor of a worldwide ministry. He had written and spoken countless times about prayer and the work of the Holy Spirit in his efforts. He could not see where events in his life would lead, any more than he knew where he would get the first $1 million donation to build the Crystal Cathedral. Any more than he could see that his ministry would one day need a massive cash infusion and big changes to survive. Ever the optimist and purveyor of Possibility Thinking, he never really grasped, some have said, the reality that he could actually lose the Crystal Cathedral.

"Others have tried to write my story," Schuller wrote. "Biographers, they're called. They have written in unforgivable print what they have wanted without my having an opportunity to correct, criticize, or applaud."[3]

Inasmuch as this text attempts a short biography, and a journalistic chronology of events, apologies go to the family of Dr. Schuller for any inadvertent inclusions or omissions that he may have found objectionable. But assuming the work of the Holy Spirit in his life and his church does not seem to be some grand leap with which to find objection. Therefore, it was possible that in the end God had other plans for what Schuller and his *Hour of Power* audience had built. It was anyone's guess before the bankruptcy court confirmed the sale.

Had Chapman University president Dr. James Doti achieved his goal of buying the Crystal Cathedral campus, he would have crafted the plan for expansion of the health-sciences department right away. He would have a little time. The move into the Crystal Cathedral Academy building would have to wait two years for the ministry's school to vacate its home. But how long it would take to turn the Crystal Cathedral itself into a performing-arts center or into something else was a question mark. It depended on the plan option that had been agreed to in court. It may have been anywhere from a few years to three decades with many variables in between, including the solvency of Crystal Cathedral Ministries.

It probably would not have gotten that far, according to Dr. Doti. The revelations about renovations, based on the costs to the diocese, particularly of the Neutra Arboretum and the Tower of Hope, likely would have triggered the cancellation of the purchase. The purchase proposal was dependent upon a due-diligence inspection of the property by experts to calculate the physical condition of the buildings.

"I believe, if we had won the bid," said Doti, "during that month of due diligence, we would have concluded we can't do this, and we would have pulled out."[4]

Where would the Crystal Cathedral be in 2020 if Chapman had first won, then pulled out? The likelihood of the diocese getting back in many months later was not strong. Bishop Kevin Vann would have had to decide, not Bishop Brown. Based on the risks involved and whatever revelations Chapman had asserted publicly, Vann was not the kind to want to leap into those waters. Of course, that all became irrelevant once the bankruptcy ended. Afterward, Doti and Chapman University did not drag their heels in taking the next steps to reach their goals.

"We still wanted the space," said Doti. "So, I got together with the trustees and moved forward."

A Chapman alumnus who had heard about the court's decision provided the first opportunity for an alternative to the Crystal Cathedral campus. He had found a building for sale in Irvine, near the Spectrum Center. The purchase of the 125-thousand-square-foot building for about $25 million led to the acquisition of surrounding buildings. It became the Rinker Health Science campus with about five hundred thousand square feet of space. Harry and Diane Rinker donated the seed money to underwrite the endowment for the campus. With $130 million invested, it was home to an accredited pharmacy program and a physician's assistant program, and there was still room for expanding.

"We have room for a medical school now, and maybe a dental school," said Doti.

Ten months after Judge Kwan's ruling, the university broke ground on Marybelle and Sebastian P. Musco Center for the Arts on its own campus property. Paul Musco was the colorful founder of Gemini Industries in Santa Ana and a well-known philanthropist who donated the seed money for the project. It cost between $64 million and $78 million, depending on the source. It was completed in 2016. At eighty-eight thousand square feet, it was a little larger than the cathedral, with 1,044 seats on three levels. The present Christ Cathedral seats 2,200. It was not a hasty reaction to falling short with Crystal Cathedral. Just like the diocese and Bishop Brown, Chapman University had been working for decades, long before the bankruptcy, to expand. Chapman had consulted with KTGY Architecture + Planning since 2001.

While the Musco Center for the Arts was under construction, the health and behavioral sciences program was split from the Schmid College of Science and Technology to create the Crean College of Health and Behavioral Sciences. Crean was a backer of Crystal Cathedral Ministries and a name invoked by Doti in bankruptcy court proceedings. By 2018, Chapman's Schmid College moved into the brand-new Keck Center for Science and Engineering—Chapman's $130 million, 140,000-square-foot, three-story building. It was the most expensive and ambitious project in the college's history, and Doti called it his crowning achievement. He retired as president shortly thereafter to return to teaching at the college. Along with "professor" he took the title "president emeritus."

"It probably turned out for the best," said Dr. Doti. "They got an architecturally distinctive cathedral of global prominence." Doti was impressed with the detail and care of the restoration. "It's a beautiful campus."

John Crean's name came up in court as one of those people buried in the Memorial Gardens who would be moved—that is, if the Catholics were awarded the sale. But not only did Crean remain buried prominently across from Robert and Arvella Schuller; his wife was buried there also.

As for the court's decision, it was not made in haste. Judge Robert Kwan had in his possession the results of a Crystal Cathedral Board vote and a letter from Dr. Schuller. Each declared support for the sale to the Diocese of Orange. Despite the endorsements for a decision, Judge Kwan heard from anyone in court who had something to say on the subject. In a final long day, Kwan heard from multiple congregants of Crystal Cathedral Ministries.

"Longtime members," said Alan Martin, who represented the diocese. "Quite a few of them would attend all the hearings." Alan often sat in the gallery with those congregants. "How often he would allow them to come up and speak and share their views, their concerns about the ministry and its legacy. I think it allowed the perspectives of the congregants to evolve and become comfortable with the end result."[5]

That end result would be the diocese taking on the responsibility of maintaining that legacy. Alan said *healing* was the wrong word but emphasized *comfortable*. There were congregants there who wanted to sell to the diocese, and those who opposed. It was important to hear all sides. Martin credited Judge Kwan for making a thoughtful, patient approach.

The diocese was responsible for preserving, as much as was reasonable, the physical campus that Schuller and the ministry built. But the ultimate legacy of the ministry was in the hands of Robert H. Schuller's grandson, Bobby V. Schuller, who found a home as full-time pastor of what became Shepherd's Grove in Irvine. He became the host and producer of *Hour of Power with Bobby Schuller*. The local congregation thrived as did the television audience.

The campus at Shepherd's Grove, now affiliated with the Presbyterian Church, was valued at about $15 million when it was handed over to Bobby Schuller's ministry. He said it was effectively just given to them in a merger. It has a preschool and a children's center among its amenities. *Hour of Power* was recorded in the church sanctuary and produced on site. They have a new twenty-four-hour suicide prevention hotline. The church provides food with "Irvine Feeds the World." They have provided over one hundred thousand meals.

"We're doing great," said Bobby Schuller.[6] "Our TV show is continuing to grow and thrive. We have millions of people watching every Sunday. International in particular is continuing to grow. We have six international offices in Europe, Asia, and Australia. Just continuing to grow and hoping to regain some of our former glory." The last part he said with a chuckle. "Just trying to recapture some of the impact that we used to have."

Schuller said he never took for granted a single moment when he stood at the podium and preached at the Crystal Cathedral. He was in awe and knew he was standing on the shoulders of a giant. Bobby Schuller had become a special person himself, with an easy way about him, a kind infectious smile, and a depth of knowledge and skill for Bible-based preaching, so it was no wonder he had gained support for his local church and a following on the new *Hour of Power*. Interestingly, if the Crystal Cathedral Ministries had somehow managed to retain the cathedral campus and stayed, Bobby Schuller would not be involved.

"Not only would I have not been asked to stay; I would not have accepted if they asked," said Schuller. He said that the family dynamic for the ministry was obviously a huge problem. He said there was a sibling rivalry, and each one had a silo with a large staff. What he learned from that was that there was a better way. At the time of this interview, he said he did not have any family members working for him and nearly an entirely new staff from the Crystal Cathedral days.

"We've got a great staff, thriving, people love to work here. It's a growing ministry. I just don't think that could have happened with the debt and the family dynamics that were happening in the end."

He called it a Catch-22.

"This opportunity is only afforded to me because it failed. So that's the Catch-22. It's like I'm so sad that it failed, and yet grateful to be able to be doing what I'm doing. Because, it's really fun and really meaningful and enjoyable."

How's that for a tapestry?

"I can't imagine doing anything else. Like if I just won the lottery, $100 million, I don't think anything in my life would change. Except maybe I would build another Crystal Cathedral."

Bobby Schuller liked nearly everything about the renovation of the cathedral campus. But inside the church, he had one complaint: the almost universally loved quatrefoils. Schuller did not like the idea of covering up the windows and blocking the view to the outside. He felt the church should be able to see the hurting world outside.

It was not an uncommon criticism. God's work may have always been perfect, but man's work was subjected to critical review. The covered windows were not appreciated by Ruby Rinker—the long-time friend of Robert and Arvella Schuller and International Ministries Board member—because it was her friend's dream to preach under the sky.

"He loved the clouds," said Rinker. "I think the right person could have done a very beautiful job, make it Catholic, and still be able to look up and see the clouds. It's theirs to do what they want to do." But she does not regret her vote supporting the sale to the Diocese of Orange. "No regrets, just disappointed that you can't see the sky."[7]

Bobby V. Schuller said the Catholic Church in the Garden Grove of the 2020s was a better fit for the Christian community. With multiple services in Spanish, Vietnamese, and even some in Chinese, it was a depth in the community that Crystal Cathedral Ministries could not match. He noted the multilingual fluency capabilities of Christ Cathedral's leadership.

"I just love Father Christopher. I think he's doing a great job," said Schuller. "I love Bishop Vann. I do believe that God has called them to be there and serve at this time. I'm so grateful they're in the right place at the right time."

When this text was written, a viral pandemic unlike anything seen since 1918 altered the way people lived and worshipped around the world. Governments closed churches, synagogues, and all places of worship over infection fears. After a couple of months, restrictions were eased, but churches were still ordered closed. Bishop Tod Brown, who shepherded the purchase of the Crystal Cathedral campus, repeatedly argued the value of a cathedral for a large diocese, so that there was a center for Catholic life in the community and a refuge in a storm. But shortly after the dedication ceremony, in a matter of months, worship services and all Masses at the newly anointed Christ Cathedral had ceased.

But then the livestreams on the internet flickered to life. Christ Cathedral, with its extraordinary video and audio capabilities, streamed over the internet—allowing people sequestered in their homes to finally enjoy Mass. Though without the Eucharist in their homes, the communion with Christ was still possible. The cathedral began to embody the purpose for which it was intended. There were twenty thousand watching one Sunday. In a few weeks, sixty thousand. By late March, there were two hundred thousand watching the livestream of Mass. Countless hours of adoration streamed live.

"So, it continues to be that kind of beacon in that outreach," said Vann, "it really does."[8]

During the pandemic, Bishop Kevin Vann continued to provide Communion to the sickest with visits to hospitals and other facilities, as did hundreds of priests across the parish. The cathedral had only a few people in it at Sunday Mass, but the comfort the services gave to tens of thousands of people at home could not be measured. The Hazel Wright Organ, which was to be dedicated in the same period, remained silent. It would be dedicated when the pandemic ended.

"I said, 'Let days speak, and many years teach wisdom.' But it is the spirit in man, in the breath of the Almighty, that makes him understand." (Job 32:7–8)

Between the cemetery and the Pastoral Center/Christ Cathedral Academy, along the promenade separating the area from the parking lot, there is a statue of Job—a fact only discovered after the title was chosen. Ask yourself, how many statues of Job have you ever seen?

AFTERWORD

Both Gabriel Ferrucci and Bishop Vann remain in contact with the Ruffatis on a regular basis. Yet, as these words are written, the work now moves toward completion on the Shrine of Our Lady of LaVang in the Marian Courtyard. It is due to be dedicated on July 17, 2021, the second anniversary of the cathedral's dedication! Likewise, the addition on the Cathedral Memorial Gardens moves ahead apace with the dedication later this year. Also, plans are now underway to complete the Undercroft Chapel, which will be dedicated to St. Callistus and will have additional cemetery crypts, including mausoleums for the bishops.

While it was emotional to leave St. Callistus for that first Mass at the cathedral campus, it truly was a moment of hope; so too now. Likewise, in these difficult days of the pandemic, the continued work on the cathedral also shows signs of new life that soon will come into bloom. As the lights of the interior of the cathedral continue to shine into the darkness of the night, the cathedral continues to be a beacon—a sign of the Faith and the "work of many hands" who helped to bring into life this "House of God" and "Temple of the Lord." We give thanks for the dedication and the "work of many hands" whose names fill these pages!

—Bishop Kevin Vann
January 2021

ENDNOTES

Ruby

[1] Thomas Curwen, "Robert Schuller's California Brand of Christianity," *Los Angeles Times*, April 2, 2015, https://www.latimes.com/local/lanow/la-me-ln-robert-schullers-california-brand-christianity-20150402-story.html.

[2] Ruby Rinker, interview by author, February 11, 2020.

The Preacher

[1] Violet Mouw, interview, "A&E Biography: Robert Schuller," 1998, video, 45:44, July 25, 2015, https://www.youtube.com/watch?v=U4nYEf8F-9g.

[2] Robert H. Schuller, *My Journey: From an Iowa Farm to a Cathedral of Dreams* (San Francisco: HarperCollins, 2001), p. 45.

[3] Ibid.

[4] Ibid.

[5] Robert H. Schuller, *Prayer: My Soul's Adventure with God; A Spiritual Autobiography* (Nashville: Thomas Nelson, 1995), p. 13.

[6] Ibid.

[7] Schuller, *My Journey*, p. 61.

[8] Schuller, *Prayer*, p. 12.

[9] Ibid.

[10] Ibid.

[11] Ibid.

The Drive-In

[1] Robert H. Schuller, *My Journey: From an Iowa Farm to a Cathedral of Dreams* (San Francisco: HarperCollins, 2001), p. 198.

[2] Ibid.

[3] Ibid., p. 199.

[4] Ibid., pp. 199–200.

[5] Ibid., p. 206.

[6] Ibid., p. 212.

[7] "Garden Grove Church to Open Unique Drive-In Church Sunday," *Orange County Register*, March 26, 1955.

[8] Ibid.

[9] Dr. George W. Crane, "Bishop Sheen and Dr. Peale," Case N-378, Syndicated Column, "The Worry Clinic," *Orange County Register*, March 26, 1955.

[10] Ibid.

[11] Ibid.

[12] Dr. George W. Crane, "Stand Upright," Syndicated Column, "The Worry Clinic," *Orange County Register*, March 26, 1955.

[13] Anne Waltz, interview, "A&E Biography: Robert Schuller," 1998, video, 45:44, July 25, 2015, https://www.youtube.com/watch?v=U4nYEf8F-9g.

The Builder

[1] Robert H. Schuller, *My Journey: From an Iowa Farm to a Cathedral of Dreams* (San Francisco: HarperCollins, 2001), p. 261.

[2] "Life Is Worth Living: Prayer," originally broadcast on the DuMont Network, 1953, video, 23:18, January 1, 2020, https://www.youtube.com/watch?v=94NH _9V499s.

[3] Robert H. Schuller, *Prayer: My Soul's Adventure with God; A Spiritual Autobiography* (Nashville: Thomas Nelson, 1995), p. 13.

[4] Christopher Smith, interview by author, February 2020. Unless otherwise noted, for the remainder of this chapter the quotes by Christopher Smith are from this interview.

[5] Randy Jackson, interview by author, November 20, 2019. Unless otherwise noted, for the remainder of this chapter the quotes by Randy Jackson are from this interview.

[6] Schuller, *My Journey*, p. 219.

[7] Ibid., p. 233.

[8] Ibid., p. 237.

[9] Ibid., p. 239.

[10] Ibid., p. 241.

The *Hour of Power*

[1] "Christ Cathedral: Inspired Architecture," *Orange County Catholic*, by staff, July 19, 2019, https://occatholic.com/christ-cathedral-inspired-architecture/.

[2] Ibid.

[3] Jim Wirick, interview by author, February 2020. All subsequent quotes by Jim Wirick are from this interview.

[4] Philip Johnson, comments in "Crystal Cathedral Bell Tower Dedication Service," recorded September 16, 1990, video, 59:04, December 9, 2016, https:// www.youtube.com/watch?v=OXyBuKF4DvI.

[5] Ibid.

[6] Deepa Bharath, "Crystal Cathedral Blames a Few Creditors for Bankruptcy," *Orange County Register*, October 19, 2010, https://www.ocregister.com/2010/10/19 /crystal-cathedral-blames-a-few-creditors-for-bankruptcy/.

[7] Rebecca Cathcart, "California's Crystal Cathedral Files for Bankruptcy," *New York Times*, October 18, 2010, https://www.nytimes.com/2010/10/19/us/19 crystal.html.

[8] Nicole Santa Cruz, "Crystal Cathedral Files for Bankruptcy Protection," *Los Angeles Times*, October 19, 2010, https://www.latimes.com/archives/la-xpm -2010-oct-19-la-me-crystal-cathedral-20101019-story.html.

[9] Bobby V. Schuller, interview by author, 2020.

[10] Comments in "Crystal Cathedral Founder's Son and Grandson Speak Out," *Orange County Register* Multimedia Video, recorded October 25, 2010, 4:35, July 28, 2015, https://www.youtube.com/watch?v=f_yVL5fR2BI.

Chapman University

[1] David Ferrell, "Jim Doti: A Man Who Climbs Mountains," *Orange County Register*, June 3, 2013, https://www.ocregister.com/2013/06/03/jim-doti-a-man -who-climbs-mountains/.

[2] Dr. Doti, interview by author, January 2020. All subsequent quotes by Dr. Doti are from this interview.

[3] "Award-Winning Sculpture Unveiled in Escalette Plaza," Chapman University Newsroom, March 1, 2011, https://news.chapman.edu/2011/03/01/award -winning-sculpture-unveiled-in-escalette-plaza/.

[4] Quotes attributed to Sherwood Oklejas are from United States Bankruptcy Court transcripts, November 17, 2011, Crystal Cathedral Ministries Debtor, Santa Ana Federal Court House.

Bishop Tod Brown

[1] "Fact Sheet and History," Diocese of Orange, accessed November 23, 2020, https://www.rcbo.org/press-room/fact-sheets-backgrounders/.

[2] William Lobdell, "Bishop Unveils Cathedral Plans," *Los Angeles Times*, June 11, 2001, https://www.latimes.com/archives/la-xpm-2001-jun-11-me-9155-story .html.

[3] Bishop Brown, interview by author, November 2019. All subsequent quotes by Bishop Brown are from this interview or from email exchanges.

[4] Orange Catholic Foundation (website), ABOUT webpage, accessed March 28, 2021, https://orangecatholicfoundation.org/our-foundation/about/.

[5] Jim Tecca, interview by author, January 2020. All subsequent quotes by Jim Tecca are from this interview.

[6] Mike Hagan, interview by author, 2020. All subsequent quotes by Mike Hagan are from this interview.

[7] Monsignor Heher, interview by author, 2020. All subsequent quotes by Monsignor Heher are from this interview.

[8] "Investment Group to Purchase Bankrupt Crystal Cathedral," *Los Angeles Daily News*, DailyNews.com, May 27, 2011, https://www.dailynews.com/2011/05/27 /investment-group-to-purchase-bankrupt-crystal-cathedral/.

[9] Ibid.

[10] Nicole Santa Cruz and Carol J. Williams, "Crystal Cathedral Ministries' Church and Campus Will Be Sold to Orange County Developer," *Los Angeles Times*, May 28, 2011, https://www.latimes.com/archives/la-xpm-2011-may-28-la-me-crystal-cathedral-20110528-story.html.

[11] "Catholic Diocese of Orange May Bid on Crystal Cathedral," *Times-Dispatch*, staff, July 9, 2011.

[12] Tim Busch, interviews by author, between November 2019 and January 2020. All subsequent quotes by Tim Busch are from these interviews.

[13] Maria Schinderle, interviews by author, between November 2019 and January 2020. All subsequent quotes by Maria Schinderle are from these interviews.

[14] Alan Martin, interview by author, 2020. All subsequent quotes by Alan Martin are from this interview.

[15] Matt Coker, "Chapman University Wants to Buy Crystal Cathedral for $46 Million," *Orange County Weekly*, July 5, 2011, https://www.ocweekly.com/chapman-university-wants-to-buy-crystal-cathedral-for-46-million-6468484/.

Meeting Dr. Robert H. Schuller

[1] Father Robert Spitzer, interview by author, 2020. All subsequent quotes by Father Robert Spitzer are from this interview.

[2] Tim Busch, interviews by author, between November 2019 and February 2020. All subsequent quotes by are from these interviews.

[3] Alan Martin, interview by author, 2020. All subsequent quotes by are from this interview.

[4] Maria Schinderle, interview by author, between November 2019 and February 2020. All subsequent quotes by Maria Schinderle are from these interviews.

[5] Reverend Schuller, as recalled by Maria Schinderle and Bishop Brown.

[6] Bishop Brown and his recollections of conversation with Dr. Schuller are from the author's interview, November 2019. All subsequent quotes by Bishop Brown and his recollections are from this interview.

An Informed Decision

[1] Maria Schinderle, interviews by author, between November 2019 and February 2020. All subsequent quotes in this chapter by Maria Schinderle are from these interviews.

[2] Rob Neal, interviews by author, between 2019 and 2020. All subsequent quotes in this chapter by Rob Neal are from these interviews.

[3] Geoffrey Mohan, "Cost of St. Vibiana Quake Safety Work Put at $20 Million," *Los Angeles Times*, October 10, 1995, https://www.latimes.com/archives/la-xpm-1995-10-10-me-55336-story.html.

[4] Berni Neal, interview by author, November 2019. All subsequent quotes in this chapter by Berni Neal are from this interview.

[5] Tim Busch, interviews by author, between November 2019 and February 2020. All subsequent quotes in this chapter by Tim Busch are from these interviews.

[6] Alan Martin, interview by author, 2020. All subsequent quotes in this chapter by Alan Martin are from this interview.

The Bids

[1] Quotes by Judge Kwan and all open-court quotes from November 14, 2011, Court Appearance, Hearing on Motion to Confirm Reorganization Plan. Unless otherwise indicated, quotes are taken from the official court transcript. Reference: In the Matter of Crystal Cathedral Ministries Debtor, Case No. SA10-24771-RK, United States Federal Court, Monday, November 14, 2011, 9:00 a.m.

[2] Unless otherwise noted, for the remainder of this chapter, quotes outside of open court and attributed to Alan Martin are from the author's interview in 2020.

[3] Maria Schinderle, interviews by author, between November 2019 and February 2020. All subsequent quotes by Maria Schinderle in this chapter are from these interviews.

[4] Tim Busch, interviews by author, between November 2019 and February 2020. All subsequent quotes by Tim Busch in this chapter are from these interviews.

The Board Votes

[1] Bishop Brown, interview by author, November 2019. All subsequent quotes in this chapter by Bishop Brown are from this interview.

[2] Tim Busch, interviews by author, between November 2019 and February 2020. All subsequent quotes in this chapter by Tim Busch are from these interviews.

[3] Father Spitzer, interview by author, 2020. All subsequent quotes in this chapter by Father Spitzer are from this interview.

[4] Associated Press, "Robert Schuller's Son Leaves Crystal Cathedral," *Whittier Daily News*, December 14, 2008, https://www.whittierdailynews.com/2008/12/14 /robert-schullers-son-leaves-crystal-cathedral/.

[5] Deepa Bharath, "Crystal Cathedral Members Launch Petition Drive," *Orange County Register*, July 18, 2011, https://www.ocregister.com/2011/07/18 /crystal-cathedral-members-launch-petition-drive/.

[6] Ruby Rinker, interview by author, November 2019. All subsequent quotes in this chapter by Ruby Rinker are from this interview.

[7] Dr. Highum, from the phone call conversation with Tim Busch as recalled by Tim Busch.

[8] Conversation constructed from the recollections of Tim Busch and Maria Schinderle.

The Lower Bid?

[1] Maria Schinderle, interviews by author, between November 2019 and February 2020. All subsequent quotes in this chapter by Maria Schinderle are from these interviews.

[2] Unless otherwise indicated, quotes are taken from the official court transcript. Reference: In the Matter of Crystal Cathedral Ministries Debtor, Case

No. SA10-24771-RK, United States Federal Court, Thursday, November 17, 2011, 1:30 p.m. Hearing on Confirmation of Chapter 11 Plan.

[3] Bishop Brown from the off-the-court record conversation with Tim Busch as compiled from the recollections of Bishop Brown and Busch.

The Hope for Sound Judgment

[1] For the remainder of this chapter, quotes attributed to Bishop Brown are from the author's interview in November 2019 or subsequent post-interview notes.

[2] Unless otherwise indicated, on-the-record quotes are taken from the official court transcript. Reference: In the Matter of Crystal Cathedral Ministries Debtor, Case No. SA10-24771-RK, United States Federal Court, Thursday, November 17, 2011, 1:30 p.m. Hearing on Confirmation of Chapter 11 Plan.

[3] For the remainder of this chapter, off-the-court record quotes attributed to James Doti are from the author's interview in January 2020.

[4] Tim Busch, interviews by author, between November 2019 and February 2020. All subsequent quotes in this chapter by Tim Busch are from these interviews.

[5] Steph Busch and the conversation with her husband, Tim Busch, about the nihil obstat was compiled from interviews with the participant in November 2011.

[6] Monsignor Cook, as recalled by Tim Busch combined with the actual text from the nihil obstat fax.

The Way Forward

[1] Bob Theirgartner, interview by author, 2020. All subsequent quotes in this chapter by Bob Theirgartner are from this interview.

[2] "About the church of Peter" and unless otherwise noted, for the remainder of this chapter, quotes attributed to Tim Busch are from the author's interviews, between November 2019 and February 2020.

[3] Rob Neal, interviews by author, 2019 and 2020. All subsequent quotes in this chapter by Rob Neal are from these interviews.

[4] "Dr. Schuller Addresses Priests," Orange Catholic Foundation, June 29, 2012, video, 5:15, August 22, 2014, https://www.youtube.com/watch?v=WVjba5stWY4. All quotes are from this speech.

[5] Father Christopher Smith, interview by author, 2020. All subsequent quotes in this chapter by Father Christopher Smith are from this interview.

[6] Monsignor Michael Heher, interview by author, 2020. All subsequent quotes in this chapter by Monsignor Michael Heher are from this interview.

[7] Ronald Campbell, "Crystal Cathedral Sold to Catholic Church," *Orange County Register*, February 3, 2012, https://www.ocregister.com/2012/02/03/crystal-cathedral-sold-to-catholic-church/.

[8] Bishop Brown, interview by author, November 2019. All subsequent quotes in this chapter by Bishop Brown are from this interview or subsequent post-interview notes.

[9] "Catholic Diocese of Orange Announces Cathedral Name," Diocese of Orange Press Release, June 9, 2012.

[10] Sharon Abercrombie, "Christian Brother Creates, Selects Art for Worship Space," *Catholic Voice* 46, no. 16 (September 22, 2008), https://catholicvoiceoak land.org/2008/08-09-22/inthisissue9.htm.

[11] Letter of Bishop Designate Vann to Rob Neal, November 29, 2012, provided by Neal.

The Wall Tumbles Down

[1] Father Christopher Smith, interview by author, 2020. All subsequent quotes in this chapter by Father Christopher Smith are from this interview.

[2] Berni Neal, interview by author, November 2012. All subsequent quotes in this chapter by Berni Neal are from this interview.

[3] Quotes attributed to Father Peter John Cameron are from his comments at the Magnificat Day of Faith, November 5, 2012, video, 1:18:59, https://www.youtube .com/watch?v=Y3iTpM9F7bY.

[4] Rob Neal, interviews by author, 2019 and 2020. All subsequent quotes in this chapter by Rob Neal are from these interviews.

[5] Joe Novoa, interview by author, 2020. All subsequent quotes in this chapter by Joe Novoa are from this interview. Conversations may be reconstructed from multiple interviewees as previously identified.

[6] Jim Wirick, interview by author, January 2020. All subsequent quotes in this chapter by Jim Wirick are from this interview. Conversations may be reconstructed from multiple interviewees as previously identified in this chapter.

[7] Bob Theirgartner, interview by author, 2020.

Bishop Vann

[1] Bishop Vann, interview by author, 2020. All subsequent quotes in this chapter by Bishop Vann are from this interview.

[2] Rocco Palmo, "From the OC, the First Word," *Whispers in the Loggia* (blog), September 21, 2012, https://whispersintheloggia.blogspot.com/2012/09/from-orange -first-word.html.

[3] Ibid.

[4] From the Apostolic Letter of Appointment as read by Archbishop Carlo Maria Viganò, Apostolic Nuncio to the United States, at the Installation Mass of Bishop Vann, December 10, 2012, video, 2:33:06, April 9, 2014, https://www.youtube .com/watch?v=lNjR3_-hrbY.

[5] Randy Jackson, interview by author, November 2019. All subsequent quotes in this chapter by Randy Jackson are from this interview.

The Neutra Arboretum

[1] Rob Neal, interviews by author, 2019 and 2020. All subsequent quotes in this chapter by Rob Neal are from these interviews.

[2] Mary Kay Westbrook, interview by author, November 2019. All subsequent quotes in this chapter by Mary Kay Westbrook are from this interview.

[3] Jim Wirick, interview by author, January 2020. All subsequent quotes in this chapter by Jim Wirick are from this interview.

History as a Guide

[1] Randy Jackson, interview by author, November 2019. All subsequent quotes in this chapter by Randy Jackson are from this interview.

[2] Rob Neal, interviews by author, 2019 and 2020. All subsequent quotes in this chapter by Rob Neal are from these interviews.

[3] Barbara Lamprecht, interviews by author, February 2020. Unless otherwise noted, all subsequent quotes in this chapter by Barbara Lamprecht are from these interviews.

[4] Barbara Lamprecht, "'Untamed Orange': Schuller, Neutra, and Semper at the Garden Grove Arboretum," *Lamprecht Architextural* (blog), September 8, 2013, https://barbaralamprecht.com/2013/09/08/untamed-orange-semper-neutra-and -schuller-at-the-garden-grove-arboretum/.

[5] Ibid.

[6] Joe Novoa, interview by author, 2020. All subsequent quotes in this chapter by Joe Novoa are from this interview.

Close the Path Behind

[1] Father Christopher Smith, interview by author, 2020. Unless otherwise noted, all subsequent quotes in this chapter by Father Christopher Smith are from this interview.

[2] Semisonic, "Closing Time," lyrics by Dan Wilson, *Feeling Strangely Fine*, MCA Records, 1998.

[3] Roxana Kopetman, "Sheila Schuller Leads Her Church to New Site," *Orange County Register*, May 30, 2013, https://www.ocregister.com/2013/05/30/sheila -schuller-leads-her-church-to-new-site/.

[4] Robert V. "Bobby" Schuller, interview by author, 2020. All subsequent quotes in this chapter by Robert V. "Bobby" Schuller are from this interview.

[5] Father Tuyen Van Nguyen, interview by author, 2020. All subsequent quotes in this chapter by Father Tuyen Van Nguyen are from this interview.

[6] Father Christopher Smith, "First Mass Christ Cathedral," Diocese of Orange, video, July 2, 2013, video, 1:12:02, https://www.youtube.com/watch?v =SrPG8wV6CGA.

[7] Ibid.

[8] Ibid.

[9] Ibid.

[10] Ibid.

[11] Ibid.

[12] *Hour of Power with Bobby Schuller*, "Crystal Cathedral: The Farewell Service," October 10, 2013, video, 57:42, https://www.youtube.com/watch?v =NdGf1JeHA9c.

[13] Ibid.
[14] Ibid.

Restoring Hope

[1] Rob Neal, interviews by author, 2019 and 2020. All subsequent quotes in this chapter by Rob Neal are from these interviews.

[2] Randy Redwitz, interview by author, 2020. All subsequent quotes in this chapter by Randy Redwitz are from this interview.

[3] Bryan Seamer and Daniel Wang, "Seismic Retrofit of the Tower of Hope—Preservation of a Masterwork of Mid-Century Modernism," TaylorDevices.com, accessed November 24, 2020, https://www.taylordevices.com/wp-content/uploads/107-Case-Study-Tower-of-Hope-13-story-Concrete-Frame-Retrofit.pdf.

[4] Jim Wirick, interview by author, January 2020. All subsequent quotes in this chapter by Jim Wirick are from this interview.

[5] Seamer and Wang, "Seismic Retrofit of the Tower of Hope."

[6] Barbara Lamprecht, interview by author, February 2020. All subsequent quotes in this chapter by Barbara Lamprecht are from this interview.

[7] Bob Theirgartner, interview by author, 2020. All subsequent quotes in this chapter by Bob Theirgartner are from this interview.

[8] Scott Johnson, interview by author, January 2020. All subsequent quotes in this chapter by Scott Johnson are from this interview.

[9] Carl Bunderson, "Two Architecture Firms Chosen to Transform Crystal Cathedral," Catholic News Agency, September 19, 2013, https://www.catholicnewsagency.com/news/two-architecture-firms-chosen-to-transform-crystal-cathedral.

[10] Ibid.

[11] Father Christopher Smith, interview by author, 2020. All subsequent quotes in this chapter by Father Christopher Smith are from this interview.

Phase One

[1] Excerpts from Brother Woeger's presentation to the selection committee are from the complete presentation report provided with permission by Brother Woeger.

[2] Monsignor Michael Heher, interview by author, 2020. All subsequent quotes in this chapter by Monsignor Michael Heher are from this interview.

[3] Scott Johnson, interview by author, January 2020. All subsequent quotes in this chapter by Scott Johnson are from this interview.

[4] Father Christopher Smith, interview by author, 2020. All subsequent quotes in this chapter by Father Christopher Smith are from this interview.

[5] Rob Neal, interviews by author, 2019 and 2020. All subsequent quotes in this chapter by Rob Neal are from these interviews.

[6] Catholic News Agency, "Renovation Plans for Orange's Christ Cathedral Aim to Uplift," September 24, 2014, https://www.catholicnewsagency.com/news/renovation-plans-for-oranges-christ-cathedral-aim-to-uplift-10392.

[7] Post-interview notes from Tim Busch, 2020.

[8] B. W. Cook, "The Crowd: Pickup Family Foundation Gives $15 Million to Hoag Neuroscience Institute," *LA Times Daily Pilot*, Opinion Column, November 9, 2017, https://www.latimes.com/socal/daily-pilot/opinion/tn-dpt-et-the-crowd -20171109-story.html.

[9] Deepa Bharath, "Rev. Robert Schuller Laid to Rest: 'He Was Much More Than a Pastor'," *Orange County Register*, April 21, 2015, https://www.ocregister.com /2015/04/21/rev-robert-schuller-laid-to-rest-he-was-much-more-than-a-pastor/.

[10] Bishop Vann, interview by author, 2020. All subsequent quotes in this chapter by Bishop Vann are from this interview.

[11] "Robert H. Schuller's Final Sermon from the Crystal Cathedral," courtesy Hour of Power, video, 16:44, December 20, 2015, https://www.youtube.com /watch?v=djNBUod3REc.

[12] "Msgr. Holquin Shares Story of Egino Weinert Tabernacle," OC Catholic TV, Diocese of Orange, video, 4:50, July 6, 2016, https://www.youtube.com /watch?v=bXmsyH5sgo0.

Phase Two

[1] Bishop Vann, interview by author, 2020. All subsequent quotes in this chapter by Bishop Vann are from this interview.

[2] Richard Heim, interview by author, 2020. All subsequent quotes in this chapter by Richard Heim are from this interview.

[3] Auxiliary Bishop Timothy Freyer, interview by author, November 2019. All subsequent quotes in this chapter by Auxiliary Bishop Timothy Freyer are from this interview.

[4] Scott Johnson, interview by author, January 2020. All subsequent quotes in this chapter by Scott Johnson are from this interview.

[5] "The Blessing of the Quatrefoils at Christ Cathedral," OC Catholic TV, Diocese of Orange, video, 3:06, posted October 17, 2018, https://www.youtube.com /watch?v=6a8WkQaaFzI.

[6] Francesco Ruffatti, "The Renovation of the Christ (Crystal) Cathedral Organ," *American Organist Magazine*, last modified April 21, 2020, https://www.agohq .org/may-2020-tao-feature-article/.

[7] "Hazel Wright Organ Installation," OC Catholic TV, Orange Catholic Foundation, video, 5:39, posted February 7, 2019, https://www.youtube.com/watch?v =h0CFo8SLRSs.

[8] Gabriel Ferrucci, interview by author, 2020. All subsequent quotes in this chapter by Gabriel Ferrucci are from this interview.

[9] Post-interview notes from Bishop Tod Brown in 2020.

[10] Brother Woeger, interview by author, 2020. All subsequent quotes in this chapter by Brother Woeger are from this interview.

[11] Dennis Jilot, interview by author, 2020. All subsequent quotes in this chapter by Dennis Jilot are from this interview.

Dedication of Christ Cathedral

[1] Biography of Cardinal Foley, Vatican (website), accessed November 25, 2020, https://press.vatican.va/content/salastampa/en/documentation/cardinali_biografie/cardinali_bio_foley_jp.html.

[2] Auxiliary Bishop Timothy Freyer, interview by author, November 2019. All subsequent quotes in this chapter by Auxiliary Bishop Timothy Freyer are from this interview.

[3] Quoted in "Cathedrals Across America, Dedication of Christ Cathedral," EWTN, video, 3:19:42, posted July 19, 2019, https://www.youtube.com/watch?v=EA1VRF5cZ8U.

[4] Cardinal Parolin, in ibid.

[5] Bishop Vann, in ibid.

[6] "Christ Cathedral Solemn Mass of Dedication," program (Portland, OR: OCP Publications, 2019).

[7] Bishop Vann, interview by author, 2020.

[8] "Dedication of Christ Cathedral."

[9] Bishop Vann, "Dedication of Christ Cathedral." Saint Augustine, Sermon 336, "The Building and Dedication of God's House within Us."

Conclusion

[1] Courtney Mares, "Pope Francis: Prayer Opens the Door to Freedom through the Holy Spirit," *National Catholic Register*, April 20, 2020, https://www.ncregister.com/daily-news/pope-francis-prayer-opens-the-door-to-freedom-through-the-holy-spirit.

[2] Ibid.

[3] Robert H. Schuller, *Prayer: My Soul's Adventure with God* (Nashville: Thomas Nelson, 1995), pp. xiii–xiv.

[4] James Doti, interview by author, January 2020.

[5] Alan Martin, interview by author, January 2020.

[6] Robert V. "Bobby" Schuller, interview by author, 2020. All subsequent quotes in this chapter by Robert V. "Bobby" Schuller are from this interview.

[7] Ruby Rinker, interview by author, 2020. All subsequent quotes in this chapter by Ruby Rinker are from this interview.

[8] Bishop Vann, interview by author, 2020.